Teaching the iGeneration

5 Easy Ways to Introduce Essential Skills With Web 2.0 Tools

Solution Tree | Press

a division of
Solution Tree

WILLIAM M. FERRITER / ADAM GARRY

555 North Morton Street
Bloomington, IN 47404

800.733.6786 (toll free) / 812.336.7700
FAX: 812.336.7790

email: info@solution-tree.com
solution-tree.com
Visit **go.solution-tree.com/technology** to download the reproducibles in this book.

Printed in the United States of America

14 13 12 11 10   1 2 3 4 5

Library of Congress Cataloging-in-Publication Data

Ferriter, William M.

  Teaching the igeneration : five easy ways to introduce essential skills with web 2.0 tools / William M. Ferriter, Adam Garry.

     p. cm.

  Includes bibliographical references and index.

  ISBN 978-1-935249-93-1 (perfect bound) -- ISBN 978-1-935249-94-8 (library binding) 1. Web 2.0--Study and teaching. 2. Web-based instruction. 3. Internet in education. 4. Educational technology. I. Garry, Adam. II. Title.

  LB1044.87.F47 2010

  371.33'44678--dc22

                    2010016077

Solution Tree

Jeffrey C. Jones, CEO & President

Solution Tree Press

President: Douglas M. Rife

Publisher: Robert D. Clouse

Vice President of Production: Gretchen Knapp

Managing Production Editor: Caroline Wise

Copy Editor: Rachel Rosolina

Proofreader: Elisabeth Abrams

Cover Designer: Orlando Angel

Text Designer: Amy Shock

To my beautiful daughter and wife, who I'll happily spend a lifetime loving. —Bill Ferriter

To my amazing son Michael and in memory of my son Max, who are the inspirations for everything I do and love. —Adam Garry

Acknowledgments

Like all pieces of writing, *Teaching the iGeneration* is the product of a thousand shared experiences. For Bill, those experiences began with Sheryl Nussbaum-Beach and John Norton, friends and colleagues from the Teacher Leaders Network. More than any single person, Sheryl has shaped Bill's thinking around good teaching and learning with technology—for adults and children alike. And more than any single person, John has shaped Bill's development as a writer and as a digital moderator. Their contributions to who Bill has become are immeasurable, rivaled only by the daily contributions made by the countless members of his personal learning network.

Bill's shared experiences continued with Mike Hutchinson, Marcy Russell, Emily Swanson, and Lyndsey Lowe, his long-time teammates and teaching partners at Salem Middle School in Apex, North Carolina. Constantly driven to grow as learners and leaders, they have never stopped imagining with Bill! Their willingness to dream about what could be—rather than get stuck in what is—have led to most of the lessons shared inside these pages. They're the forgotten heroes of his professional career: constantly pushing, constantly prodding, constantly polishing, constantly improving.

Adam's shared experiences began many years ago in an elementary school in Pasco County, Florida. One man, Dr. John Mann, believed in him and invested the time to support his growth as an educator and a leader. Adam has had the pleasure of learning with and from Dr. Mann since he first stepped into a classroom, and he is forever grateful.

Adam's work as a consultant around comprehensive school reform focused on project-based learning and technology has afforded him many tremendous opportunities, but none more valuable than the people he has met and learned from for all these years. Some of his mentors include Dr. Chris Corallo and Eric Jones in Henrico County, Virginia, and Dr. Mike Looney in Williamson County, Tennessee. Chris and Eric have been the driving force in Adam's growth as a leader and a consultant and have helped him develop the craft of asking the right questions and listening to learn. And while Dr. Looney and Adam haven't always seen eye to eye on education issues, Dr. Looney's ability to craft a compelling argument and make others think have afforded Adam some of his best learning opportunities.

For both Bill and Adam, the staff of Solution Tree has been a tremendous support throughout the writing of *Teaching the iGeneration*. In less than a year, Douglas Rife and Gretchen Knapp helped shepherd this book from an idea to the final product that you hold. Rachel Rosolina took a rough first draft to a much-improved final copy—with kind words at every step of the way—in the same short window of time.

And while Adam and Bill don't have enough space to name every single superintendent, principal, teacher, or student that they have had the pleasure to work with over the past sixteen years, both take a small piece of them everywhere that they go. It isn't very often that someone gets to say that they love what they do, but both Adam and Bill can. After all, they have been blessed to work with some of the most amazing educators and students in this country. Those educators and students give both Adam and Bill hope that we can—and will—transform learning to meet the needs of the iGeneration.

Solution Tree Press would like to thank the following reviewers:

Steven Anderson
Instructional Technologist
Clemmons Middle School
Winston-Salem, North Carolina

Russ Goerend
Sixth-Grade Language Arts Teacher
Waukee Middle School
Waukee, Iowa

Paul Cancellieri
Seventh-Grade Science Teacher
Durant Road Middle School
Raleigh, North Carolina

Kevin Jarrett
K–4 Computer Teacher and Technology Facilitator
Northfield Community School
Northfield, New Jersey

Howie DiBlasi
Technology and Educational Consultant
Digital Journey
Georgetown, Texas

Meg Ormiston
Professional Development Specialist
Tech Teachers, Inc.
Burr Ridge, Illinois

Michael Fisher
Instructional Coach and Educational Consultant
Amherst, New York

Alan Veach
Principal
Bloomington New Tech High School
Bloomington, Indiana

Table of Contents

Reproducible pages are in italics.

Visit **go.solution-tree.com/technology** to download the reproducibles in this book.

About the Authors

William M. Ferriter—@plugusin on Twitter—is a sixth-grade language arts and social studies teacher in a professional learning community (PLC) near Raleigh, North Carolina. A National Board Certified Teacher, Bill has designed professional development courses for educators nationwide. His trainings include how to use blogs, wikis, and podcasts in the classroom; the role of iTunes in teaching and learning; and the power of digital moviemaking. Bill has also developed schoolwide technology rubrics and surveys that identify student and staff digital proficiency at the building level. He is a founding member and senior fellow of the Teacher Leaders Network and has served as teacher in residence at the Center for Teaching Quality.

An advocate for PLCs, improved teacher working conditions, and teacher leadership, Bill has represented educators on Capitol Hill and presented at state and national conferences. He is among the first one hundred teachers in North Carolina and the first one thousand in the United States to earn certification from the National Board for Professional Teaching Standards. He has been a Regional Teacher of the Year in North Carolina, and his blog, the Tempered Radical, earned Best Teacher Blog of 2008 from Edublogs.

Bill has had articles published in the *Journal of Staff Development*, *Educational Leadership*, and *Threshold Magazine*. A contributing author to two assessment anthologies, *The Teacher as Assessment Leader* and *The Principal as Assessment Leader*, he is also coauthor of *Building a Professional Learning Community at Work.*™

Bill earned a bachelor of science and master of science in elementary education from the State University of New York at Geneseo.

Adam Garry is a former elementary school teacher. He is currently the manager of Dell's global professional learning organization. He has presented and keynoted at technology conferences around the world, including Alan November's conferences and National Education Computing Conferences. He has published many articles on technology integration for several education magazines and authors his own blog. Since 2001, he has consulted in school districts across the country on school change, professional development, 21st century skills, technology integration, curriculum and instruction, and leadership. He is also a facilitator for the Partnership for 21st Century Skills' Professional Development Affiliate program and the International Society for Technology in Education's School 2.0 workshops. Adam received a BA in elementary education, a master's in teaching and learning with a technology emphasis, and a certificate in administration and supervision from Johns Hopkins University.

The iGeneration

They have never known a life without the internet, let alone computers, and many don't know a world without mobile phones.

—Sarah Cornish, *Total Girl* magazine

For most of the students gathered in the Davis Drive Middle School library in the late 1990s, school could not have been more exciting. Invited by NASA to participate in a global project, small groups of eighth-grade scientists were following the orbital path of the space shuttle Discovery as it traveled around the world. Because the space shuttle's onboard cameras could snap pictures of landforms on Earth, student experts were responsible for using the Internet—a relatively new tool for teachers and students at the time—to track world weather patterns, geographical features, and daylight hours.

When students realized that the space shuttle would be traveling over interesting areas of our planet—the Horn of Africa, the Strait of Gibraltar, the Black Sea, the Aleutian Islands—during daylight hours on a clear day, electricity would ripple through the media center regardless of the time. Students would quickly write up a photo request form and draft an email to NASA. If the request arrived in time—and if it was not buried under a pile of other requests made by different student groups scattered across the United States—the reward would be a digital copy of an orbital photo, something no student of the '70s had ever experienced.

For Dan—the teenage project manager selected by his peers because of his obvious passion for all things digital—the entire project was an experience in frustration, however. "I can't believe how slow these pages load!" he'd shout at anyone who would listen. "If I was at home, I'd have this work done already, and we'd have a better shot of getting our picture requests in on time. The Internet at school just plain stinks." No matter how hard his teachers worked to remind Dan that he was experiencing something new and unique—*"You're talking to the space shuttle, Dan. You couldn't have done that when I was in school. The Internet didn't even exist. Neither did the space shuttle!"*—he was inconsolable. He was, after all, standing at the leading edge of the iGeneration.

Whether you call them the Net Generation, Generation Y, Generation Z, the Gen Nexters, the Look-at-Me Generation, the Millennial Generation, the Echo Generation, the ADHD Generation, or the iGeneration, the students born between the early 1990s and the year 2000 have taken over our schools—and they are nothing like their predecessors!

Inheriting a world with nearly universal access to the Internet, *iGeners*—a term used throughout this text to describe the children of today's classrooms and tomorrow's workplaces—are almost universally plugged in. Earbuds hang from backpacks, and cell phones are stuffed into nearly every pocket. Instant communication has replaced listening to messages, streaming video has replaced waiting for television shows to start, Xboxes have replaced Ataris, digital images have replaced negatives, and high-speed connections have replaced the dial-up modems that nearly pushed Dan over the edge. Even emailing NASA—so exciting in 1997—would be considered old-fashioned by iGeneration standards.

iGeners see technology as a tool for participating. They follow the lives of peers electronically, posting messages, videos, and pictures for one another in social networking forums like Facebook and MySpace. They join together to tackle video games with players from around the world. They rate everything from their teachers to their favorite songs. They organize around causes and start online petitions. Where their parents and teachers see the Internet as a place for gathering *information*, the iGeneration sees the Internet as a place for simply gathering *together* (boyd, 2008).

Statistically speaking,

- 97 percent of college-aged iGeners own computers.

- 94 percent own cell phones, and 56 percent own mp3 players.

- 76 percent of iGeners use instant messaging for upwards of eighty minutes every day, and 92 percent of those same users report doing other tasks on their computers while engaged in conversations with peers.

- 59 percent of school-aged iGeners are already sharing their artwork, creating videos, designing Web pages, maintaining blogs, and remixing content created by others online.

- 55 percent have created profile pages on social networking sites like Facebook or MySpace, and 47 percent have posted images on photo-sharing sites where others could comment on them. (Junco & Mastrodicasa, 2007; Lenhart, Madden, Smith, & Macgill, 2007)

You know what the iGeners look like in your classrooms. They're the ones willing to experiment their way through anything, confident that trial and error can crack the code better than reading manuals or following directions. They're turning to the Internet first and the library second when assigned research projects. Their minds are working fast, but not always as deeply or as accurately as the adults in their lives would like (Oblinger & Oblinger, 2005).

To you, iGeners seem like professional infosnackers—flitting through sites looking for information that is easy to access, loading their papers with citations from Wikipedia, and filling their writing samples with Internet shorthand. Text-heavy passages intimidate iGeners, who are more comfortable with images and videos as sources for learning (Oblinger & Oblinger, 2005). Graphic novels, manga, and magazines have replaced novels on the iGeneration's bookshelves.

iGeners are more emotionally open than anyone from previous generations. They're comfortable building relationships online, sharing the kind of information that makes their parents uncomfortable. They like working in teams better than working alone, and they use digital opportunities for interaction to try on new identities and personalities. The introverts in your classroom often become extroverts online, finding safe opportunities to connect with peers—both in their community and around the world. For iGeners, technology is less important than the action that it enables. They're passionate about networking with others; digital tools simply make that passion possible (Oblinger & Oblinger, 2005).

Portable—and instant—communication is what matters the most to iGeners, who crave interaction and tune out the teachers who aren't engaging or whose classes move too slowly (Oblinger & Oblinger, 2005). Often bored in school, iGeners spend their days texting under their desks, snapping pictures and recording videos with their cell phones, and (im)patiently waiting for the bell to ring so they can plug themselves back in.

And if you're like many of today's teachers, the students of the iGeneration may have you completely frustrated!

The Dumbest Generation

For Dina Strasser, seventh-grade teacher and author of the widely acclaimed blog the Line (http:// theline.edublogs.org), the technology-driven lives being led by today's students carry costs that few educators or parents have ever really taken the time to consider. Students who are constantly connected end up disconnected, Dina argues, losing out on "real" experiences with other human beings or the environment around them. Local issues become irrelevant to teens that see the world as their audience. Ignoring diverse opinions is easy online.

"My worry is the fundamental concept of aloneness the Internet fosters," writes Dina, "disconnected not only from each other, but from our physical world. In terms of our *actual* human needs . . . the idea that we are, and can exist healthily, completely under our own steam is a pure falsehood. It's that simple" (Dina Strasser, personal communication, March 30, 2008).

Tom Huston—the senior associate editor for *EnlightenNext* magazine—agrees, arguing that anyone under the age of thirty tends to swim in superficiality. "Members of my generation," he writes, "lock and load our custom iTunes playlists, craft our Facebook profiles to self-satisfied perfection, and, armed with our gleefully ironic irreverence, bravely venture forth into life within glossy, opaque bubbles that reflect ourselves back to ourselves and safely protect us from jarring intrusions from the greater world beyond" (Huston, 2009).

Spend any time digging through the growing heaps of research churned out each year on the screen and media behaviors of the iGeneration, and you'll better understand how intellectually bereft Huston's "glossy, opaque bubbles" really are. Begin with the almost shocking reality that the typical U.S. teenager spends almost 325 minutes behind a screen—whether it be a television, computer, or gaming system—*per day*, a number that has been steadily increasing since 2003 (Nielsen Company, 2009). What's more, constant connectedness is rapidly spreading beyond the plug as more teens carry mobile devices with Internet capabilities.

While connected, our kids surround themselves with content that is difficult at best to admire. Despite having access to more educational media sources than previous generations (think the Discovery Channel and PBS Online), today's teens tune in to *Family Guy* and *American Dad*—close cousins of *The Simpsons*—and *American Idol*. Google, YouTube, and Yahoo! are their favorite Web destinations, and *Halo 3*—a violent first-person shooter video game rated Mature by the Entertainment Software Rating Board—was the most anticipated release by thirteen- to seventeen-year-olds since 2005 (Nielsen Company, 2009).

As anyone working with or raising teenagers can attest, gaming has become nearly ubiquitous among members of the iGeneration, with 97 percent of twelve- to seventeen-year-olds self-identifying as gamers. In fact, gaming has become one of the most prominent fixtures in the social lives of iGeners, replacing the neighborhood activities of previous generations. Groups of teens now gather—either in person or online—to play titles ranging from *Call of Duty* and *Devil May Cry* to *World of Warcraft* and *Half-Life*. Fewer than one in four teens play video games alone, spotlighting the central role that games hold in the social development of today's teens. Reasoned parents and educators have to question the significance of the time that our kids spend with controllers in their hands, especially considering the lack of evidence that collective gaming encourages civic behavior (Lenhart et al., 2008).

Social networking services like Facebook and MySpace play an equally important role in the lives of iGeners. With over half of all teens checking their social networking profiles more than once a day—and almost a quarter checking their profiles more than ten times a day—it is impossible to deny that virtual interactions are as important as face-to-face relationships for today's teens and tweens (Common Sense Media, 2009). Not surprisingly, however, these interactions aren't always positive. On social networking sites, 54 percent of teens complain about teachers, 37 percent pick on their peers, and 28 percent share personal information that they would not have shared in other forums (Common Sense Media, 2009).

Academic Performance in the iGeneration

Equally discouraging is the academic performance of the iGeneration. Despite living in a world of cutthroat global competition for knowledge-based work, American students continue to underachieve in the classroom. As McKinsey & Company demonstrated in a 2009 review of Programme for International Student Assessment results, the mathematical and scientific abilities of U.S. children lag behind students in countries that compete with the United States for high-value jobs. What's more, the gap between American teens and their international peers only grows larger the longer they stay in school. "In other words," report authors write, "American students are farthest behind just as they are about to enter higher education or the workforce" (McKinsey & Company, 2009, p. 8). A closer look at evidence of learning on the domestic front spotlights additional concerns. Only 34 percent of eighth graders demonstrated "solid" or "superior" reading abilities on the most recent National Assessment of Educational Progress (Lee, Grigg, & Donahue, 2007). Perhaps we shouldn't be surprised, though, considering that only 20 percent of seventeen-year-olds report reading for fun daily, and that fifteen- to twenty-four-year-olds spend just under nine minutes a day reading for any reason (Hess, 2008). Scholars have increasing concerns about critical thought expressed through writing—due, perhaps, to the kind of inarticulate expression found in the ninety-six text messages the average American teen sends and receives per day, a statistic that caused James Billington, the librarian of Congress, to declare the sentence the "biggest casualty" of the Internet age (Nielsen Company, 2009; Weeks, 2008).

Knowledge of the core historical events and defining pieces of literature that have shaped thinking for generations is also waning. Less than half of our teens can place the Civil War in the proper century, almost 40 percent are unsure of when World War I happened, and almost 30 percent don't know that Columbus sailed for America before 1750. While 97 percent of our teens can tie Martin Luther King Jr. to his "I have a dream" speech, only 71 percent know that John F. Kennedy once entreated Americans to "ask not what your country can do for you; ask what you can do for your country." Only 50 percent of our teens know of Job's patience, 52 percent know that George Orwell warned against tyranny, and 77 percent know that *Uncle Tom's Cabin* depicts the evils of slavery (Hess, 2008).

Statistics and trends like these led Mark Bauerlein—a professor of English at Emory University and one-time director of research and analysis at the National Endowment for the Arts—to declare the iGeneration America's dumbest generation:

> Whatever their other virtues, these minds know far too little, and they read and write and calculate and reflect way too poorly. However many hours they pass at the screen from age 11 to 25, however many blog comments they compose, intricate games they play, videos they create, personal profiles they craft, and gadgets they master, the transfer doesn't happen. The Web grows, and the young adult mind stalls. (Bauerlein, 2008, Kindle location 1683–1685)

Moving Learning Forward

Bauerlein is particularly hard on teachers and other technology advocates, arguing that the millions of dollars districts have invested in digital tools to support learning have been largely ineffectual. Combating the view that schools should provide students with more time to explore and create online, Bauerlein writes:

> Ever optimistic, techno-cheerleaders view the digital learning experience through their own motivated eyes, and they picture something that doesn't yet exist: classrooms illuminating the wide, wide world, teachers becoming twenty-first-century techno-facilitators, and students at screens inspired to ponder, imagine, reflect, analyze, memorize, recite and create. (Bauerlein, 2008, Kindle location 1900–1906)

And a closer look at the technology integration efforts in most schools might just reaffirm Bauerlein's doubts. After all, most schools are investing their professional-development technology budget in training teachers to use computers for noninstructional purposes even though new tools allow for a significant shift in pedagogy. Instead of exploring how new digital opportunities can support student-centered inquiry or otherwise enhance existing practices, today's schools are preparing their teachers to use office automation and productivity tools like Microsoft Word and PowerPoint. While fewer than half of America's teachers believe that they can use technology to plan individualized lessons, almost 70 percent feel comfortable with using technology to complete administrative tasks, resulting in digital change efforts that achieve nothing more than "adding power to a marginal teaching approach" (National Education Association, 2008, p. 29).

How does this underpreparation play out in our classrooms? The numbers are discouraging. Even as 95 percent of our teachers believe that technology improves student learning, only 40 percent report using technology to monitor individual student progress, only 37 percent report using technology to research and gather information, and only 32 percent report using technology in their daily instruction. Fewer than one classroom in five sees students engaged in collaborative work around shared digital projects (National Education Association, 2008).

Moving learning forward, then, begins by introducing teachers to ways in which digital tools can be used to encourage higher-order thinking and innovative instruction across the curriculum. iGeneration students, regardless of demographics, have shown an excitement for digital opportunities to learn, and technologists all over the world have created a range of tools that make collaboration, innovation, and individual exploration possible. Despite Bauerlein's skepticism and a mountain of statistical doubt, today's students can be inspired by technology to ponder, imagine, reflect, analyze, memorize, recite, and create—but only after we build a bridge between what they know about new tools and what we know about good teaching.

Focusing on the Verbs

Building that bridge begins by revisiting exactly what it is that we know about good teaching. While the calendar may have pushed us into the 21st century, the same traits have always defined inquisitive learners, haven't they? As noted educational historian and critic of the 21st century–skills movement Diane Ravitch writes:

> I . . . have heard quite enough about the 21st century skills that are sweeping the nation. Now, for the first time, children will be taught to think critically (never heard a word about that in the 20th century, did you?), to work in groups (I remember getting a grade on that very skill when I was in third grade a century ago), to solve problems (a brand new idea

in education), and so on. Let me suggest that it is time to be done with this unnecessary conflict about 21st century skills. Let us agree that we need all those forenamed skills, plus lots others, in addition to a deep understanding of history, literature, the arts, geography, civics, the sciences, and foreign languages. (Ravitch, 2009)

This discovery—that learning depends on skills instead of tools—is one that many educators are struggling to make. Instead of recognizing that tomorrow's professions will require workers who are intellectually adept—able to identify bias, manage huge volumes of information, persuade, create, and adapt—teachers and district technology leaders wrongly believe that tomorrow's professions will require workers who know how to blog, use wikis, or create podcasts. As a result, schools sprint in new digital directions with little thought, spending thousands on technology before carefully defining the kinds of learning that they value most. The consequences are high-tech classrooms delivering meaningless, low-level instructional experiences. "You can't *buy* change," argues Sylvia Martinez of Generation YES. "It's a process, not a purchase. The right shopping list won't change education" (smartinez, 2010).

Successful digital integration projects, on the other hand, build on the foundational belief that new technologies are nothing more than tools that can be used to teach the kinds of old-school skills that have been important in the academic and social growth of all children, regardless of what generation they were born in. For Marc Prensky, digital learning expert and author, refocusing our instructional attention requires a dedicated effort to separate nouns from verbs in conversations about teaching with technology (Prensky, 2009). Verbs are the kinds of knowledge-driven, lifelong skills that teachers know matter: thinking critically, persuading peers, presenting information in an organized and convincing fashion. Nouns are the tools that students use to practice those skills. As Prensky writes:

> In teaching, our focus needs to be on the verbs, which don't change very much, and NOT on the nouns (i.e. the technologies) which change rapidly and which are only a means. For teachers to fixate on any particular noun as the "best" way (be it books or blogs, for example) is not good for our students, as new and better nouns will shortly emerge and will continue to emerge over the course of their lifetimes.
>
> Our teaching should instead focus on the verbs (i.e. skills) students need to master, making it clear to the students (and to the teachers) that there are many tools learners can use to practice and apply them. (2009)

Following Prensky's advice by placing verbs first in instructional decision making should make 21st century learning more approachable for every teacher, including those who are uncomfortable online. While today's nouns—social bookmarking services, content aggregators, blogs, Web conferences, personal learning networks, asynchronous discussion forums, instant messaging applications—can be intimidating, educators have spoken the language of higher-order thinking since our first pedagogy classes in which we were introduced to Benjamin Bloom's *Taxonomy of Educational Objectives* (1956). We inherently recognize the difference between—and have a polished collection of strategies to support—experiences ranging from those that require simple application of knowledge to those that ask students to synthesize information or to make judgments.

A quick review of the literature around 21st century learning reveals—just as Prensky and Ravitch argue—that today's verbs bear a striking resemblance to the essential skills that Bloom described over fifty years ago. Will Richardson, instructional expert and author of *Blogs, Wikis, Podcasts, and Other Powerful Web Tools for Classrooms* (2006), detailed one set of critical verbs in a 2008 post on his blog, where he wrote:

> Our kids' futures will require them to be:
>
> - **Networked**—They'll need an "outboard brain."
> - **More collaborative**—They are going to need to work closely with people to co-create information.
> - **More globally aware**—Those collaborators may be anywhere in the world.
> - **Less dependent on paper**—Right now, we are still paper training our kids.
> - **More active**—In just about every sense of the word. Physically. Socially. Politically.
> - **Fluent in creating and consuming hypertext**—Basic reading and writing skills will not suffice.
> - **More connected**—To their communities, to their environments, to the world.
> - **Editors of information**—Something we should have been teaching them all along but is even more important now. (Richardson, 2008)

The Partnership for 21st Century Skills—an advocacy organization of business and education leaders brought together "to define a powerful vision for 21st century education and to ensure that students emerge from our schools with the skills needed to be effective citizens, workers, and leaders in the 21st century" (2009)—developed a similar set of skills in their often-cited *Framework for 21st Century Learning*. Along with a set of information, media, and technology skills, the *Framework* describes three primary learning and innovation skills (Partnership for 21st Century Skills, 2009):

1. **Creativity and innovation**—The ability to generate, evaluate, revise, and act on original ideas, both as an individual and as a member of a collaborative group.

2. **Critical thinking and problem solving**—The ability to make effective judgments based on evidence, to make connections between ideas, to reflect on learning experiences, and to evaluate potential solutions to critical issues.

3. **Communication and collaboration**—The ability to articulate clearly, listen effectively, and select communication tools appropriately while making meaningful contributions to diverse groups.

These skills are echoed in standards documents developed by national organizations representing teachers in nearly every content area. The standards of the National Council for the Social Studies (1994) call for students to explore the ways that humans organize in order to exert influence. Generating questions, synthesizing information, and participating in a community of learners are emphasized by the National Council of Teachers of English (1996), developing arguments and using reasoning to investigate are spotlighted by the National Council of Teachers of Mathematics

(2004), and thinking critically about alternative explanations is stressed by the National Academy of Sciences (1996). Even the standards set by the National Association for Sport and Physical Education (2004) highlight higher-order verbs, requiring that students learn responsible behavior and respect for others during physical activities.

So rest assured. Instead of requiring a complete overhaul of the instructional practices in your classroom or building, 21st century learning depends on nothing more than identifying the ways that new digital tools can facilitate authentic, student-centered experiences with the same enduring skills that you've been teaching for years.

Getting Started

Our purpose for writing *Teaching the iGeneration* is a simple one. Our hope is to help you find the natural overlap between the work that you already believe in and the kinds of digital tools that are defining tomorrow's learning. Each chapter introduces one of five enduring skills and abilities necessary for success in any knowledge-based enterprise. These skills include the following:

1. **Information fluency**—Intellectual discoveries rest at the heart of any true learning experience, which means that students must be able to systematically study content and question their own preconceived notions about the world around them. Questioning requires an ability to sort knowledge, identify sources of valuable information, and make frequent connections between ideas.

2. **Persuasion**—In a world in which new content can be created and published easily, students should understand the strategies used to influence audiences. They must be able to craft convincing arguments, recognize unsubstantiated claims, and find ways to raise their voices as individuals and as members of collective groups.

3. **Communication**—Collective action, regardless of the circumstance, requires skilled communicators that can create meaning and work through conflict together. Students must be able to listen, to summarize and draw conclusions, to express positions, and to see interactions with others as learning opportunities.

4. **Collaboration**—Collaboration is a defining skill of knowledge-based workplaces. To succeed in these workplaces, students must be able to appreciate alternative viewpoints, to build consensus in the face of interpersonal conflict, and to coordinate their efforts with other members of a team.

5. **Problem solving**—Our world is faced with a greater collection of borderless challenges than at any point in history. Drought, poverty, and global warming press nations to find international solutions to widespread problems. Students of the 21st century must be able to operate within this culture, constantly imagining, designing, implementing, and evaluating new approaches, regardless of the field in which they work.

Next, each chapter will detail the digital solutions that can be used to enhance—rather than replace—traditional skill-based instructional practices. Readers will study the characteristics of different types of digital tools, explore teaching tips for overcoming common challenges associated with each tool, and examine a list of free services currently available that teachers can incorporate into their instruction immediately. The tools introduced include the following:

- **Blogs**—Since the early 1990s, writers have been creating content for the Internet using blogs, one of the simplest Web 2.0 tools. Designed to make publishing instant and easy for everyone, blogs have become one of the first tools that many digital teachers embrace.

- **Wikis**—Originally created in 1995 as a tool to facilitate communication between computer programmers, wikis are public websites that allow all visitors to be editors. In innovative classrooms, wikis are providing forums for collaboration between groups of students working on shared projects.

- **Content aggregators**—The greatest challenge in a world in which digital content is being created quickly and easily by experts and amateurs alike is efficiently sifting through information to find reliable resources worth exploring. Content aggregators make this kind of targeted information filtering possible.

- **Asynchronous discussion forums**—Classroom conversations have always been a staple of intellectual development, providing students with opportunities to refine and revise their thinking about topics of interest. Asynchronous discussion forums can extend classroom conversations beyond the school day.

- **Web conferencing software**—Prime Minister Gordon Brown of the United Kingdom recently described a "global ethic" and sense of togetherness defining the character of all humans that can develop across geographic boundaries because of digital connections. Web conferencing software can make these kinds of real-time, action-oriented connections possible in any classroom.

- **Video editing applications**—With almost 80 percent of the U.S. Internet population viewing online videos each month (Lipsman, 2009), and with twenty hours of video being uploaded to YouTube each minute (Junee, 2009), it is essential for students to develop skills at creating, manipulating, and interpreting visual messages.

- **Social bookmarking and annotation tools**—Like many high school teachers, Carol Porter-O'Donnell (2004) knew that her students needed practical strategies for attacking nonfiction reading materials. As a result, she began teaching students a set of skills for annotating texts. Social bookmarking and annotation tools make it possible for students to work together to make sense of challenging classroom content that they find online.

Finally, every chapter of *Teaching the iGeneration* will end with a set of sample projects and supporting materials tailored to each enduring skill and tool type. Readers will learn how students can practice persuasive skills by writing open letters to world leaders and collaborative skills by building shared warehouses of information connected to a topic of deep personal interest. They will see how the conversation skills taught in traditional classroom settings translate to online forums focused on controversial topics. They will explore the collective intelligence that develops when information fluency tools help student groups to study together and investigate the steps that effective teachers take when introducing their classes to visuals as a medium for crafting influential messages.

It is important to note that while the print version of *Teaching the iGeneration* includes dozens of tangible handouts designed to support these activities, you can visit **go.solution-tree.com/technology** for an equally impressive and ever-changing collection of resources. There, you will find detailed sets of step-by-step directions for using some of the most popular Web 2.0 services and screencast tutorials that can guide you—or your students—through everything from publishing blog entries to editing video. You will also find updated lists of suggested services and materials for additional lessons and activities.

By extending the *Teaching the iGeneration* collection to the Web, we are hoping to avoid the all-too-common pitfall of books focused on technology: content that ends up outdated as tools and services change over time. While readers must understand that some of the resources mentioned in this book may someday be obsolete, a quick visit to **go.solution-tree.com/technology** should always connect readers to cutting-edge information about teaching with digital tools.

Better yet, all of the resources posted online—including digital versions of every handout in this text—are interactive and available for download. You will be able to fill out tables and checklists right on your computer. You will also be able to share files with your students that they can fill out electronically, save, and then turn back in to you. Over time, you are likely to find that the resources available at **go.solution-tree.com/technology** are as valuable as anything included directly in this text.

Global Poverty's Role in *Teaching the iGeneration*

It is also important to note that we designed many of the sample projects presented in *Teaching the iGeneration* to focus student attention on global poverty, largely because middle and high school students—the target audience for our text—are often highly motivated by the idea of fairness. Novels connected to justice and injustice like *To Kill a Mockingbird*, *The Adventures of Huckleberry Finn*, *Where the Lilies Bloom*, and *Roll of Thunder, Hear My Cry*, and topics connected to justice and injustice like animal cruelty, the Holocaust, and racism have formed the cornerstone of the curriculum in the American classroom for generations.

Global poverty stands as the single greatest contemporary issue connected to the theme of fairness and justice. Despite remarkable advances in the quality of life in developed nations during the past century, over 80 percent of the world's population continues to live on less than ten dollars a day (World Bank, 2008). Infant mortality rates remain more than ten times higher in developing countries than in the industrialized world, life expectancies remain more than ten years shorter in developing countries than in the industrialized world, and residents of industrialized nations will make almost $3 million more in the course of their lifetimes than their neighbors in the developing world (United Nations Children's Fund, 2008).

Examine state standards for social studies instruction, and you'll find natural connections to the themes of worldwide poverty echoed in the required curriculum across grade levels. In North Carolina, sixth graders are expected to identify connections between different levels of economic development and quality-of-life indicators like purchasing power, literacy rates, and life expectancy (North Carolina Department of Public Instruction, 2006). Texas ninth graders are asked to use political, economic, social, and demographic data to study the standard of living in nations around the world (Texas Education Agency, Curriculum Division, 1998). Juniors in New York State must use data to develop new approaches and solutions to economic problems (New York State Education Department, Curriculum, Instruction and Instructional Technology, 1998).

Poverty also plays a prominent role in the global citizenship curriculums being developed and delivered in public schools and universities. Many of those curricula draw ideas from Oxfam, a British organization that encourages students to take action on world issues such as poverty and injustice. For Oxfam, thinking about poverty begins between the ages of five and seven when students are introduced to the concepts of rich and poor. As students get older, the conversations become increasingly more complex. Eleven-year-olds study the inequalities between regions, fourteen-year-olds study the implications that poverty has on world peace, and sixteen-year-olds develop an awareness of the primary positions in world debates about issues connected to poverty (Oxfam Development Education Programme, 2006).

For all of these reasons, global poverty can provide a natural context for digital projects that have meaning and motivate kids. Remember, though, that global poverty is not the only motivating topic for today's students. The materials in this text that address global poverty directly can easily be tailored to any contentious issue—global warming, cloning, year-round schooling, banning of books, the systematic elimination of the arts in schools—that connects to your curriculum and is appropriate for your students.

Chapter Overviews

There is no one right way to read *Teaching the iGeneration*. Some readers will begin from page one and work their way straight through until the end. Others will identify an enduring skill, tool, or project that can be easily integrated into their current work. To help you decide on the strategy that is right for you, here is an overview of each of the five chapters.

Chapter 1: Managing Information in the 21st Century

In just a few short years, the way that researchers interact with content has fundamentally changed. A reliance on the Internet, in which a seemingly endless pile of sources awaits, has replaced our reliance on libraries and encyclopedias as homes for information. With nothing more than a few quick clicks, students can find everything from articles and research studies to blog entries, interviews, photos, and videos on nearly any topic. The challenge rests in sifting through this content quickly and reliably, identifying sources worth trusting and eliminating sources that aren't.

Chapter 1 introduces teachers to several strategies, resources, and tools that can help students fluently manage and evaluate online information. Specifically, teachers will learn how student search efforts can be structured, how Web-based resources can be evaluated for reliability, how RSS feed readers can provide instant access to customized collections of organized information, and how social bookmarking and shared annotation tools can be integrated into any classroom's research efforts.

Chapter 2: Writing Open Letters to World Leaders

Persuasion has always been a skill that defined the most influential individuals in our society, whose convincing messages gain traction with powerful audiences and lead to direct change. Digital tools for publishing, however, make it possible for more people to be noticed—a new reality that hasn't gone *unnoticed* by governments. In a 2009 TED Talk, Gordon Brown—serving as the prime minister of the United Kingdom—argued that our wired world is allowing regular citizens to join together around ideas and to put pressure on their governments like never before (Brown, 2009).

In chapter 2, teachers will study several strategies for introducing written persuasion—the most approachable forum for gaining influence—to students. Specifically, teachers will examine the critical elements of persuasion, learn how microlending projects designed to support entrepreneurs in developing nations can provide opportunities to practice persuasion, and explore how blogs can be used to elevate student voice. All of the materials included in this chapter are designed to walk students through the process of creating an online open letter to a world leader addressing a controversial issue.

Chapter 3: Telling Powerful Visual Stories

While the text-based persuasive strategies introduced in chapter 2 are both essential and effective, visual content—still images and streaming video—is becoming an increasingly common tool for gaining influence in today's world. Knowing that the iGeneration has been surrounded by visual messages for a lifetime, everyone from politicians and educators to corporate executives and army recruiters is working to use still images and video-based content to communicate important messages. It is important to understand, however, that while the medium for communicating persuasive messages may have changed, the characteristics of the most influential ideas remain the same.

Chapter 3 introduces the important role that surprising, concrete, and emotional stories have always played in crafting memorable ideas. Then, teachers learn how these same traits can be used to create powerful still images and simple videos. We explore the difference between traditional and digital storytelling, discuss the role that Creative Commons content can play in responsible digital authoring, and introduce a scaffolding process for digital video projects. Finally, we share a series of templates, study guides, samples, and rubrics for structuring visual influence projects.

Chapter 4: Studying Challenging Topics Together

One of the most important lessons for teachers interested in integrating technology into their instruction is to meet students where they are. Learning experiences that incorporate the kinds of technology habits and behaviors that the iGeneration has already embraced beyond school are far more likely to generate high levels of enthusiasm, investment, and motivation. For most teachers, this means finding ways for students to use new media tools to communicate with one another.

Chapter 4 is designed to show teachers how to pair their students' natural desire to communicate with learning-based outcomes. Specifically, teachers will study the differences between collaborative and competitive dialogue and learn more about the role that Socratic circles can play in developing responsible communication habits in students. They will also examine how students are already using digital tools to facilitate social interactions, reflect on the implications that these behaviors have for teaching and learning, and examine a series of materials and suggestions for systematically structuring student-centered synchronous and asynchronous conversations around controversial issues.

Chapter 5: Collaborating to Solve Problems

While evaluating information, elevating awareness, and attempting to influence thinking about controversial issues create many opportunities for meaningful learning experiences, productive global citizens must also be skilled at developing shared solutions to the challenges facing our planet. They must see value in crafting ideas together and in collecting multiple perspectives. They must be willing to open their own work to review and recognize that groups are inherently smarter than individuals when tackling particularly knotty issues. To put it simply, collaborative problem solving must be embraced in order for our world to survive.

Chapter 5 begins by introducing teachers to the critical elements of any attempt to promote problem solving in their classroom. It then explores the important role that groups can play in solving the most complex problems and how companies are using wikis—one of the most approachable digital tools—to promote collaborative problem solving in the workplace. Finally, it provides a series of handouts, templates, tips, and tricks for starting classroom-based wiki projects that give students opportunities to experiment with developing solutions together.

■ ■

However you choose to tackle our text, remember that the purpose of *Teaching the iGeneration* is not to introduce you to new gadgets and gizmos. Instead, our goal is to help you find ways in which today's tools can support the kinds of experiences that encourage students to learn. As Peter Cookson writes, learning is a

> continuum of cognitive and expressive experiences that range from gathering data for the purpose of understanding the world; to organizing data into useful and coherent informational patterns; to applying information to real questions and problems and, in the process, creating knowledge; to developing wisdom that offers the hope of transcendent unity. (2009, p. 8)

Reintroducing that sense of rigorous and systematic study to the iGeneration—a generation that has grown up connected but has failed to understand the power of connections—requires nothing more than a teacher who is willing to show students how the tools that they've already embraced can make learning efficient, empowering, and intellectually satisfying.

Are you ready to be that teacher?

CHAPTER ONE

Managing Information in the 21st Century

One key point often forgotten in conversations about teaching and learning in the 21st century is that many of the concepts important to learners of earlier generations are equally important today. Students still explore the ways that governments interact with people and examine the connections between organisms and their environments. Challenging studies of controversial topics still define civics classes, and creative problem solving has always been a constant in the math classroom. Famous citizens—politicians, artists, scientists, and mathematicians—serve as reminders of the character traits we most admire, and ancient civilizations allow students to draw conclusions about life today.

What's more, the core instructional techniques of most classrooms remain unchanged. Students are still crafting written reports and position statements on topics of personal interest and global importance. Powerful conversations give students the opportunity to polish foundational beliefs. Teachers continue to expose students to the content of their curricula in the hopes of challenging preconceived notions; hands-on experiences are as essential to real learning today as they have been for generations. In all of these circumstances, information—whether it is collected beyond the classroom or generated independently by students—remains at the center of the learning experience.

That's where the similarities between learning yesterday and today end. While the students of previous generations interacted with information by poking through card catalogs, manageable handfuls of books from the local library, or sets of encyclopedias purchased one volume at a time from the local grocery store, today's students are surrounded by seas of online content. By July of 2008, Google had indexed 1 trillion unique URLs on the Internet, returning thousands of search results on almost any topic (Alpert & Hajaj, 2008). By November of 2009, eighty-five thousand active Wikipedia contributors had created nearly 20 million pages of content written in 260 languages and covering over 3 million unique topics (Wikipedia, 2009). Even nontraditional content is being published and consumed in seemingly impossible numbers. Consider the nearly 15 billion videos that U.S. Internet users watched in March 2009, or the nine hundred thousand blog posts that are generated every single day, and it's easy to see how *too much* information can become a serious problem for today's student (Lipsman, 2009; Winn, 2009).

To make matters worse, content posted online can suffer from the kinds of issues that traditional media sources—generally scrutinized carefully for reliability and quality before publication—have worked diligently to police. Websites can be outdated, contain inaccurate information, or be created by amateurs with little professional experience. Authors can attempt to influence their audience by posting biased information intentionally designed to deceive. While digital publishing has made content creation possible for more people, it has also removed the conventional barriers to publishing—high costs, trained writers, limited access to content—that traditionally served as reliability filters (Shirky, 2002).

Success in today's digital world, then, requires students to be fluent with information. Before students can even begin to interact with content in a meaningful way, they must be able to search efficiently by picking out reliable information and eliminating sources that stretch the truth. They must also be able to organize resources into collections that are easy to navigate and return to. Finally, they must be able to collaborate around research collections, taking advantage of the collective intelligence found whenever groups work together on information-based tasks (Surowiecki, 2004).

Luckily for learners, just as the volume of information available online has multiplied exponentially in the past decade, so has access to digital tools that can make managing information easy. The resources presented in this chapter are designed to introduce teachers and students to a handful of these tools—and to the core behaviors that are necessary before students can effectively navigate new digital landscapes.

Readers will learn about improved search engine features such as Google's Wonder Wheel (www .googlewonderwheel.com), a tool that can help users break broad topics—and the search results that go with them—into sets of specific and manageable subcategories. They'll also learn about content aggregators such as Pageflakes (www.pageflakes.com) that automatically monitor sets of frequently updated websites, and collaborative research tools such as Diigo (www.diigo.com) that allow groups to build shared collections of resources and to have conversations around the ideas they are exploring together. Finally, they'll learn how to identify reliable websites, an essential skill for becoming a knowledgeable consumer of online content in the 21st century.

Searching Efficiently

We've chosen to start *Teaching the iGeneration* with a study of the skills necessary for managing information because every skill, conversation, and project spotlighted later in this book will require students to collect research. The first step in preparing students to pull together information in a media landscape dominated by digital content should always be to introduce strategies for searching the Web efficiently—a practice that 49 percent of all Internet users tackle on a daily basis and that 87 percent of digital kids engage in at least once per week (Fallows, 2008; Horst, Herr-Stephenson, & Robinson, 2009).

Internet searching may seem like a straightforward task, but anyone working in today's class-rooms knows that students approach Web searches in an apparently haphazard manner, jumping from link to link looking for information in a process that researchers Heather Horst, Becky Herr-Stephenson, and Laura Robinson (2009) call *fortuitous searching*. "Fortuitous searching represents a strategy for finding information and reading online that is different from the way kids are taught to research and review information in texts at school," write Horst et al. "Students are taught to use tools such as identifying a purpose for reading, activating prior knowledge, predicting the content of a text before and during reading . . . By contrast, fortuitous searching relies upon the intuition of the search engine and the predictive abilities of the reader" (p. 55).

While fortuitous searching may be a successful strategy for students exploring topics that they know well, it collapses whenever researchers lack the background knowledge that makes intuition and effective prediction possible. Young researchers studying new concepts enter generic terms—*volcanoes, World War II, famous mathematicians*—into search engines and are forced to sift through pages of websites unconnected to the topic of study or too sophisticated to understand. Inexperienced students also select topics that are too narrow for a research project—the average temperature of magma, the color of Allied uniforms during World War II, the birthplace of Pythagoras—ending up with limited content that cannot support an interesting and extensive final product.

The traditional solution to this challenge—and one that still works well—is to show students how to identify subcategories related to their research before turning to the Web. Identifying subcategories can be done by generating lists of questions about a topic of study, or by writing personal statements expressing individual reasons for pursuing a research project. Researchers can also focus on the chronologies, technologies, geographies, or biographies connected to particular themes—or even use the subheadings in common encyclopedias to set direction (Samuels, 2009). While methodically adding this kind of structure to research projects may seem to constrict the natural research practices of tweens and teens, predetermined subcategories increase the likelihood that students will identify sources of value once they've started searching.

A digital solution to the challenge of focusing research efforts is to introduce your classes to the Google Wonder Wheel. Designed specifically to break large concepts, events, and ideas into manageable groups of related websites, the Wonder Wheel—a feature found under the Show Options tab at the top of any Google search page—can quickly point student researchers in new directions and help organize thinking around almost any issue. Students using the Wonder Wheel to study World War II, for example, would see Google's initial 101 million search results sorted into the eight subcategories shown in figure 1.1 (page 20).

What makes the Wonder Wheel even more valuable is that as each link on the original web is selected, Google refines the search results further, generating new subcategories and providing access to smaller collections of websites that are more likely to contain useful information (see fig. 1.2, page 20).

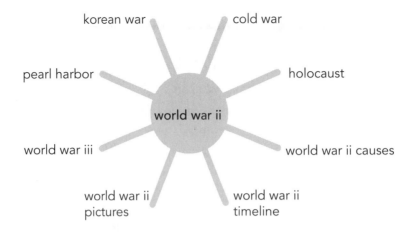

Figure 1.1: World War II in Google's Wonder Wheel.

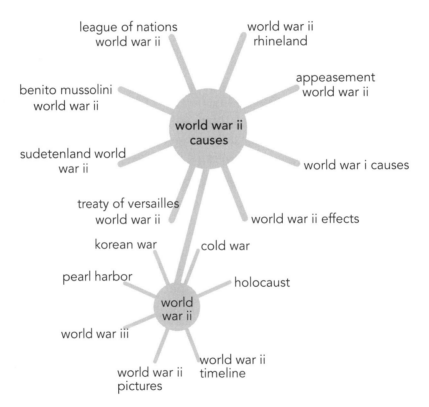

Figure 1.2: World War II subcategories in Google's Wonder Wheel.

By instantly categorizing search results in an interactive web, the Wonder Wheel models the process that skilled researchers use to narrow topics and introduces students with little background knowledge to the key concepts connected to any subject. The "Google's Wonder Wheel" handout (pages 32–34) included at the end of this chapter encourages students to use the Wonder Wheel to search for information on a controversial topic, to track the work that Google does when sorting search results into subcategories, and to reflect on the Wonder Wheel as a tool for facilitating research.

Rating the Reliability of Websites

While Google's Wonder Wheel can help students narrow topics and efficiently predict new directions for research projects, it offers no guarantees that the search results returned come from reliable sources. Just like researchers in any generation, your students must become adept at identifying the characteristics of sources that can't be trusted—and if the results of a 2006 study by the New Literacies Research Lab at the University of Connecticut are any indication, this skill can be harder to master than you think. After introducing one of the Internet's most famous hoax websites to twenty-five seventh graders identified as accomplished online readers, researchers found that all but one believed the site was credible (Krane, 2006). In a related project in South Carolina, the New Literacies Research team found that nearly 60 percent of students surveyed report never bothering to check the accuracy of websites they are using for research (Bettelheim, 2007).

As intimidating as these numbers may seem, teaching your students to ask four questions while working online will leave them prepared to spot all but the most sophisticated hoaxes.

1. **Does the information on this website make sense?** The single best tool that researchers have for spotting sources that can't be trusted is their own common sense! Teach students to approach online content with healthy skepticism—and to find new sources whenever a site seems suspicious. With thousands of pages of content available online, there is never a good reason to settle on a source that contains questionable claims.

2. **What kinds of sources does this website link to?** Have you ever visually skimmed a Wikipedia entry? If you have, you've probably noticed that most entries include dozens of links. That's because responsible website authors understand that linking to sites containing proof of their claims earns respect and increases the credibility of their content. For student researchers, this means doubting sites that fail to provide readers with external sources to explore—or that link to sites that seem equally suspicious.

3. **Can I find any evidence of bias on this website?** Authors of sites studying controversial issues often have strong opinions about the topics that they are tackling. As a result, they tend to rely on emotionally loaded words and phrases that suggest unusual levels of urgency, passion, or action. While emotionally loaded words and phrases do not automatically mean that content is unreliable, they do suggest that an author is biased—and biased authors may intentionally fail to tell readers "the whole truth" about an issue.

4. **What does the fine print say?** Few students really read the fine print on any website. In fact, it's likely that they rarely even notice the small links titled "Disclaimers," "Terms of Service," "Frequently Asked Questions" (FAQs), or "Contact Us" buried in the header or the footer of most sites. That's a recipe for disaster considering that this often-hidden content is usually the best place to rate the reliability of any website. People looking to protect themselves from being tricked online have to take the time to poke through the fine print—and to learn more about the authors—of the sites that they are studying.

These questions are introduced in the activity "Spotting Websites You Just Can't Trust" (pages 35–37), which asks students to look at the same website spotlighted by the New Literacies Research team: an effort to save the endangered—and completely fictional—Pacific Northwest Tree Octopus.

Organizing Information

While independent searches will always play an important role in the study habits of today's learners, success in a world in which thousands of pages of new content are posted daily and sites are changed almost hourly depends on a more proactive approach to information management. Success depends on the ability to fluently sift through digital noise and get ready access to information of interest. Content aggregators—also called feed readers—can help anyone consume online information more efficiently.

Feed readers are free, Web-based applications that automatically check sites with frequently updated content. Users begin their work with feed readers by creating customized collections of interesting sites they'd like to follow, a simple process that involves nothing more than copying and pasting Web addresses into the appropriate menu bar of a content aggregator. Each time any of the sources in a user's customized collection changes, feed readers retrieve links to the new content, making it possible to instantly skim additions to dozens of websites in one place and at one time. For the 43 percent of online consumers using feed readers in the United States (Rotman-Epps, 2008), managing information goes from a frustrating search through thousands of sites to an efficient review of several trusted sources.

Classroom teachers are using content aggregators for three primary purposes, the first of which is to create resource collections for student researchers. Facilitating classroom research projects almost always begins by pointing students to sets of sources that are reliable. Feed readers, which often allow users to make their customized collections of sites publicly visible, can automate this process. Each time that you begin a new unit of study, track down several current sources and organize them on a new page in a feed reader. By doing so, you can give students an online destination for accurate—and constantly updated—content covering the topic that you are studying in class. Need an example of what this could look like in action? Then check out this collection of current events websites that is being used by sixth graders to study the geography of Europe and Africa: www.pageflakes.com/wferriter/16714925

Second, teachers can use content aggregators to monitor sites on which students are creating content or collaborating with one another online. Ask teachers new to digital tools about their greatest fears, and you're likely to hear one answer time and again: "How am I supposed to monitor all of the content that my kids are creating? What happens if they post something inappropriate for the world to see?" Thankfully, feed readers make digital monitoring easy. Paste the Web address for online projects—collaborative wikis, classroom blogs, asynchronous conversations between students—into your feed reader, and you'll be notified every time new content is added by students.

Finally, teachers can use content aggregators to follow the thoughts and ideas of other teaching professionals. For classroom teachers, the most meaningful professional development opportunities begin and end with exposure to like-minded colleagues who are willing to make their practice transparent. While finding job-embedded time for this kind of collaborative reflection has always been a challenge, digital forums are breaking down the traditional barriers to learning in the schoolhouse (Ferriter, 2009). Each day, educators are joining together in online discussion groups or writing blogs that freely share resources and ideas with the world. If you are willing to invest a bit of time and effort into tracking down these conversations—and organizing them into feed readers—you can create a differentiated tool for your own personal growth. Visit www.pageflakes.com/wferriter/16618841 to explore one teacher's customized collection of professional feeds.

Like any digital application, there are literally dozens of different feed reader programs to choose from, each with unique strengths and weaknesses. While it is impossible to predict which aggregators will remain popular and available over time, three have currently caught the attention of educators. Many teachers are drawn to the Google Reader (www.google.com/reader) because it can be accessed with the same login as other Google services like Gmail and Google Docs. Others are drawn to the clean, advertisement-free layout of the pages provided by Netvibes (www.netvibes.com). Finally, Pageflakes (www.pageflakes.com) has worked to develop a teacher version of their tool (http://teacher.pageflakes.com) that includes an online grade tracker, a task list, and a built-in writing tutor. Pageflakes users can also embed blogs and discussion forums directly into their customized feed collections, creating an all-in-one digital home that students can use to study content together.

The online-only handout "Using Feed Readers to Organize Student Thinking"—posted at **go.solution-tree.com/technology**—introduces readers to Pageflakes and explains how teachers can design resource pages for student study groups complete with to-do lists and message boards. Also visit **go.solution-tree.com/technology** for links to all the websites in this text.

Collaborating Around Research

Learning to search the Web efficiently, identify the characteristics of reliable websites, and use feed readers to organize information are largely independent tasks, aren't they? And while they are essential skills for navigating a digital landscape, today's students also need to learn to work collectively around research. That's where social bookmarking and shared annotation tools come in.

Becoming increasingly important for managing shared collections of information, social bookmarking and annotation tools allow groups of users to follow one another's Web-based discoveries. For teachers willing to push the digital envelope, these tools can make collaborative research even more efficient and interesting for students. The challenge, however, is that social bookmarking and annotation are research practices that many students—and most teachers—have little experience with.

Social Bookmarking

Designed to allow users to categorize Web finds through the use of tags—keywords that allow for easy searching and grouping of content—social bookmarking applications take advantage of the wisdom of millions of users to identify resources worth exploring. In their simplest form, social bookmarking applications allow users to organize their own personal bookmarks in an online forum accessible from any computer connected to the Internet.

When users share their bookmarks and tag collections with a group, however, their favorite resources become instantly available—and searchable—to anyone who cares to look. That means if your students are working with peers on a research project, they can see what their partners are reading related to their topic of study. Essentially, users of social bookmarking applications can help one another sift through the volumes of content available online. Rather than starting from Google, social bookmarking users narrow their focus by first exploring links their peers have bookmarked.

Like any collaborative school-based experience, successful social bookmarking projects depend on a teacher's ability to introduce productive group structures and behaviors. Clearly defining the tasks that students are expected to complete while working with one another helps reduce the kinds of frustrations that arise when students wrestle with new responsibilities and work patterns. Teachers that require students to brainstorm lists of common tags, create digital forums for communication, and set clear starting and ending dates for participation take the ambiguity that leads to friction out of social bookmarking projects.

Initial social bookmarking efforts also thrive when teachers assign specific roles to each member of student research groups. Specific roles assigned in advance serve as a tangible introduction to the kinds of unique practices that effective participants in social bookmarking communities engage in. They also ensure that the early efforts of student groups are successful, both in creating reliable collections of shared content and in learning to collaborate electronically, which builds classroom confidence. While the adult users of social bookmarking applications are unlikely to identify specific tasks for individual participants to complete, their behaviors generally fall into the same broad categories. Those categories can be introduced to students through the following six roles: Original Thinkers, Connectors, Reliability Cops, Mind Readers, Johnny Opposites, and the Cleaning Crew.

Original Thinkers

Any group of students working together with social bookmarking applications depends on having a healthy collection of Web links worth exploring. The Original Thinker's role in a social bookmarking group is to bring content to the collective table by searching for websites connected to the current topic of study.

While volume matters (Original Thinkers should plan to bookmark upwards of twenty sites for each research thread in order to ensure a measure of reliability in the information stream that a group studies), quality of content counts, too. Original Thinkers are essentially information filters for their partners. Careful selections can help groups make quick work of shared assignments.

Connectors

During the course of any research project, new strands of thought will naturally arise. The group studying Woodstock will want to learn more about acoustics. The group studying the Vietnam War will want to learn more about Cambodia. The group studying prime numbers will want to learn more about Euclid and ancient Greece.

The Connector's role in a social bookmarking group is to be on the constant lookout for links related to these kinds of secondary themes. Without Connectors, social bookmarking groups will struggle to build the background knowledge necessary for understanding their primary topics.

Reliability Cops

While online resources have definitely made researching easier, they have also made researching riskier. That's because anyone can write anything online, whether or not it is true. Bogus websites filled with untrustworthy information can be found in any set of search results that groups study.

That's where Reliability Cops come in. Reliability Cops must know everything there is to know about sniffing out websites that can't be trusted, and they must be willing to review every website that social bookmarking groups spotlight as worthy of continued study. Reliability Cops should delete any fishy sites from a group's shared collection. The handout "Judging Quality Web Links" (pages 38–39) provides students with a checklist to help rate Web resources.

Mind Readers

Some of the most valuable sources for finding new articles in social bookmarking applications are the libraries of links automatically generated by popular services like Diigo and Delicious. Generally organized by tag, these libraries—which Diigo calls "bookmark lists" (www.diigo.com/list/home), and which Delicious calls "popular tags" (http://delicious.com/?view=tags)—sort every tag used by every user, creating a catalog of potential sources that groups can use when researching.

The Mind Reader's role in a social bookmarking group is to poke through these tag libraries looking for sites that may be valuable. Essentially, Mind Readers are looking into the collective brain of other users of social bookmarking services to tap into materials that their groups may have missed.

Johnny Opposites

Collections of Web links built with social bookmarking tools are inherently inclined to bias. After all, individual users make personal choices about the overall value of a site before adding it to a group's growing resources. Tackling controversial topics can result in one-sided studies. Deeply religious students may select different information to spotlight about natural selection and adaptation than students whose parents are university biology professors. Conservative students may select different information to spotlight about the 2008 U.S. presidential election than students who have recently joined the High School Democrats of America.

The role of Johnny Opposites in social bookmarking groups is to make sure that personal biases don't taint a set of links by intentionally searching for sites that represent alternative viewpoints on any hot-button issue that their groups are exploring.

The Cleaning Crew

Social bookmarking efforts often collapse for one reason: group members get lazy and fail to annotate the shared links or to follow any kind of common tagging language. The result: haphazard collections of seemingly random Web links that are no easier to explore than simple Google searches.

That's where members of the Cleaning Crew come in. Understanding the important role that accurate titles, clean descriptions, and common tags play in efficient learning, the Cleaning Crew constantly reviews the bookmarks added to shared collections and polishes incomplete entries.

■ ■ ■ ■ ■ ■ ■ ■ ■ ■ ■ ■ ■ ■ ■ ■ ■ ■ ■

At the end of the chapter, we've included the checklist "Social Bookmarking as a Research Tool" (pages 40–41) that student research groups can use to guide their social bookmarking efforts; in addition, visit **go.solution-tree.com/technology** for a series of handouts and tip sheets that can help introduce students to social bookmarking. Directions for setting up student accounts and class groups in Diigo (www.diigo.com)—one of the most popular social bookmarking applications—can be found in the online-only handout "Diigo Social Bookmarking Directions for Teachers." Simple Diigo user directions—adding bookmarks, using tags effectively, starting conversations about research collections—are included in the online-only handout "Diigo Social Bookmarking Directions for Students." Finally, a note-taking guide designed to introduce students to common roles in social bookmarking groups is included in the online-only handout "Social Bookmarking Roles."

Shared Annotation

For students—who are inherently social creatures—the shared annotation features of Diigo are the most motivating, because they make ongoing conversations around content possible. After installing a simple toolbar to their Internet browser, Diigo users can add highlights and text annotations to any Web-based resource. For student research groups exploring content for classroom projects, this option provides a measure of targeted exploration between like-minded thinkers. Questions can be asked, thoughts can be challenged, and collective conclusions can be drawn quickly, easily, and transparently. No longer are novice researchers left to make sense of their studies alone. Instead, from any computer at any time, students can actively engage in a kind of "new reading" that adds real value to the research experience—a value that instructional expert Will Richardson believes will change the way that all of us interact with text:

> More and more I'm finding Diigo annotations and notes cropping up on the articles and essays that I read, and by and large I've found the commenters to be serious, thoughtful and articulate. . . . Those of us who are mucking around in these new reading and writing spaces have no formal training in it, obviously, just a passion to connect and a willingness to experiment and engage in conversations around the topics that interest us. (2009)

While there has been little effort to formally train students to work in new reading and writing spaces thus far, formal training can certainly help the shared annotation efforts in your classroom. Much like the structures suggested for social bookmarking projects, groups engaged in early attempts at shared annotation need clear tasks and timelines for their work. More importantly, students need training in the kinds of comments that add value to shared annotation projects. The language of productive, content-driven conversations needs to be systematically introduced in classrooms, otherwise students will revert to the informal interactions that define their online lives beyond school. Specifically, teachers structuring successful shared annotation projects introduce three conversation behaviors to their students: spotlighting key content, responding to peers, and asking questions.

Spotlighting Key Content

Shared annotation efforts depend on the ability of group members to identify content in online sources that will stimulate conversation. Group members who spot potentially valuable information must first highlight it and then add thoughtful annotations explaining the role that the content can play in a group's research efforts. Initial annotations must include sufficient detail to make a researcher's thinking clear and should be written using age-appropriate standards for grammar and spelling. To do otherwise makes communicating with digital group members inefficient and frustrating.

The pitfall for spotlighting key content in online annotation projects will resonate with any teacher who has taught note taking in their classrooms: students tend to add too many highlights, obscuring content that is truly valuable. To avoid this common trap, emphasize selective highlighting skills in your classroom. Require students to read an entire selection before adding any highlights. Then, encourage students to single out words and phrases rather than complete paragraphs of text. Finally, ask students to explain how the text they have chosen to highlight will benefit their group's research efforts (Santa, Havens, & Valdes, 2004).

Responding to Peers

Early efforts at shared annotation almost always reveal the same pattern: students act in an egocentric manner, adding their own highlights and comments to a text but failing to read and respond to the thoughts of others. This is a natural pattern both for younger students who aren't developmentally ready to think beyond themselves, and for older students who have inadvertently learned to act as individuals when it comes to schoolwork. It is also a pattern exacerbated by the novelty of new technologies. Students can be so excited about experimenting with digital tools that they overlook the content generated by other members of their research groups.

To avoid this trap, teachers must emphasize the important role that responses play in shared conversations around text. Start by encouraging students to read and react to the thoughts of their peers before adding new annotations or highlights to shared texts. Introduce the language of good responses by sharing simple sentence starters (*I wonder if . . . This reminds me of . . . This will be important to us when . . . I think this connects best to . . . I'm concerned that . . . I'm not sure I agree with . . .*) that can be used in conversations with classmates (Copeland, 2005). Model the kinds of comments that students can make when responding to peers by joining conversations around articles that research groups are studying. Shared annotation projects become truly productive only after students embrace the opportunity to react to the thinking of others.

Asking Questions

A third and final lesson that students tackling shared annotation projects must learn is that questions are the lifeblood of any learning experience. Without questions, good conversations simply die. That means almost every comment added to a shared text should end with a provocative question—or a series of questions—designed to elicit further conversation. Students can use questions to ask for specific feedback from group members, to push against the thinking of peers, to set new directions for research, or to clarify misunderstood positions.

Make questioning a more important part of your classroom's annotation efforts by celebrating the best questions added by peers to conversations. Create question banks for students to explore that include samples of the kinds of questions that continue conversations. Most importantly, model openness to being questioned by spotlighting instances in shared annotation efforts when students push back against your thinking. Practicing interaction with questions will increase the depth and quality of the conversations that your students are having in shared annotation projects.

■ ■ ■ ■ ■ ■ ■ ■ ■ ■ ■ ■ ■ ■ ■ ■ ■ ■ ■

Ensuring that these kinds of conversation behaviors become second nature in your classroom starts by assigning specific roles to members of student research groups working on shared readings for the first time. Rotating students through roles—and publicly spotlighting outstanding performances in class—can help guarantee that effective annotation habits take hold in your classroom. Five fun potential roles covering the kinds of behaviors essential to successful annotation efforts include Captain Cannonball, the Provocateur, the Middle Man, the Author's Worst Nightmare, and the Repo Man.

Captain Cannonball

Good conversations only begin with participants who are willing and able to find interesting ideas to talk about. That is Captain Cannonball's role in a shared annotation group. With a critical eye and an understanding of a group's interests and responsibilities, Captain Cannonball should find four or five key points in a shared reading to highlight and should craft initial questions for other readers to consider. Captain Cannonball's choices are important. The success of a shared reading often depends on the quality of the first comments and questions added.

The Provocateur

The best conversations always include a bit of passion. Disagreements, after all, are really nothing more than evidence of deep thinking as participants work to defend, explain, revise, or refine their personal beliefs. Sadly, these opportunities for genuine learning are few and far between in school conversations because everyone plays nice, not wanting to make waves or rock the boat. The Provocateur's role in a shared annotation group is to stir things up a bit, challenging the thinking of peers in the conversation. Directly responding to the comments made by others, the Provocateur reminds everyone that there are two sides to every story.

The Middle Man

Participants who are skilled at finding the common ground between different positions are just as important to successful conversations. Pointing out the overlap between two seemingly contradictory points of view helps all members of a group remain connected to one another and highlights areas for continued study. The Middle Man's role in a group annotation is to carefully consider the different perspectives being shared, looking for connections. Middle men are often the glue that holds contentious conversations together.

The Author's Worst Nightmare

Shared annotation tools like Diigo allow groups to do something that was once unheard of: with a few digital clicks, users can challenge statements and ideas made by any author. No longer are readers required to simply accept that authors are experts who have the final word on topics being studied. Instead, readers can publicly push back against the assertions and ideas of authors.

That's the role of the Author's Worst Nightmare in a shared annotation group. Armed with a healthy dose of skepticism, the Author's Worst Nightmare questions statements made and conclusions drawn throughout a shared reading. While groups may eventually decide that an author's assertions are spot-on, the Author's Worst Nightmare's primary responsibility is to make sure that every point is put through the fires of reflection.

The Repo Man

Shared conversations are only successful if groups walk away with a collection of shared ideas that can be used to focus future work. That's where the Repo Man comes in. The Repo Man's role in a shared annotation group is to carefully monitor conversations, looking for summary points that define exactly what it is that a group is learning together during the course of a collective reading. While the Repo Man's real work begins as a conversation is ending, he or she must stay in tune with the thoughts and ideas being shared as a conversation develops in order to identify important "takeaways" that a group can learn from.

■ ■

Along with a checklist that can guide student groups tackling shared annotation projects for the first time ("Shared Annotation Checklist," pages 42–43), an activity designed to encourage students to reflect on the characteristics of quality annotations ("Reflecting on Diigo Annotations," pages 44–45), and the rubric "Scoring Shared Annotation Efforts" (pages 46–47) that are included at the end of this chapter, a series of handouts, tutorials, and tip sheets—posted online at **go.solution-tree .com/technology**—can help you deliver shared annotation training to your classes. Much like the resources provided for teachers interested in social bookmarking, you will find step-by-step advice in the online-only handouts "Diigo Shared Annotation Directions for Teachers" and "Diigo Shared Annotation Directions for Students." You will also find "Shared Annotation Roles," an online-only handout students can use to take notes on the different roles and responsibilities in shared annotation groups.

Final Thoughts

Since the 1990s, researchers have been attempting to describe a potential social crisis caused by inequitable access to new tools and technologies. According to this thinking, poor and minority communities would only fall further behind in a world working online. This *digital divide*—a term coined in the mid-1990s—exacerbated a condition that Pippa Norris, the McGuire Lecturer in Comparative Politics at the John F. Kennedy School of Government, Harvard University, once described as "information poverty." She wrote:

> As the Internet evolved, a darker vision has been articulated among cyber-pessimists who regard digital technology as a Pandora's box, unleashing new inequalities of power and wealth, reinforcing deeper divisions between the information rich and poor, the tuned-in and the tuned-out, the activists and the disengaged. (2001, p. 13)

Today, however, the low cost of both computers and access to the Web has nearly eliminated this traditional view of the digital divide. Statistics collected from the 2008 Pew Internet and American Life Project survey (Fox & Vitak, 2008) show that 73 percent of the population of the United States are actively using the Internet, including:

- 90 percent of Americans between the ages of eighteen and twenty-nine

- 85 percent of Americans between the ages of thirty and forty-nine

- 63 percent of the rural residents of the United States

- 63 percent of Americans whose formal schooling ended with a high school diploma

What's more, 55 percent of Americans have a high-speed connection to the Web, and 56 percent of Americans are using mobile devices—laptops, cell phones, game consoles—to access the Internet wirelessly (Horrigan, 2008, 2009).

A new digital divide, however, is developing between those using new tools and technologies to collect information and those who fail to move beyond traditional research and study practices. As *Edutopia* writer Richard Rapaport writes:

> Those stuck on the dark side of the new media digital divide will be as out of luck and out of touch as those who cursed Johannes Gutenberg as an agent of the devil when that first printed Bible came off the press in 1452. Gutenberg's invention offered a new, and to some, an intimidating, way of collecting, storing, disseminating, and even thinking about knowledge. More than five and a half centuries later, the rise of Web 2.0 and the new social media offers perhaps an even more profound method to expand the way people interact, communicate, and collectively create. (2009)

To put it simply, human patterns for interacting with ideas are changing dramatically. Making sure that your students end up on the right side of this new digital divide starts with intentional efforts to introduce the kinds of tools, strategies, and behaviors that make information management, fluency, and evaluation easy. Systematically teaching strategies for searching the Web and for identifying reliable content—as well as embracing content aggregation, social bookmarking, and shared annotation—will leave your students better prepared to succeed in a rapidly changing information landscape.

Authors' Note: Interested readers can find a handout titled "Additional Information Management Tools and Resources" posted online at **go.solution-tree.com/technology** that details additional Web-based information management tools available to teachers and students. Here, you can learn about Delicious (www.delicious.com), one of the first social bookmarking services to gain attention. If you are a fan of Google products, you can learn about Google Reader (www.google.com/reader), which is a content aggregator that works much like Pageflakes, and Sidewiki (www.google.com/sidewiki), a Google product that allows readers to interact with one another around websites. By exploring these tools, you'll be prepared to continue your work with information fluency even if the specific products spotlighted in this chapter—Pageflakes and Diigo—are blocked by your district's firewall.

Google's Wonder Wheel

Often, the most challenging step in researching any controversial topic is defining the most important subcategories—or strands of study—that broad ideas can be broken down into. Type a topic like "poverty" into any popular search engine, and you'll be buried by millions and millions of websites, which makes identifying valuable information almost impossible. Even searching for books on poverty at the local library will leave you overwhelmed. But breaking broad topics into subcategories is really hard when that topic is new to you, right? Until now, understanding the themes connected to ideas generally required a pretty complex understanding of the main ideas to begin with!

With Google's Wonder Wheel, however, breaking a controversial topic into subcategories and sifting through Web-based resources is a breeze. Use the following handout to identify a collection of categories and resources that may be worth exploring about the topic that we're currently studying in class.

Wonder Wheel Steps	Your Results
Begin by visiting Google (www.google.com) and searching for your broad topic—poverty, global warming, drought, crime, hatred—the same way that you always have. In the "Your Results" column of this handout, record the total number of Web resources that Google finds related to your topic.	Total number of Web resources connected to this topic:
Click the **Show Options** tab found at the top of your Google search window. Then, select **Wonder Wheel** from the **Standard View** menu on the left-hand side of your screen. Google will automatically generate a web that includes several subcategories connected to your broad topic.	Wonder Wheel web for this subcategory:
Click the link for one subcategory that you think is important to explore. Draw the Wonder Wheel web that appears in the "Your Results" column of this handout. Also, record the number of Web resources that Google finds related to this subcategory.	Total number of Web resources connected to this subcategory:
Review the subcategories included in the new Wonder Wheel web generated by Google. Are there any that you think would logically fit into your research project? If so, list them in the "Your Results" column of this handout.	New subcategories that may be connected to my research project:

Wonder Wheel Steps	Your Results
Each time that you click on a new link in Google's Wonder Wheel, a collection of new search results sorted by subcategory will appear on the right-hand side of your screen. This narrows your research and quickly points you to resources that are likely to be more valuable. Spend some time exploring the subcategories and Web resources that you believe are directly connected to your research project. In the "Your Results" column of this handout, record the number of search results Google returns for each subcategory as well as the Web addresses of research sites in each subcategory that you want to explore further. Consider using SnipURL (www.snipurl.com) to shorten any long addresses before adding them to this handout.	Name of subcategory 1: Number of search results returned: Websites to explore: Name of subcategory 2: Number of search results returned: Websites to explore: Name of subcategory 3: Number of search results returned: Websites to explore:

Wonder Wheel Steps	Your Results
Now that you've used Google's Wonder Wheel to sort through search results connected to the topic that we are studying in class, reflect on the Wonder Wheel's strengths and weaknesses in the "Your Results" column of this handout.	Your general thoughts about the Wonder Wheel as a research tool:
How did the Wonder Wheel help you as a researcher? Do you think it saved you time? Why? Did it have any impact on the direction that you will take when writing about our controversial topic?	Strengths of the Wonder Wheel as a research tool:
Were there any weaknesses of the Wonder Wheel as a research tool? Are there any negative consequences for student researchers when Google does the sorting for them?	Weaknesses of the Wonder Wheel as a research tool:

Spotting Websites You Just Can't Trust

Now that you've learned to use Google's Wonder Wheel to sort through information connected to the controversial topic that we're studying in class, it is important that you understand that *you can't automatically trust everything that you find online*—especially when you're studying a topic that can get people all riled up! In today's world, people are using the Internet to share their opinions and to try to persuade readers to think a certain way.

As a researcher, though, it is your job to find facts and to avoid being fooled by people who aren't telling you the whole truth. This activity will help you spot websites that aren't trustworthy by looking at one of the most famous hoax websites of all time—http://zapatopi.net/treeoctopus/—an effort to save the endangered Pacific Northwest Tree Octopus!

Lesson 1: Common Sense Matters

One of the best defenses against falling for half-truths told online is your own common sense! If something just doesn't sound right, you should automatically be suspicious!

The first thing that should catch your attention on the Save the Tree Octopus website is the very animal it is claiming to protect! Have you ever heard of an octopus living in a tree? Right—and your common sense should automatically make you doubt the rest of the information shared on this page.

Spend a few minutes working with a partner to gather other statements from this website that just don't make sense. Record your discoveries here.

Lesson 2: Look for Links

The sad fact of the digital age is that anyone can write anything at anytime online, whether it is true or not. Knowing that they've got to build the confidence of readers, legitimate online content creators supply you with sources for their information; and online readers should explore multiple sources before deciding what is worth believing.

Working with a partner, look for links in this website. Has the author included any? Where would you expect to see more links added if this were a reliable website? Are there any claims made in the text that responsible writers would prove true by including links to evidence?

Lesson 3: Links Don't Automatically Equal Credibility

While links are a good sign that a website's author might be telling the truth, the presence of links doesn't automatically mean that a site can be trusted. Links—just like anything online—can be faked, too!

Teaching the iGeneration © 2010 Solution Tree Press • solution-tree.com
Visit **go.solution-tree.com/technology** to download this page.

To quickly check how reliable links really are, hover over them individually and look in the gray navigation bar at the bottom of your Web browser. You will see the Web address of the site that the link would take you to.

Good website authors will always include links to a diverse range of websites. When *every* link in an online article takes you to the same site, chances are good that you shouldn't trust the information being shared.

Working with a partner, explore the Sasquatch link in the "Why It's Endangered" section and the Demonstration by Students link in the "How You Can Help" section of this website.

What makes them suspicious?

Lesson 4: Always Look for Additional Resources

On almost every website dealing with controversial issues, you'll be able to find a collection of links to additional resources. Sometimes these resources will connect to research reports covering the topic you are studying. Other times, they will connect to groups that share similar perspectives or viewpoints as the author of the website that you are currently exploring.

Most of the time, you'll be able to find this collection of links in the sidebar of a website. They can also be found under pages titled "Related Links" or "Additional Resources." To judge the reliability of a website, always explore these additional sources. If they seem reliable, chances are good that the website's author is a responsible thinker. If they seem biased or comical, you probably shouldn't trust the information you're currently exploring!

Working with a partner, explore the "Links to a Better Tomorrow" section of the Pacific Northwest Tree Octopus website. What do you notice? Do the sites included seem to connect to reliable sources? How do you know?

List three or four of the most questionable resources included in this link collection and explain what makes them worthy of skepticism.

Lesson 5: Look at the Fine Print

Let's face it, few of us ever notice the small links titled "Disclaimers," "Terms of Service," "Frequently Asked Questions" (FAQs), or "Contact Us" buried in the header or the footer of most sites. That's a recipe for disaster considering that this often-hidden content is usually the only place where hoaxsters bother to tell the truth. Anyone looking to protect him- or herself from being tricked online must take the time to poke through the fine print.

Working with a partner, explore both the green FAQ tab found at the bottom of the content section of the website *and* the FAQ link found in the gray footer of the entire webpage. List some of the comical statements included on both of these pages that prove the Pacific Northwest Tree Octopus is nothing but a funny prank that this author is pulling on readers.

Lesson 6: Look Out for Loaded Words

Whenever you are exploring websites about controversial topics, you are bound to come across words and phrases packed with emotion. Getting involved is urgent, and sitting on the sidelines is a crime. Tragedies happen every day, and we can't wait a minute longer to act. Devastation is possible. Carelessness is a cause.

While these kinds of emotionally loaded words and phrases don't automatically mean that the author is lying, they are a sign of bias. Authors who use loaded words and phrases have a strong opinion that they just can't hide—and that means they may willingly fail to tell readers how others feel about the issue. When you see loaded words and phrases, it is important to do a bit more digging so that you learn "the whole truth" about an issue.

Working with a partner, read through the Pacific Northwest Tree Octopus website. Do you see any loaded words or phrases? Are there places where the author lets his emotions about this issue show?

Now that you've had a chance to explore the strategies for spotting untrustworthy websites, put those skills to the test by visiting another popular hoax website: Free Forever, Dog Island (www .thedogisland.com).

Judging Quality Web Links

Because online authors earn credibility with their readers by linking to external sources that support their positions and verify the facts they've included in their arguments, it is important for you to identify several logical places to include links in the piece you are writing. You should also evaluate the overall quality of the sources that you intend to link to. This handout will guide you through that process.

Use the column on the left to list statements from your writing where you'd like to insert a link to evidence. In the next column, include the links. Use www.snipurl.com to shorten links. The three columns on the right are a rubric used to rate the quality of the resources you are linking to.

Statement	Link Address	Poor Resource	Average Resource	High-Quality Resource
		☐ Doesn't include links to any external sources ☐ Is full of emotionally loaded words and phrases ☐ Includes statements that don't make sense ☐ Is out of date ☐ Comes from a source—an individual, group, or business involved in this issue—that may be biased	☐ Includes a handful of reliable links ☐ Isn't overly biased, although it is easy to tell how the author feels about this issue ☐ Shares current information that can be verified, but fails to provide multiple viewpoints ☐ Includes contact information for the author	☐ Comes from a trustworthy source—university, well-known news source, business, or expert ☐ Shares current information that can be verified through embedded links ☐ Provides multiple viewpoints about the issue being studied ☐ Includes contact information for the author

Statement	Link Address	Poor Resource	Average Resource	High-Quality Resource
		☐ Doesn't include links to any external sources ☐ Is full of emotionally loaded words and phrases ☐ Includes statements that don't make sense ☐ Is out of date ☐ Comes from a source—an individual, group, or business involved in this issue—that may be biased	☐ Includes a handful of reliable links ☐ Isn't overly biased, although it is easy to tell how the author feels about this issue ☐ Shares current information that can be verified, but fails to provide multiple viewpoints ☐ Includes contact information for the author	☐ Comes from a trustworthy source—university, well-known news source, business, or expert ☐ Shares current information that can be verified through embedded links ☐ Provides multiple viewpoints about the issue being studied ☐ Includes contact information for the author
		☐ Doesn't include links to any external sources ☐ Is full of emotionally loaded words and phrases ☐ Includes statements that don't make sense ☐ Is out of date ☐ Comes from a source—an individual, group, or business involved in this issue—that may be biased	☐ Includes a handful of reliable links ☐ Isn't overly biased, although it is easy to tell how the author feels about this issue ☐ Shares current information that can be verified, but fails to provide multiple viewpoints ☐ Includes contact information for the author	☐ Comes from a trustworthy source—university, well-known news source, business, or expert ☐ Shares current information that can be verified through embedded links ☐ Provides multiple viewpoints about the issue being studied ☐ Includes contact information for the author

Social Bookmarking as a Research Tool

One of the best ways for your research group to begin collecting and organizing information on the topic we are studying in class is to use a social bookmarking tool called Diigo (www.diigo.com). After your teacher creates student accounts for everyone in your class and introduces you to the basics of Diigo, use the following checklist to organize the work of your group.

1. Has your group brainstormed a list of common tags that you will use when bookmarking websites for your research project? Does every group member have a copy of this tag list?

   Your Response/Next Steps:

2. Does your group have an Original Thinker, who will bookmark at least twenty websites connected to your topic of study?

   Your Response/Next Steps:

3. Does your group have a Connector, who will identify and bookmark resources on secondary topics? (Example: *Life expectancy is a secondary topic for poverty.*)

   Your Response/Next Steps:

4. Does your group have a Johnny Opposite, who will ensure that the links you are collecting represent both sides of controversial topics?

   Your Response/Next Steps:

5. Does your group have a Reliability Cop, who will rate the overall value of *every* Web resource bookmarked based on how trustworthy it appears to be?

   Your Response/Next Steps:

6. Does your group have a Mind Reader, who will dig through the Diigo bookmark lists (www.diigo.com/list/home) searching for sites that may be useful in your research project?

   Your Response/Next Steps:

7. Does your group have a Cleaning Crew, who will ensure that every link in your shared collection has tags and short descriptions?

   Your Response/Next Steps:

8. Has your group worked out a plan for communicating during your initial efforts to identify and bookmark sites for your research project?

   Your Response/Next Steps:

9. Will you use the Topic option in Diigo? If so, has a new strand been posted already?

   Your Response/Next Steps:

10. Has your group set a starting date and an ending date for researching that everyone can agree to?

    Your Response/Next Steps:

Shared Annotation Checklist

Once your group has started a healthy collection of websites to explore for your research project, you can use the shared annotation features of Diigo (www.diigo.com) to take notes and wrestle with key ideas together. After your teacher has introduced social bookmarking and shared annotation to you, use the following checklist to organize and evaluate your shared annotation efforts.

1. Has your group used the social bookmarking feature of Diigo to create a healthy collection of websites to explore together?

    Your Response/Next Steps:

2. Does your group have a Captain Cannonball who will craft initial comments and add initial highlights to your collection of shared websites?

    Your Response/Next Steps:

3. Does your group have a Provocateur who will challenge the thinking of his/her peers in shared annotation conversations?

    Your Response/Next Steps:

4. Does your group have a Middle Man who will find common ground and draw conclusions based on the range of statements made in a shared annotation conversation?

    Your Response/Next Steps:

5. Does your group have an Author's Worst Nightmare who will challenge statements and ideas made by the authors of your articles?

    Your Response/Next Steps:

6. Does your group have a Repo Man who will create a list of summary statements at the end of a shared annotation conversation?

    Your Response/Next Steps:

7. Do all of the comments in your shared conversation use proper annotation language? Are they proofread carefully? Do they begin with lead statements and end with questions? Do they demonstrate deep thinking? Do they add value to your studies?

   Your Response/Next Steps:

8. Have you created a plan for deleting highlights or annotations that are throwaways? How will you hold your peers accountable for posting quality thoughts to your conversation? For fulfilling their role in your shared annotation group?

   Your Response/Next Steps:

9. Has your group set a starting date and an ending date for commenting that everyone can agree to?

   Your Response/Next Steps:

Reflecting on Diigo Annotations

One of the keys to really taking advantage of Diigo (www.diigo.com) as a student research tool is learning to make quality contributions to the conversations that your peers are having around articles. Use this handout—which includes a strand of conversation between sixth-grade students—to reflect on the characteristics of quality annotations and Diigo conversations. This strand addressed a current event article about a U.S. company's work in the South American country of Peru.

Original Text Highlight: U.S.-owned Doe Run Resources Corporation bought the smelter from the state in 1997 on the condition that it would reduce toxic emissions.

Comments Added to Highlight

- Interesting—this is another example of a US company owning a factory in South America. Remember that South American countries often have natural resources but they don't have the tools to do anything with those natural resources, so companies from countries like ours come in to do the work. So the question is should we feel bad about the fact that a US company is polluting heavily in Peru? (comment by William Ferriter)

- I think that we should feel bad for the fact that we're putting other children at risk so we can earn more money. Just because those children aren't our children, doesn't mean we shouldn't care about their health. Also, these factories emit lead into the air. So do you think it's ok for the U.S. to ban lead in our country, but then go and buy a factory that basically pumps lead into other children? Do you think it's fair that we're shortening these children's lives so our country can get more money? (comment by Caroline W)

- Caroline said: Do you think it's fair that we're shortening these children's lives so our country can get more money?

  Absolutely not! We have enough money already. As one of the wealthier countries in the world, we don't have the right to 'bully' the underdeveloped countries. We should be helping them not hurting them. If we want to make world peace, helping underdeveloped countries is a good start. The poor countries tend to fight more because they are in major need of money, natural resources, land, or something other than that. We also don't want the poor Peruvians to get mad at us. On the flip side, we are in an economic crisis. Do you think that the people leading the business need money or want to provide jobs. I still don't think that matters as much as helping out other countries. What do you think about this situation? (comment by Anna E)

- I think the people that lead the business don't really care about the health of the people in Peru, near the smelter. They probably only care that they get money from the job that it provides. If they did care, they wouldn't even be over there pumping lead into the air and peoples' bodies. The US banded this for a reason: it was harming the peoples' health that live around it. For us to go over there and do it to the people of Peru just isn't right. We already know what it does to our health and we don't care. Do you think the extra money for the US is worth harming other peoples' health? (comment by Kristen W)

Questions for Reflection

1. What do you notice about each of these comments? Are there any shared strengths to the comments? Shared weaknesses? What impresses you? What turns you off?

2. What kinds of things do each of the participants in this conversation do to encourage their peers to share their thoughts? How important do you think that is for groups reflecting on articles together?

3. Which comment in this strand of conversation adds the most value to the thinking and work of the group? Why?

Scoring Shared Annotation Efforts

Improving shared annotation efforts requires regularly reviewing the content that groups are creating together. Students and teachers alike can use the following rubric to judge the quality of the work done around any shared reading.

Above Average
The highlighting on this shared reading draws attention to ideas that are essential for this group's research efforts. There is no evidence of excessive highlighting or of decisions to spotlight unimportant information. This group does a great job using annotations to carry on a conversation with one another! Questions are asked and answered, ideas are raised and challenged, and new thinking is generated together. I'm impressed because the researchers used proper grammar and spelling in all situations, making it easy to understand their ideas. There weren't any places where I struggled to understand what annotations meant. *Overall, this shared annotation project was amazing! I learned a ton just by reading through the thoughts shared by the members of this group.*

Average
While this group has definitely highlighted valuable information, in places it was hard for me to sift through all of the highlights to figure out what exactly was important. Many of the annotations in this shared reading seem like first drafts to me. They include enough information to catch my attention, but not enough information to really make me think. What's more, I don't always understand how each annotation is going to help the researchers. There aren't enough conversations between researchers in the annotations around this shared reading. I see a lot of people doing a great job making their own thinking clear, but there aren't many questions being asked or answered. It just doesn't seem like the members of this research group are working with one another very well. One strength of this shared reading is that I had no trouble understanding the writing in any of the annotations added by researchers. Students used proper grammar and spelling in almost every situation—which meant that I knew exactly what they were trying to say even when I thought that they could have written more. *Overall, this shared annotation effort left me interested, but wanting to know more.*

Needs Improvement
I really struggled to understand the highlights added to this text. At times, there were entire paragraphs highlighted that didn't seem to have anything to do with the topic being researched. Other times, there were highlights that seemed important but there were no annotations to explain exactly why that text mattered. I was left guessing by a lot of the highlights on this reading.

page 1 of 2

Most of the annotations in this shared reading were really disappointing. They rarely included enough detail for me to understand exactly what the research group was thinking. Worse yet, there were way too many playful annotations that weren't connected to the project that this group was working on. I'm not convinced that this group took the idea of shared reading seriously.

Worse yet, I'm not sure I saw any examples of meaningful conversations between researchers in the annotations around this reading. No one asked any really good questions or responded to the thoughts of their peers. When partners did interact with each other, their responses were too brief to be valuable for learning.

The quality of the grammar and spelling in this shared reading was also poor! There were way too many places where I had to work to understand exactly what student researchers were trying to say in their annotations.

Overall, this shared annotation effort left me frustrated and confused.

Questions for Reflection

1. If you had to defend the score that you've given this group, what evidence from their highlights and annotations would you use? Can you find any specific highlights and annotations that support your final rating?

2. Which individual members of this student research group made the most meaningful contributions to their team's efforts? What was it about their contributions that were impressive to you?

3. What specific suggestions for improvement would you make to the members of this student research group? How can they improve their shared annotation efforts?

CHAPTER **TWO**

Writing Open Letters to World Leaders

For students, one of the most powerful opportunities provided by the tools in today's media environment is the chance to be heard. While the students of earlier generations felt just as passionately about controversial issues as the students who currently sit in our classrooms—the civil rights movement, the Vietnam War, and the Iran hostage crisis moved teens of the 1960s, 1970s, and 1980s to action—today's teens can use digital tools such as blogs, podcast programs, and video programs to easily join together with thinkers from across continents, gaining a level of influence and awareness equal to (or even greater than) the influence and awareness held by adults.

The challenge is that today's students are not automatically prepared to be any more influential than peers from earlier generations. While they may have access to tools that allow them to be heard, being heard is only valuable when the messages shared are worth listening to. In a world in which anyone connected to the Web has instant access to millions of perspectives on controversial topics, thinkers who do a poor job differentiating their ideas and articulating compelling points of view remain powerless.

As a result, the initial resources presented in this chapter have little to do with technology. Instead, readers begin by exploring materials designed to introduce students to the traditional practices that authors use to sway readers. We introduce the characteristics of convincing evidence and share examples of persuasive pieces, laying a foundation for effective argument that can translate across any genre for communication. We also provide handouts that can be used to track and evaluate the proof collected for persuasive pieces. Then, we discuss microlending—extending credit to entrepreneurs in the developing world—as a motivating, real-world opportunity for practicing persuasion. Working through these materials can help ensure that your students understand the role that evidence plays in developing credibility.

Only then will readers investigate one of the most approachable digital tools for persuasion: blogs. Readers will explore a series of structures, handouts, and suggestions designed to ensure classroom blogging efforts are successful. We include checklists for organizing blogging projects, along with tips and tricks for addressing the most common questions faced by teachers using blogging as a forum for elevating student voice. Finally, we provide directions for using Blogger (www.blogger .com)—one of the easiest read/write applications available to educators.

All of this work takes place within the context of one classroom activity: writing open letters to world leaders on controversial issues. Teachers who tackle this sequence of learning experiences can pair students together to both research a contentious topic connected to the curriculum and write a classroom blog entry designed to change the way a politician, millionaire, or celebrity entertainer thinks about that issue.

Social studies teachers can encourage their students to persuade world leaders to actively address challenges like global poverty and child labor. Science teachers can have students focus on topics like global warming and deforestation. Physical education students can write about childhood obesity, and students in dance, drama, or band classrooms can argue against the kinds of budget cuts that leave visual and performing arts programs decimated. Even students in math classrooms can write open letters, experimenting with the role that statistics and graphs play in attempts to communicate influential messages.

Why Open Letters?

One needs to look no further than the 2004 presidential election to understand the role that the Internet can play in driving conversations around controversial topics. Senator John Kerry, touting his military service in Vietnam as a personal trait that would enhance his ability to serve as the president of the United States, was publicly challenged by several officers he'd served with who argued that his claims of heroic deeds were simply untrue (Dobbs, 2004). Immediately, Kerry's critics joined together to form the Swift Boat Veterans for Truth (www.swiftvets.com), a group committed to drawing attention to "the gross exaggerations, distortions of fact, contradictions and slanderous lies" that they believed Senator Kerry was telling the American people (Hoffman, 2004).

Recognizing the power of collective voice, the Swift Boat Veterans turned first to the Internet, creating a website complete with downloadable video advertisements, online petitions, and quotes from noted military leaders—both those who knew Kerry as a soldier and those who simply questioned his ability. Readers could sign up for email updates each time new content was created and join together in discussion forums with other interested participants. Before long, the actions of the Swift Boat Veterans caught the attention of bloggers and the mainstream media, successfully making Kerry's war service the centerpiece of the presidential campaign.

The lesson to be learned from the Swift Boat Veterans is simple: world leaders no longer live in isolated bubbles, removed from the masses. Instead, they must constantly feel the pulse of the general population and be ready to make quick adjustments to positions, ideas, and core beliefs. This shift in governing was acknowledged by British Prime Minister Gordon Brown, who spoke publicly in a 2009 speech about the leverage gained by citizens using digital tools to organize. "Foreign policy can never be the same again," he argued. "It cannot be run by elites; it's got to be run by listening to the public opinions of peoples who are blogging, who are communicating with one another around the world" (Brown, 2009). Brown's point: *anyone* passionate enough about a topic can craft convincing messages and build powerful coalitions that attract political attention and drive change.

For teenage students who are typically deeply committed to justice, this is a powerful lesson providing the motivation for producing impressive final products. Students who understand that their ideas can become the impetus for large-scale change are more likely to invest considerable time into looking at issues from all angles. They are also more likely to research diligently, write carefully, and proofread methodically because they are publishing with a purpose. As National Writing Project teachers involved in a 2006 study of writing as a vehicle for social action discovered, "In learning any set of skills, whether personal, athletic, or academic, engagement mattered. Young people cannot learn what they won't engage with" (Berdan et al., 2006, p. xvi).

Perhaps the best evidence that writing open letters on contentious issues can engage students is a joint effort between the National Writing Project and Google conducted in the fall of 2008 and the spring of 2009. The Letters to the Next President project encouraged middle and high school students to write letters to the presidential candidates of the United States expressing their perspective on topics they cared most about (www.letters2president.org). Students in 217 different schools (National Commission on Writing, 2009) submitted almost seven thousand letters covering everything from abortion and the economy to education and the environment. Motivation levels were high in classrooms in which students embraced the real-world opportunity for persuasion. As high school teacher Ellen Shelton explained, "There was a larger context for their work. They really had a voice in this discussion. Someone outside of a teacher, someone on the national level, wanted to know what they were thinking about" (National Writing Project, 2008).

Teachers can learn valuable lessons from the Letters to the Next President project. First, today's students are unsatisfied with learning experiences that are divorced from the world they will one day inherit. Instead, they want to investigate—and to articulate perspectives about—the kinds of significant issues that are shaping the direction of their countries. What's more, with systematic efforts to teach both the elements of persuasion and to introduce students to the tools that make digital publishing possible, any classroom can create their own influential forums for public expression.

Understanding Persuasion

To begin your own open-letters projects, you should start by introducing your students to the characteristics of effective persuasion. One of the most articulate advocates for written persuasion is Don Rothman, senior lecturer emeritus at the University of California, Santa Cruz. Rothman has spent the past thirty years teaching students how writing can be used as a tool for public discourse and civic engagement. "I have come to see quite vividly literacy's potential to enhance democracy," argues Rothman, "especially around the intellectual and social practices that make nonviolent persuasion possible. Literacy, of course, doesn't guarantee freedom of expression, but writing, in particular, offers opportunities for people to counter alienation, isolation, and selfishness that undermine democracy" (Brown, 2005, p. 43).

In an interview with Dan Brown—editor of the *Higher Education Exchange*—Rothman described three key factors on which successful written persuasion depends (Brown, 2005):

1. **A respect for other people's views**—Persuasion, argues Rothman, is often misinterpreted as "bad manners" primarily because of a resistance on the part of public figures to acknowledge how their own beliefs have been shaped by the thoughts, ideas, and opinions of others. Making room in persuasive arguments to show an appreciation for diverse viewpoints can earn influence and allies. Convincing others to embrace novel ideas requires a willingness to highlight the natural connections between their core beliefs and new directions.

2. **A willingness to sustain conversations**—The most effective arguments are built only after careful listening. Meaningful conversations between individuals who disagree result in a collective intelligence around controversies. Silencing opponents—inadvertently or intentionally—only leads to underinformed positions, and underinformed positions are rarely persuasive. That means writers who learn to sustain the thinking of others are in a better position to understand complex issues.

3. **An ability to accurately, and civilly, describe sources of disagreement**—Divergent ideas are inevitable in persuasive conversations, and the approach that thinkers take when addressing disagreement often determines how influential they will be. While today's culture celebrates aggressive responses designed to humiliate perceived "opponents," effective persuasion depends on the ability to disagree agreeably. "It means being able to describe quite accurately what you disagree with," writes Rothman, "presenting respectfully the logic of a misguided argument" (Brown, 2005, p. 48).

Like many of the skills presented in *Teaching the iGeneration*, today's teens are unlikely to embrace Rothman's key points without regular instruction. While the traits of effective written persuasion can definitely be learned, they are rarely modeled by public figures. To ensure that your students reflect on multiple perspectives before developing an open letter to a world leader on a controversial topic like global poverty, introduce the "Recognizing Different Perspectives" handout found on pages 62–63. Then, use the "Collecting and Respecting Different Perspectives" handout (pages 64–65) to structure meaningful conversations between students with divergent viewpoints on the controversial topic that you are studying. Finally, the "Exploring Misguided Arguments" handout (page 66) can help students craft thoughtful responses to people holding on to faulty core beliefs.

Characteristics of Convincing Evidence

While successful persuasive projects must always begin by developing a clear understanding of opposing viewpoints, thinkers must eventually craft independent positions. Scaffolding this process starts by sharing the characteristics of convincing evidence with novice learners. Three approachable evidence categories that can be introduced to the students in your classroom are statistics, star statements, and stories.

Statistics

Statistics are facts or pieces of information expressed as a number or a percentage. Statistics are some of the most convincing bits of evidence in persuasive pieces because they make abstract concepts concrete and tangible. What's more, statistics allow readers to make simple comparisons between new topics and their own lives. Finally, statistics can be presented visually in charts and graphs—and visual representations of abstract concepts can be interesting and easier to understand.

Star Statements

Star statements are direct quotes from experts, eyewitnesses, world leaders, or popular celebrities. Star statements lend credibility to persuasive pieces, proving to readers that an author's core beliefs are recognized and respected by outside authorities. Star statements also add a sense of voice to written pieces, which provides engaging content and convincing language that have already been polished and perfected. The most effective persuaders carefully select statements from the kinds of stars admired by their target audiences. While the thoughts and opinions of elected officials are likely to carry weight with adults, statements from athletes, celebrities, or musicians would be more convincing in pieces designed to persuade teens.

Stories

Stories share direct experiences with the topic being studied. Like statistics, they provide concrete examples of the impact that abstract concepts have on individuals and communities. What's more, stories are teaching tools that every reader has experienced. Patterson, Grenny, Maxfield, McMillan, and Switzler (2008) write, "People change how they view the world through the telling of vibrant and credible stories. Concrete and vivid stories exert extraordinary influence because they transport people out of the role of critic and into the role of participant" (p. 61). While finding credible stories about controversial topics can sometimes be challenging for novice writers, the efforts invested almost always result in written pieces that are far more persuasive.

■ ■

At the end of this chapter, you will find a collection of materials designed to introduce the characteristics of convincing evidence to your students. The first handout, "An Introduction to Convincing Evidence" (page 67), asks students to find examples of statistics, star statements, and stories used in persuasive pieces posted online. The second, "Evaluating Persuasive Letters" (page 68), allows students to rate two persuasive letters—written by middle grades students—focused on global poverty and designed to influence U.S. President Barack Obama. The last, "Convincing Evidence Tracking Sheet" (pages 69–70), can be used by student research groups to ensure that persuasive pieces include a nice balance of statistics, star statements, and stories. When you believe that your students are ready to begin crafting open letters to world leaders on controversial issues, you may find the "Persuasive Letter Organizing Template" (page 71) and "Persuasive Letter Scoring Rubric" (pages 72–73) helpful as well.

Using Microlending to Experiment With Persuasion

Microlending—making small loans ($25–250) designed to extend economic independence to entrepreneurs living in poverty—is an idea with a long history. In the 20th century, microlending drew international attention due to the work of Muhammad Yunus and the Grameen Bank of Bangladesh. Today, many international organizations work to pair interested lenders in the developed world with motivated small business owners in South America, Africa, and Asia. One of the most notable microlending organizations, Kiva (www.kiva.org), enables tens of thousands of users to loan millions of dollars every week.

What makes Kiva projects exciting is that they are loans, not gifts. The average loan is repaid within six to twelve months, giving lenders the chance to continually support new entrepreneurs. Each Kiva loan is overseen by a Kiva Field Partner—organizations on the ground in developing nations that manage loans, collect repayments, and report on progress. Many schools have embraced microlending as a tool for empowering students to take real action on an important global issue. Some—like the Meadows School in Las Vegas, Nevada, and Bellevue High School outside of Seattle—have even accumulated huge lending accounts by approaching local businesses with sponsorship requests and proposals. "They are gaining experience in managing assets and researching the geographies where we loan," says Meadows School MicroBank faculty adviser Kirk Knutsen (Boss, 2009).

For classes studying persuasion that plan to write open letters to world leaders on global poverty, microlending projects can form the basis of motivating initial efforts at being influential. After introducing students to facts and statistics about worldwide poverty, studying the ways that people around the world work to make their living, and explaining the role that microlending can play in improving life in developing nations, teachers and students can brainstorm plans for raising money to be loaned out through Kiva. Approaching businesses for sponsorships or donations, holding raffles and selling baked goods, or offering students the opportunity to earn "free periods" by raising money are all strategies that successful teachers have used to build initial lending funds. Sums as small as fifty dollars are often enough to get microlending clubs off of the ground. "It's not a cliché to say that little amounts of money do make a difference," argues Justin Blau, student founder of the Meadows School MicroBank (Boss, 2009).

And that's when the practice with persuasion begins! Students can be broken into lending teams responsible for researching potential loans and making "pitches" to their classmates designed to convince others that their entrepreneur is worth supporting. Quality of life indicators can be collected, country profiles can be explored, and lending terms can be evaluated. Students can make decisions based on the continuing stability of nations, the stated goals of entrepreneurs, and the perceived reliability of the Kiva Field Partner responsible for managing funds, and can use the collected evidence to deliver persuasive arguments to their peers during classroom sessions in which final lending decisions will be made collectively.

Unlike traditional classroom projects focused on persuasion—reflecting on school uniform policies, convincing administrators to extend extra privileges in the cafeteria, making cases for favorite bands, foods, or movies—microlending projects resonate with today's students, who tend to be more globally aware than students of previous generations (Tapscott, 2009). "It's real money and real people we're lending to," says Blau. "That's why we're so motivated . . . We are able to know the names and see the faces of the people receiving the loans" (Boss, 2009). What's more, microlending projects provide natural sources for statistics, star statements, and stories—the kinds of convincing evidence students will need before developing effective persuasive letters to world leaders on global poverty.

Visit **go.solution-tree.com/technology** for an extensive collection of handouts designed to help teachers interested in using microlending projects to experiment with persuasion. They include:

- **Studying Poverty: Infonation Comparison Activity, Studying Poverty: Infonation Comparison Summary Notes**—These handouts, designed to introduce the differences between living conditions in the developed and developing world, ask students to use the United Nations' Infonation tool (www.un.org/cyberschoolbus/infonation3/menu/advanced .asp) to study quality of life indicators ranging from GDP per capita and unemployment rates to infant mortality and crude death rates.

- **Do Something Funny for Money Day**—The first step that teachers must take to start microlending clubs is to raise funds that can be loaned to entrepreneurs in developing nations. This handout introduces teachers to Do Something Funny for Money Day, a fundraising project that is easy to implement and has proven to be successful in middle and high school classrooms.

- **Lending to a Woman, Lending to a Group, Giving a Gift Certificate to Another Class, Which Country Should We Loan To?**—Student microlending clubs must make several decisions before selecting entrepreneurs to support. These handouts help students think through four of the most common decisions: making loans to women, making loans to groups of entrepreneurs, giving gift certificates to other microlending clubs, and determining which countries need immediate support.

- **Kiva Loan Questions, Kiva Loan Questions: Your Notes**—For student microlending clubs using Kiva, the best lending decisions are made after reflecting on the country, entrepreneur, and lending term profiles available on each loan's information page. These rubrics help students reflect on this information while researching potential loans.

- **Persuasive Speech Organizer**—In successful school-based microlending projects, loans are made only after student lending teams deliver persuasive speeches to the entire club designed to convince peers that their entrepreneur is worth supporting. This template can be used to help lending teams organize a convincing persuasive speech based on the criteria that they've studied together.

■ **Rating Kiva Loan Opportunities**—Students listening to the persuasive speeches delivered by their peers have the opportunity to practice critical evaluation by making active judgments about positions based on personal beliefs. This handout can be used by students to identify a set of "Lender Belief Statements" and then rate potential loan opportunities against these guiding principles.

Structuring Classroom Blogging Projects

Once your students are comfortable with the characteristics of written persuasion, they will finally be ready to share their personal opinions with a larger audience—and there isn't a more popular tool for sharing ideas and opinions than blogs, one of the original Web 2.0 tools. With millions of authors posting new content to the Web each day, blogs have been embraced as a nearly ubiquitous tool for reaching audiences. Politicians blog to share ideas about running governments, CEOs blog to share ideas about running their companies, educators blog to share ideas about effective instruction, and students blog to share personal reflections and public works.

What makes blogs so popular is that they make Web-based publishing easy. No longer do users have to understand complicated computer programming languages to post their ideas online. Instead, they can simply choose from a range of free blogging services, create an account, and begin writing! The windows and toolbars that users see after signing in to blogging services look identical to the windows and toolbars of most popular word processing programs. Icons for changing the color and size of text are paired with icons for inserting pictures, bulleted lists, and Web links. Users can even tag posts—much like websites can be tagged in the social bookmarking applications introduced in chapter 1—to create categories for their writing. After entries have been polished, publishing to the Web is a one-click process that opens student ideas to a broader audience than they've ever had the opportunity to write for previously.

Classroom blogging projects require a measure of structure before they will be successful, however. Before creating a digital home for your students' open letters to world leaders, consider the following school-based blogging tips and tricks.

Posting All Content on One Classroom Blog

One of the first questions that teachers ask when starting classroom blogging projects is, "Should I have each student in my class create his or her own blog?" The answer is a resounding no! For blogs to survive and thrive, they need a constantly updated stream of content. Blogs that are not updated on a regular basis lose the attention of readers, who have plenty of other options in today's digital world. Because most K–12 students will struggle to generate content over a long period of time—and because monitoring the content posted on fifty or more blogs can be an overwhelming challenge for any teacher—it is best to start a classroom blogging project with one blog that every student in your class can post to.

While you'll have to work with one username and password—which could lead to inappropriate or unpolished entries being posted by students who you don't completely trust—your chances of generating an audience for your classroom blog are far greater when your students are working together to generate content instead of working alone.

Encouraging Students to Become Regular Readers of Others' Blogs

Believing that blogs are *only* opportunities for students to practice writing skills is a fatal flaw for most classroom blogging projects. Instead of digital soapboxes, teachers and students must begin to see blogs as interactive forums for continuing conversations around topics of interest—and interactive forums require two-way participation. That means your students need to become avid readers of blogs, too. Consider organizing a collection of student blogs in a public feed reader that your students can visit during silent reading time or while surfing the Web at home.

Encouraging students to read blogs written by other students serves three primary purposes. First, students who read blogs are likely to see models of persuasive writing that can be used as comparisons for their own work. Second, students who read blogs are likely to be exposed to ideas for interesting topics they may want to explore in new entries of their own. Finally, students who read blogs connect with potential audiences. While it might take some time and energy to track down age-appropriate blogs that are tackling topics of interest to your students, the effort is well worth your time.

Promoting Student Blog Entries to Parents and Colleagues

While writing for the Web ensures that your students will eventually have readers from every corner of the globe, the vast majority of your blog's readers—and almost all of your commenters—are going to be your students' parents, the students of your colleagues, and educators that you have made connections with in faraway locations, because parents, colleagues, and students in classrooms just like yours have a stake in the learning your students are doing online. That's what makes them willing to read what your kids are writing and to leave a comment every now and then.

Don't let this discourage you! In fact, work hard to *promote* your students' writings with parents and colleagues. Send out links to pieces that you're particularly proud of or that are likely to stimulate exciting conversations. Ask parent volunteers to stop by once a week and leave feedback for students who have posted new entries. Not only do students need to receive feedback in order to remain motivated by your classroom blogging efforts, but feedback from those who matter—moms, dads, teachers, and best friends—is often far more meaningful than the occasional comment left by an outsider, regardless of where they are from.

Teaching Students to Comment on Entries Written by Others

As your students begin reading blog entries, you should systematically teach the skills necessary for writing effective blog comments because comments give students opportunities to practice reacting to ideas in writing. What's more, comments left on entries written by other authors can serve as first drafts for future posts on your classroom's blog. Finally, commenting emphasizes the community nature of blogging and draws reciprocal readers—people interested in looking closer at the ideas expressed by your students—to your classroom's blog. The handout "Leaving Good Blog Comments" (pages 74–76) can be used to introduce your students to the language of blog commenting.

Reminding Students to Respond to Comments

As your project to write open letters to world leaders begins to draw attention and receive comments from readers, remind your students to respond to each comment directly, either in the comment section of their original entry or in a new post on your blog. By responding to readers, your students are showing their audience that they are listening—a key to encouraging return visits!

More importantly, however, responding to comments allows your students to take advantage of the primary benefit of writing for an audience: the ability to have thinking challenged over and over. Writers who make their core beliefs transparent are often introduced to new perspectives, and responding to those new perspectives—pushing back, refining original positions, articulating misunderstandings—is a critical part of the cycle of true learning.

Emphasizing the Role That Quality Writing Plays in Online Credibility

Because writing and publishing online is so easy—and because interactions between students in electronic forums are often defined by casual grammar and language use—many students approach blogging with a careless attitude, failing to invest significant time in crafting polished entries and comments. While they crave an audience, they misunderstand the message that mistakes send to readers.

Not only should teachers encourage students to work through the steps of the writing process (brainstorming, drafting, revising, and editing) before publishing open letters to world leaders on classroom blogs—just as they would on traditional tasks—they should also reinforce time and again that the credibility of digital writers is dependent on the quality of their written work. Students *must* know that the potential for influence exists only when students present ideas in ways that will impress readers.

Naming and Training Student Editors

Teachers who are starting classroom blogging projects often enthusiastically jump in with two feet, encouraging classes to churn out dozens of entries, promoting posts with parents and peers, and building new lessons with their blogs in mind. Then, they end up buried by entries that are poorly written or by students who need technical help posting new pieces. Eventually, they begin to question whether the time they are investing in monitoring student work and in facilitating digital novices is really worth it. Enthusiasm is replaced by exhaustion.

That's why student editors are so important for successful classroom blogging projects. Training a handful of super-motivated students to proofread new entries and to support students struggling with technical skills can ensure that teachers don't suffer from "monitoring burnout." Over time, you'll have veteran student editors who take great pride in the blog that your class is producing. Not only will they continue to write for you once they've left your class, but they'll also serve as competent gatekeepers by polishing entries that aren't quite ready to be published, monitoring comments that are being posted, and generating enthusiasm for the work that you are doing online.

Requiring Students to Use Pseudonyms While Working Online

For many schools and districts, the risks involved in introducing students to tools for communicating, collaborating, and publishing content far outweigh the rewards. Frightened by stories of Internet predators, restrictions are placed on the kinds of information that students can reveal and the kinds of opportunities that students can be engaged in online.

One step you can take to keep your students safe—and to comfort district leaders who question your decision to begin a classroom blog—is to teach your students about the importance of remaining confidential online. Resist the urge to include the name of your school or yourself in your blog's title. Refuse to link directly to any sites that readers could connect back to your classroom, and require that students use pseudonyms to sign their writing.

As "cloak and dagger" as these efforts at Internet safety may seem to you, students enjoy them! Pseudonyms and confidentiality allow them to try on different identities and to be judged based on their thoughts instead of their age or their social groups. And the first time that their work is mistaken for that of someone older, your students will be electrified!

Scheduling Regular Readers for Videoconference Feedback Sessions

If you carefully cultivate parents, peers, and colleagues as regular readers who stop by to comment on the work that your students are publishing online, consider scheduling videoconferences to connect your students to real members of their audience. By inviting readers "into" your classroom, you automatically reinforce the idea that student voice really does matter.

Have your digital guests describe what it is that they like the best about your open letters project. Encourage them to share specific entries that they enjoyed and content strands that were motivating. Ask for areas of improvement. Nothing can be more powerful to student writers than hearing from their readers—and hearing from readers is one digital step away!

Including and Regularly Exploring Visitor Maps and Page View Statistics

As motivating as local readers can be for student bloggers, discovering that visitors from all over the world stop by to read their work never fails to amaze tweens and teens. To prove to your students that their open letters are reaching readers in faraway locations, be sure to include a visitor map in the sidebar of your blog.

While there are many services that will track the location of the visitors that land on your site, ClustrMaps (www.clustrmaps.com) is one of the most popular because it highlights each visitor with a red dot on a digital image of the world. Before long, red dots will cover entire continents, reinforcing the idea that your students are being heard! ClustrMaps also reports the number of page views that your website receives on a regular basis—and can break those page view statistics down by continent. Consider asking students to track this information carefully in their notebooks or on a classroom bulletin board. Watching your readership grow over time will be just as motivating to your students as seeing where their readers are coming from.

■ ■

This chapter ends with a collection of handouts that teachers starting classroom blogging projects may find useful, including "Teacher Checklist for Blogging Projects" (pages 77–80)—designed to help teachers think through the technical and pedagogical preparations that go into successful classroom blogging projects—and "Blog Entry Scoring Checklist" (pages 81–82). Visit **go.solution-tree.com/technology** for the online-only handout "Directions for Posting Blog Entries" based on Blogger, Google's free blogging application, as well as the online-only handout "Additional Blogging Tools and Resources," which details the strengths and weaknesses of three other popular blogging applications—TypePad, Edublogs, and Pageflakes.

Final Thoughts

For many teachers, classroom blogging projects are a risky move they are unwilling to take because they lack faith in the quality of work that their students can produce. As Mike—a high school English teacher and regular reader of the Tempered Radical blog (http://snipurl.com/temperedradical) explained in the comment section of a 2007 blog post:

> I'm usually amused, but more dismayed when a colleague informs me that they've just discovered the internet . . . and blogging software and plan to use it to transform the lives of their students. I'm dismayed because what they commonly end up doing is wasting huge amounts of class time as their students write poorly, with little evident reasoning, in a medium that exposes their lack of ability to a much wider audience. (Ferriter, 2007)

Classroom blogging efforts, however, are only a huge waste of class time when they are poorly structured affairs in which teachers place technology before teaching—or when students are forced to write about topics that they have little passion for. "Nobody can be forced to do this," write Charlene Li and Josh Bernoff (2008), authors of *Groundswell* and experts on the use of social media tools to drive change. "Blogging is too personal, and requires too much effort, to be crammed down anybody's throat. The result of that, inevitably, will look and feel lame, and it's worse than not having a blog at all" (Kindle location 1208–1211).

To avoid the same pitfalls, focus first on the kinds of content likely to leave your students jazzed—in this case, persuasive letters designed to influence world leaders to take action on controversial topics. Then, help students collect, evaluate, and collaborate around information connected to their topic of study. Finally, explore samples of effective writing and the characteristics of convincing evidence. Only then will your students be ready to produce the kinds of persuasive content that you can be proud of.

Recognizing Different Perspectives

One of the keys to being persuasive is the ability to understand the full range of perspectives that people may hold on the issue you are studying. Before crafting the final copy of your persuasive piece, use this handout to think through how others may feel about the same topic. The sample responses are based on the topic of global poverty. Responses can be built on student predictions, conversations with peers, or evidence collected while researching. Remember to focus your response on the controversial issue that you are studying in class and to include as much detail as possible when defining differing viewpoints.

Questions to Consider	Sample Response	Your Response
How do **you feel** about the controversial topic that we are studying?	I believe that global poverty is a serious issue that we should all decide to take action on, whether our country is poor or not. Not only should governments take steps to solve global poverty, individuals should be involved, too. Solving poverty is the responsibility of everyone.	
How would people who are **completely opposed** to your point of view feel about the controversial topic that we are studying?	They would argue that the responsibility for solving global poverty belongs only to the countries in which people are poor—and that it is not the job of countries like ours to fix the world's problems. Finally, they would say it was all right for individuals to get involved, but they wouldn't see the need to get involved themselves.	
Is it possible for people to **mostly disagree** with your point of view, but see at least something positive in your positions? How would they feel about the controversial topic that we are studying?	They would argue that while solving global poverty is a noble goal, it's just not possible for countries like ours to tackle such a huge problem. Trying to solve global poverty could end up hurting people in nations like ours. They would believe that we need to take care of ourselves before taking care of others.	

page 1 of 2

Questions to Consider	Sample Response	Your Response
Is it possible for people to **mostly agree** with your point of view, but see some weaknesses in your positions? How would they feel about the controversial topic that we are studying?	They would argue that solving global poverty is a challenge worth tackling and that everyone in the world deserves the right to live in a country in which their basic needs are met. They would also think it is the job of countries and individuals to get involved in fighting poverty. They would want to see every country helping, though—not just big countries like ours. They would want to see the people and governments of poor countries working to solve poverty, too.	

The most persuasive thinkers seek out conversations with individuals who have different positions, hoping to learn as much as possible about the issue they are studying. Use this table to identify two friends or family members to talk to who are likely to see things differently than you do.

Name of friend or family member	How are they likely to feel?	When will you speak with them?
	☐ Completely opposed ☐ Mostly agree ☐ Mostly disagree	
	☐ Completely opposed ☐ Mostly agree ☐ Mostly disagree	

Collecting and Respecting Different Perspectives

Now that you've thought through a range of different perspectives about the global issue that we are studying in class, it's time to seek out real voices from real people who disagree with you. Engaging in conversations with those who think differently will help you understand the issue you are studying better. Use this handout to collect viewpoints that don't align with your own. Remember to show respect in any face-to-face conversations that you have. Sustaining conversations and thinking together will help everyone learn more.

Conversation Planning Steps

1. Who do you intend to speak to? (This can be any classmate, family member, or friend who you know thinks differently than you do.)

2. When do you plan to speak to this person? (Do you have time to meet during the school day? Will you have to make any travel arrangements to meet with this person? Is there a due date that you must be aware of? How will you get in touch with this person?)

3. How do you expect this person to feel about the controversial issue that you are studying? (Have you heard this person speak about the issue you are studying before? Are they likely to completely disagree with your point of view? Will there be any common ground between your perspectives?)

4. Is there anything about this person's age or experiences that might shape the way they think about the topic you are studying? (Are they likely to have first-hand experience with the topic that you are studying? Will their experience—or inexperience—influence their point of view? Will their age, family background, or hometown influence their point of view? How?)

5. What questions do you most want to ask this person? How will you challenge their thinking? What do you most want to understand? (The best conversations are built on questions! If you want to encourage other people to talk, you've got to concentrate on asking and listening instead of talking and telling. Brainstorming good questions now will help you sustain conversations later.)

Taking Notes During Your Conversation

1. What key points does this person make about the issue that you are studying? (Are there ideas that they repeat time and again? Do they use phrases like, "What I really believe . . ." or "Most importantly . . . ?")

2. What kinds of attitudes or emotions does this person display during your conversation? (Do they seem open to new ideas? Are they angry? Excited? Emotional? How do they respond to challenges that you pose? Which ideas "fire them up"? Which ideas do they seem the least interested in?)

3. How does this person answer the questions that you ask? (Remember that you came into this conversation hoping to understand new perspectives. Record as many details as you can.)

Reflecting on Your Conversation

1. What new ideas did you learn about your topic during this conversation? (Careful thinkers can always learn something new from people who have different points of view. What caught your attention during this conversation? What points caught you by surprise? What hadn't you considered before?)

2. What new ideas did you learn about your opponents during this conversation? (Are there specific points that they feel particularly strongly about? Are there specific points they might be convinced to change their mind about? What kinds of language do they use?)

3. Are there parts of this person's point of view that resonate with you? What is impossible for you to agree with? (Persuasion often depends on finding common ground between different points of view. Where is the overlap between your thinking and the positions of this person? What are the flaws in their thinking? How can you respectfully convince them that their ideas are flawed?)

Note: While speaking with an actual person will be far more meaningful, it is not required to gather different perspectives. You can also search the Internet to collect multiple viewpoints on the issues you are studying. Consider visiting www.letters2president.org to explore the perspectives of other middle and high school students who are thinking about global issues like poverty, war, the environment, and the economy.

Exploring Misguided Arguments

Often, people who think differently about topics than you do will base their opinions on inaccuracies. While they may passionately believe that they have shaped their positions carefully, there are flaws in their thinking. The best persuaders can accurately describe the sources for disagreements and respectfully point out misguided arguments. Use this handout to structure your responses to individuals who hold inaccurate ideas about the topic you are studying.

1. What core belief does this person hold that you think is flawed? (Be as specific as possible when describing their point of view. Include statements that they have made or facts that they have used to defend their point of view.)

2. Why would a reasonable person think this way? (What is it about the flawed point of view that would resonate with reasonable people? Do these ideas reflect common fears in your town? In the United States? Have there been any major events recently that would make this flawed point of view seem accurate?)

3. Are there any public figures who agree with this flawed point of view? If so, what kinds of messages are they sending to listeners? (Politicians, movie stars, musicians, television show hosts, authors, and athletes can be very influential—and very wrong! Use the Internet to track down any comments being made by public figures that might influence the way people think about the topic you are studying.)

4. Specifically, what is wrong with the core belief you are questioning? What evidence can you provide to prove that this core belief is flawed? (Questioning the emotions and personalities of the people you disagree with is unproductive and disrespectful. Instead, stick to the facts. What is it that you think your opponents have failed to think through carefully? What clear and convincing evidence can you provide to call their flawed thinking into question?)

5. What strengths can you find in this core belief to compliment or celebrate? Was it well intentioned? Inventive but impossible? Did it make you think differently? Challenge you? (Remember that your opponent feels as strongly about their core beliefs as you feel about yours. Effectively challenging flawed thinking often means finding the admirable qualities in another position. Doing so makes it clear that you don't doubt the intentions or the competence of another thinker.)

An Introduction to Convincing Evidence

Over the next few weeks, you'll be working with a group of students to craft an open letter to a world leader convincing him or her to take action on the controversial topic we are studying in class. Being persuasive will require that you collect and share a range of different types of evidence in your letter. Use this handout to begin exploring the characteristics of three main types of convincing evidence.

Type of Evidence	Your Task	Your Response
Statistics are facts or pieces of information that are expressed in a number or a percentage. Example: *The people of Niger live on less than $700 per year.*	Visit the following global issues website and collect three convincing statistics that could be used in a persuasive piece on poverty. http://snipurl.com/sgzht	
Star statements are direct quotes from experts, eyewitnesses, world leaders, or popular celebrities. Example: *"Our world has an obligation to protect its poorest citizens," said Reverend Margaret Duncan of the human rights organization Pastors for Poverty.*	Visit the following *Washington Post* article and find a star statement from President Barack Obama that could be used in a persuasive piece on poverty. http://snipurl.com/sgzmu	
Stories share someone's direct experiences with your topic. They may explain the impact that your topic has had on an individual or a community or provide examples of the consequences of your topic in action. Example: *Yusuf's dreams as a Somali boy were simple: a second set of clothes, a radio, the chance to go to school. The poverty and violence in his country had left him with almost nothing.*	Visit the following Oxfam website, which details the story of one woman working to fight poverty in her hometown. Copy down three or four convincing sentences that could be used in a persuasive piece on poverty. http://snipurl.com/sgzvx	

Question for Reflection

1. Now that you've studied three main types of persuasive evidence, which do you think is the most convincing? Why? Which do you think is the least convincing? Would your answer change depending on the audience for your piece? Explain your thinking in three to five sentences.

Evaluating Persuasive Letters

Convincing evidence can make all of the difference when you are trying to be persuasive. Need proof? Then check out the following two sample letters designed to convince President Barack Obama to take action on global poverty, and answer the reflection questions found at the bottom of this page.

Persuasive Letter 1

Dear President Obama,

Imagine if you had grown up in the same Angolan town as Jonas, a twelve-year-old boy who is struggling to survive even as we speak. You see, his country is being destroyed by a civil war that has been raging for nearly twenty-five years.

For Jonas, that means a lack of clean water and safe shelter. It means that schools are rarely open and that his father has spent more time away from home fighting than he has with his son. It means fear and hunger and, most of all, poverty.

If you were Jonas, your life expectancy would be thirty-seven years—barely old enough to even run for president here in the U.S.—and there would be a 40 percent chance that you couldn't even read or write.

Is helping people who live in poverty the kind of change you were talking about when you were elected, Mr. Obama?

Jonas hopes so . . . and so do I.

Persuasive Letter 2

Dear President Obama,

Do you realize how lucky you were to be born in the United States of America? After all, you could have been born in a million different countries on a million different continents, and there's not a single place that would have been better than here.

Think about it. What would your life be like if you were born somewhere else? Would you be the president? Probably not. Would you be able to read? Probably not.

You probably wouldn't even have food to eat or a roof over your head. You certainly wouldn't have the fancy homes and cars that you have now.

That's why you should care about poverty. I do.

Questions for Reflection

1. If you were to rate the two persuasive letters on a scale of one to five—with five representing the highest score possible—what scores would you give? Why?

2. Working with a partner, identify and provide an example of each of the different types of convincing evidence—statistics, star statements, and stories—used in persuasive letter 1. Circle the piece of evidence used in persuasive letter 1 that you think is the most convincing.

3. Working with a partner, list three places in persuasive letter 2 where the author could have inserted a statistic, star statement, or story. Explain what type of evidence you would have tried to find had you written this piece.

Convincing Evidence Tracking Sheet

Now that you have had the chance to explore three of the main types of convincing evidence used in persuasive pieces—statistics, star statements, and stories—and to evaluate two persuasive letters written to a world leader on the topic of poverty, it is your turn to begin collecting convincing evidence for your own open letter to a world leader. Use this handout to begin organizing the convincing evidence that you find while you are researching. In the first column, write the evidence you plan to include in your persuasive piece. Be accurate with numbers and names. In the second column, select the type of evidence you are collecting. Tracking the types of evidence used will ensure your piece is interesting to readers. In the last column, include the title, author, and page number of your source. If the source is a website, use www.snipurl.com to shorten the address.

Evidence	Type	Source
	☐ Statistic ☐ Star Statement ☐ Story	
	☐ Statistic ☐ Star Statement ☐ Story	
	☐ Statistic ☐ Star Statement ☐ Story	
	☐ Statistic ☐ Star Statement ☐ Story	
	☐ Statistic ☐ Star Statement ☐ Story	
	☐ Statistic ☐ Star Statement ☐ Story	

Teaching the iGeneration © 2010 Solution Tree Press • solution-tree.com
Visit **go.solution-tree.com/technology** to download this page.

Tasks for Reflection

Now that you have finished collecting a set of convincing statistics, star statements, and stories, spend a few minutes completing the following reflective tasks.

1. Rank your evidence in order from the most convincing to the least convincing. Explain your thinking.

2. Generate a list of evidence that you'd still love to find. What statistics, star statements, or stories would make your letter even more convincing?

3. Rank your list of sources in order from the most valuable to the least valuable. Which sources should you return to first if you need to find more convincing evidence to add to your persuasive letter? Why?

4. Have a peer or a partner check your ranked lists. Do they agree with you? Why or why not?

Teaching the iGeneration © 2010 Solution Tree Press • solution-tree.com
Visit **go.solution-tree.com/technology** to download this page.

Persuasive Letter Organizing Template

Once you've gathered multiple perspectives and collected convincing evidence to support your point of view on the controversial issue that you are studying in class, it is time to create an open letter to a world leader that is designed to persuade. This organizing template can help you structure your first draft. Remember that you can find sample letters covering a range of topics on the Letters to the Next President website (www.letters2president.org).

Introduction
Introductions have one primary purpose: you must convince readers that the world issue we are studying is important enough to deserve their attention. Often, this is best done by sharing moving stories. Can you show how your issue is influencing life? Can you make suggestions about how the reader is—or will be—influenced by this issue? Don't assume that your reader has enough background knowledge to recognize that this issue is worth caring about. Instead, provide clear and convincing evidence here.

Detail Paragraph 1	Detail Paragraph 2	Detail Paragraph 3

Persuasive letters include anywhere from one to three detail paragraphs designed to introduce readers to evidence that is directly connected to the issue being studied. You should include quotes from experts in the field, convincing statistics, or stories of your issue in action.

Conclusion
The conclusions of persuasive letters have two primary purposes: first, you must show your readers that you have considered the perspectives of people who are likely to disagree with you. Start by mentioning the biggest concern that an opponent is likely to have and then either (1) show why this concern is flawed or (2) explain why your world leader should move forward despite this concern. Finally, your conclusion must be motivating and memorable. Appealing to a sense of right and wrong, describing the positive outcomes of getting involved, and describing the negative outcomes of a refusal to act are all strategies that can leave readers inspired.

Persuasive Letter Scoring Rubric

Parents, students, and teachers can use the following rubric to rate persuasive letters designed to influence world leaders.

Above Average
You have definitely taken a stand on the issue we are studying—and you've supported your position with some of the most convincing points that I've ever seen! It would be impossible for readers to be unmoved by your writing because you've focused on concepts that are likely to be convincing to everyone. More importantly, you've addressed all of the "complaints" that opponents are likely to have with your point of view, detailing the flaws in their thinking and/or leaving readers convinced to move forward anyway. I'm really impressed by the evidence that you've found to persuade your readers. You've done a great job balancing statistics, star statements, and stories in your piece, and your evidence works together nicely, making your piece seem more like a story than a nonfiction letter on a controversial topic. Your writing is also top-notch. It is clear and easy to understand, with no spelling or grammar errors. Your paragraphs are all approachable—none are too long and none are too short—and your use of varied sentence lengths, figurative language, and interesting vocabulary makes your piece fun to read. *Overall, your piece changed the way that I feel about this issue. Not only am I convinced that I need to take action, but I'm also convinced that I need to get others involved in taking action, too. This is a topic that is too important to overlook.*

Average
You have definitely taken a stand on the issue we are studying—and more importantly, you've supported your position with several good points. Readers will be able to follow your thinking and will probably be nodding their heads in agreement as they work through your piece because you've focused on important concepts that matter. In places, you've done a good job using convincing evidence—statistics, star statements, and stories—to persuade your readers. In other places, though, you make statements that are not backed up with evidence. While the reader might be able to guess why the points you are making matter, the best persuaders never make their readers fill in the blanks. While there's nothing particularly fancy about your sentence structure or vocabulary, there are few mechanical errors in your piece that are going to leave your readers confused. Your writing is solid—and that means you've done a good job communicating with readers. *Overall, your piece convinced me that this issue mattered and that your point of view makes sense. I'm not sure that I have enough information to convince me to take action yet, but I definitely want to know more and will probably research on my own.*

Teaching the iGeneration © 2010 Solution Tree Press • solution-tree.com
Visit **go.solution-tree.com/technology** to download this page.

Needs Improvement

I'm not sure I know what your point of view is on the issue we're studying in class. I struggled to follow your thinking, and I'll bet that other readers will struggle, too. I wish that you had focused on a few key points because the ideas you shared seem to wander. They just don't fit together very well in my mind.

I'm also not sure that you've chosen the most convincing evidence for your piece. While you've included a few statistics, star statements, and stories, they don't always seem connected to the topic we are studying. What's more, the bits of evidence you've included that do connect to our topic don't seem very important to me.

Some of my biggest struggles, though, were caused by grammar and spelling mistakes. At times, just understanding your writing was difficult. I felt like I was working really hard to make sense of your piece—and readers who have to work hard to understand are probably not going to be persuaded.

Overall, your piece didn't convince me that this issue mattered. I can't imagine that I'm going to go take any action based on what I've read.

Leaving Good Blog Comments

The best blogs are truly interactive, with users listening and responding to one another. They are interesting digital conversations! Highly accomplished commenters are constantly thinking while interacting with others who are leaving comments. They come to the conversation with an open mind, willing to reconsider their own positions—and willing to challenge the positions of others. The following tips will help you craft great blog comments.

Gather Your Thoughts

To be an active blog commenter, start by carefully reading the original post. Then, take the following steps while working your way through the comments left by others.

Tasks	Your Response
Gather facts. Jot down things that are interesting and new to you. Facts often become the source for fascinating questions or new strands of conversation.	
Make connections. Relate and compare things you are hearing to things you already know from your personal life or your studies.	
Ask questions. What confuses you about the comments that have already been made? What don't you understand? Remember that there will *always* be questions in an active thinker's mind.	
Give opinions. Make judgments about what you are viewing and hearing. Do you agree? Do you disagree? Like? Dislike? Do you support or oppose anything that you have heard or seen? Why?	

Tasks adapted from Santa, Havens, & Valdes, 2004

Craft Your Comment

Good blog comments require the same skills as any piece of writing—careful proofreading, solid elaboration, and accurate punctuation. Use the following steps to craft a good blog comment.

Task	Your Response
Include an opening quote. While commenting, try to respond directly to other readers. Begin by quoting some part of the comment that you are responding to. That will help other readers know what it is that has caught your attention. Example: *Jack K. posed a wonderful question: "Do adults hate more than children do?"*	
Elaborate—even if you don't agree. Next, explain your own thinking in a few short sentences. Elaboration is important when you're trying to make a point. When responding to another reader, don't be afraid to disagree with something that they have said. Challenging another reader will help them reconsider their own thinking—and will force you to explain yours! Just be sure to disagree agreeably; impolite people are rarely influential.	
Answer questions. Point out places where you are confused. Raise perspectives that haven't been considered. Make comparisons to topics that you've already studied. Share what surprises you—either about the topic or the thoughts of your peers. Example: *I think that we all hate the same but the hate starts with parents, teachers, and others in authority. It's really hard not to adapt to what everyone else is thinking or doing. Hate is a strong feeling toward a certain person because they're different—and we all know people who are different.*	
Finish with a question. Digital conversations are like any good conversation—they depend on interesting questions and new strands of thought to keep them alive. That means the best blog comments end with a question designed to keep people talking. Your question should be open-ended, which means participants shouldn't be able to respond with a yes or no answer. They should also be related to the body of your comment. Finally, they should be interesting enough to make others want to respond!	

Teaching the iGeneration © 2010 Solution Tree Press • solution-tree.com
Visit **go.solution-tree.com/technology** to download this page.

Task	Your Response
Example: *That idea poses another question for me: Do you think that people who hate are afraid of difference or are they really just afraid of change? Isn't it more comfortable to stay the way we are than to try to become something new?*	
Prepare to be challenged. If another reader challenges your thinking in a blog conversation, don't be offended. Listen to your peers, consider their positions, and decide whether or not you agree with them. You might discover that they've got good ideas you hadn't thought about. Either way, respond—let your challengers know how their ideas have influenced you.	

General Reminders
Don't ever use your real name or the name of your school when commenting! Remaining anonymous is the safest way to add comments to blogs. Don't respond to anyone who says something inappropriate to you in a blog comment. Find your teacher if this happens! Be sure to proofread your posts carefully. Tons of errors will make people think that you don't know what you're talking about.

Reference

Santa, C. M., Havens, L. T., & Valdes, B. J. (2004). *Project CRISS: Creating independence through student-owned strategies* (3rd ed.). Dubuque, IA: Kendall/Hunt.

Teacher Checklist for Blogging Projects

Blogging is one of the most accessible digital projects to tackle. Because it mirrors work that most teachers are already having students do in class—producing written content—blogging projects are a natural first step for digital novices. These checklists will help you structure successful blogging experiences for your students. The following yes or no questions will help you determine whether or not you are prepared to facilitate blogging projects in your classroom. Be sure to list what needs to be done along with a date for when this action should be completed. Consider including the names and contact information of anyone who can help you complete this action step, as well.

Technical and Procedural Preparations

1. Does your school or district's technology services department have a preferred blogging service? Have they made arrangements for students or teachers to have blogs using a particular service?

    Your Response/Next Steps:

2. Have you checked with your school or district's technology services specialists to learn more about any restrictions that they have placed on the creation of digital work by students?

    Your Response/Next Steps:

3. Are you aware of any Internet safety policies or procedures in place at the school or district level that may influence your blogging project?

    Your Response/Next Steps:

4. Have you introduced your students to basic Internet safety practices—using pseudonyms, refusing to give away locations, never posting pictures of individuals? Are you convinced that they are prepared to write online responsibly?

    Your Response/Next Steps:

5. Have you informed parents that their children will be maintaining an online forum for reflection? Are you planning on asking parents to sign a permission slip before students can participate in your blogging project?

    Your Response/Next Steps:

Teaching the iGeneration © 2010 Solution Tree Press • solution-tree.com
Visit **go.solution-tree.com/technology** to download this page.

6. Have you created a Blogger user account?

   Your Response/Next Steps:

7. Have you made a decision about whether to create one classroom blog or individual blogs for each of the students in your class or on your team?

   Your Response/Next Steps:

8. If you are creating one classroom blog, have you worked with students to decide on a name and checked to see if it is available?

   Your Response/Next Steps:

9. If you are allowing the students in your class or on your team to have their own blogs, have you introduced the steps for creating individual accounts at the blog service you intend to use?

   Your Response/Next Steps:

10. Are you planning on using a feed reader (content aggregator) to organize a collection of blogs for your students to read and respond to?

    Your Response/Next Steps:

11. Have you developed a comfort level with the basic steps involved in crafting and posting entries in Blogger? Do you know how to add images and links? Are you comfortable with embedding content?

    Your Response/Next Steps:

12. Have you created a plan for tracking visitors to your website? Are you planning on using visitor map and stat tracker services like ClustrMaps (www.clustrmaps.com)?

    Your Response/Next Steps:

Pedagogical Preparations

1. Have you thought through the kinds of entries you would like to see students making on your classroom blog?

    Your Response/Next Steps:

2. Have you introduced students to the characteristics of each category of entry? Are you planning on developing samples and templates for each category of entry?

    Your Response/Next Steps:

3. Do your students understand the important role that links play in blog entries? Are they capable of identifying reliable sites to include as sources in their blog posts?

    Your Response/Next Steps:

4. Do your students have a collection of other blogs to follow? Are they reading blogs written by other students on a regular basis? Have you created regular opportunities to talk about the characteristics of quality blog entries in class?

    Your Response/Next Steps:

5. Do your students understand the important role that commenting can play in student blogging projects? Have you introduced the characteristics of good blog comments to your classes?

    Your Response/Next Steps:

6. Have you modeled the steps involved in starting posts, adding links, inserting pictures, and posting final copies in the blog service that you've chosen to use with students?

    Your Response/Next Steps:

7. Have you created handouts that detail the basic digital steps involved in posting entries on your classroom blog?

    Your Response/Next Steps:

8. Have you considered training a small cadre of student technology leaders to serve as student editors? Do these editors have a clear sense of their responsibilities? Will there be any rewards for filling this role?

    Your Response/Next Steps:

9. Are you planning on advertising student blog entries with the parents of your students and your professional colleagues in order to drive traffic to your site?

    Your Response/Next Steps:

10. Do your students understand that their thinking may be challenged by the readers of their entries? Are they comfortable with—and open to—being challenged? Have you taught them how to challenge the thinking of other online writers?

    Your Response/Next Steps:

11. Have you encouraged parents to leave comments on your students' blog entries? Are they comfortable with challenging the thinking of their children?

    Your Response/Next Steps:

12. Have you worked with your students to set realistic and measurable goals—number of posts, number of comments, number of page views, visitors from foreign countries—for your classroom blogging project?

    Your Response/Next Steps:

Blog Entry Scoring Checklist

As your class begins to craft blog entries connected to controversial issues or classroom content, you can use this checklist to evaluate blogging assignments.

Questions to Consider

1. Has the author tackled a topic that is interesting or appropriate for his or her intended audience? Does the topic connect to something being studied in class? To a broad theme running across content areas?

   Your Response/Next Steps:

2. Is there evidence that the author has thought deeply about the topic of study? Are you convinced that he or she is clearly and transparently wrestling with new ideas here?

   Your Response/Next Steps:

3. If the author is tackling a controversial issue, has he or she expressed his or her position in an articulate, convincing, and responsible manner?

   Your Response/Next Steps:

4. Has the author used statistics, quotations, anecdotes, and stories effectively to express his or her point of view? Are readers likely to be influenced by this post?

   Your Response/Next Steps:

5. Has the author included extensive links to reliable outside sites that are designed to provide readers with evidence for central claims or sources for continued study?

   Your Response/Next Steps:

6. Has the author used age-appropriate grammar and mechanics? Has the piece been carefully proofread to ensure that mistakes don't interfere with the reader's understanding?

   Your Response/Next Steps:

Teaching the iGeneration © 2010 Solution Tree Press • solution-tree.com
Visit **go.solution-tree.com/technology** to download this page.

7. Does the author spark conversations with readers by asking provocative questions or expressing interesting positions in this post?

Your Response/Next Steps:

8. Will readers want to respond to this blog entry? Can they work in new directions, generating posts that build from the strands of conversation introduced by this author?

Your Response/Next Steps:

9. As comments are added to this entry, has the author worked to continue the conversation by responding to readers? Do his or her responses ask questions, challenge thinking, or demonstrate a willingness to be challenged?

Your Response/Next Steps:

10. Will readers walk away from this blog post and ongoing comment conversation knowing more about the topic being studied?

Your Response/Next Steps:

Final Thoughts

What makes you proud about this blog entry? How can this author improve his or her final product?

CHAPTER **THREE**

Telling Powerful Visual Stories

Few thinkers have been more prominent in the past decade than the team behind VitalSmarts, a corporate training group that has spent almost thirty years helping Fortune 500 companies make the kinds of rapid behavioral changes that result in growth. Drawing from their experiences as leaders of nonprofit organizations, researchers studying management theory, and consultants charged with improving team dynamics, Kerry Patterson, Joseph Grenny, David Maxfield, Ron McMillan, and Al Switzler combined their collective experiences to coauthor two *New York Times* bestsellers since the year 2000—*Crucial Conversations* (2002) and *Crucial Confrontations* (2004)—that are changing the way humans interact with one another. Their most recent book tackles a different topic, though. *Influencer: The Power to Change Anything* (2008) examines what it takes to be persuasive.

What Patterson et al. discovered about influential individuals and arguments carries implications for teachers interested in introducing their classes to persuasion in today's new media environment. "When it comes to altering behavior," they write, "you need to help others answer only two questions. First: Is it worth it? (If not, why waste the effort?) And second: Can they do this thing? (If not, why try?)" (Patterson et al., 2008, Kindle location 879–884). Any persuasion attempt that does not address these two simple questions is destined to fail.

More importantly, while persuasive arguments built from the kinds of carefully crafted written messages explored in the previous chapter are by far the most convenient and effective in most circumstances—after all, written messages require little more than our own knowledge, credibility, and voice—the most influential thinkers depend on skills that are more nuanced and sophisticated. *"When it comes to resistant problems,"* writes the VitalSmarts team, "verbal persuasion rarely works. Verbal persuasion comes across as an attack. It can feel like nagging or manipulation" (Patterson et al., 2008, Kindle location 890–895, emphasis in original).

So what *does* work when attempting to persuade around resistant problems? The key is a teaching tool as old as time: well-told stories! Stories provide listeners with opportunities to work through imaginative rehearsals, seeing situations through the eyes of participants instead of simply attempting to understand as outsiders. What's more, stories appeal to human emotions—and human emotions increase individual investment in deeply personal ways. While statistics appeal to logic and reason, they are far less effective at provoking action than emotions—and they are far less memorable. Good stories can move people from a position of knowledge to a position of empathy—from appreciating a situation to actually caring about outcomes (Patterson et al., 2008). Patterson and his partners argue that "stories provide every person, no matter how limited his or her resources, with an influence tool that is both immediately accessible and enormously powerful" (2008, Kindle location 1259).

In this chapter, we look at the characteristics of memorable stories. First, we explain how simplicity, unexpectedness, concreteness, credibility, and emotions can be used to create influential narratives. Then, we explore how new media tools—handheld cameras, video editing applications, and online image and video collections—are changing the ways that content creators attempt to influence audiences. Finally, we introduce a set of tips and tricks designed to help teachers effectively integrate digital storytelling and visual persuasion into their classrooms.

Ideas That Are Made to Stick

Chip and Dan Heath—the brothers who wrote *Made to Stick: Why Some Ideas Survive and Others Die* (2007)—are adamant defenders of Halloween, a holiday, they argue, spoiled because of one persistent story that started in the late 1960s: evil individuals crawl from dark corners each year to wreak havoc by sliding razor blades inside apples and handing out tainted candy to kids. Communities acted immediately, and have been acting ever since. Each fall, news reporters and child safety experts express disgust that anyone could be coldhearted enough to poison children. Church groups organize fall festivals billed as risk-free alternatives to Halloween. Police departments and hospitals x-ray goodie bags, parents force children to carefully inspect each sweet treat before it's eaten, and thousands of perfectly good pieces of fruit are thrown away annually. Trick-or-treating has never been quite the same (Heath & Heath, 2007).

What may surprise you is that there has *never* been an intentional attempt by a stranger to harm a trick-or-treater with razor blades or poisoned candy. In fact, the only two cases in which children died due to Halloween-related events were caused by relatives—a heartless father attempting to collect on an insurance policy and an uncle whose heroin stash was inadvertently discovered and eaten. "The candy-tampering story has changed the behavior of millions of parents over the past thirty years," write Heath and Heath. "Sadly, it has made neighbors suspicious of neighbors. It has even changed the laws in this country" (2007, Kindle location 231–236). And it is a complete myth.

For Heath and Heath, the lesson to be learned from the destruction of Halloween is a simple one: some ideas are just plain sticky. They are uniquely resistant and retold time and time again. They convey powerful messages and change the way people act. Even the most ridiculous ideas—urban legends and old wives' tales—are believed long after they are told (Heath & Heath, 2007). Remember when your mother warned you that the chewing gum you swallowed would stay in your stomach for seven years? She was wrong. Your gum may not have been fully digested when it left your body, but it definitely left your body before seven years were up! The warning that your friend passed along about gang members killing drivers who flashed their lights after dark was a myth, too—so you can start using your high beams again; and chances are good that the next six junk emails that land in your inbox warning of the catastrophic effects of nail polish, the plot to blow up the local shopping mall next Friday, or the robbers using eggs to blind the vision of unsuspecting motorists before stealing their cars are also wrong.

But that won't stop your colleagues from forwarding them along and believing them with an almost foolhardy conviction, will it? So what is it about these ideas that can cause otherwise intelligent people to suspend logic and believe? Research done by Chip Heath at Stanford University suggests that the best stories—and the most influential individuals—apply the following five principles to actively create stickiness and staying power (Heath & Heath, 2007):

1. **Simplicity**—Too many ideas get bogged down in the details. By trying to say everything, we end up saying nothing at all. Stickiness depends on our willingness to strip away our thinking until we find a small handful of core principles to share with audiences.

2. **Unexpectedness**—Audiences, particularly in the information-soaked world that we live in today, rarely pay attention. Why listen to a speaker or follow a presentation when you're convinced that you can find the same information in half the time online? Capturing attention depends on appealing to curiosity—and curiosity is peaked by the unexpected.

3. **Concreteness**—Any teacher who has ever struggled to understand his or her school's mission statement understands that ambiguity kills ideas. While lofty ideals and language can sound really good on paper, messages that define tangible actions or appeal to the senses are more likely to have a long-term impact.

4. **Credibility**—Advertising agencies learned long ago that celebrity can add credibility to any message. The result: a never-ending parade of product endorsements and commercials. The average person crafting messages for audiences, though, must rely on a more practical version of credibility. Their ideas must be approachable and ready to test.

5. **Emotion**—Can you really blame your mother for making you throw away pounds of Halloween candy based on nothing more than an elaborate lie? Fear for your safety—perhaps the strongest emotion that mothers hold for their children—drove her actions. The best messengers recognize that when audiences feel, rather than simply think, they are more likely to remember.

Like Patterson et al., Chip and Dan Heath argue that the best way to communicate simple, unexpected, concrete, credible, and emotional messages is through stories. "Research shows that mentally rehearsing a situation helps us perform better when we encounter that situation in the physical environment. Similarly, hearing stories acts as a kind of mental flight simulator, preparing us to respond more quickly and effectively" (Heath & Heath, 2007, Kindle location 288–298).

The Visual Content Explosion

The challenge for the modern storyteller is that digital media has fundamentally changed both the medium through which stories are told and the minds of today's listeners. Paralleling the rapid expansion of broadband Internet access, the availability of mobile devices, the rise of digital video recorders, the growth of the gaming industry, and the decreasing costs of personal video and photography equipment, access to—and engagement with—visual content exploded in the first decade of the 21st century.

YouTube (www.youtube.com)—the first online video warehouse to gain widespread popularity with Internet users—sees nearly twenty hours of new content uploaded to its servers every minute. Their 90 million monthly visitors watch an average of eighty-three video clips—a number that has grown steadily since 2008—and YouTube's consistent efforts to make customized recommendations of new videos has meant that the average user spends twice as much time browsing today as they did a year ago (Helft, 2009). Still, YouTube sees itself as an underdog when it comes to the world of visual influence. "Our average user spends 15 minutes a day on the site," argues Hunter Walk, YouTube's director of product management. "They spend about five hours in front of the television. People say, 'YouTube is so big,' but I really see that we have a ways to go" (Helft, 2009).

Hulu (www.hulu.com)—YouTube's main competitor—also saw remarkable growth in 2009, adding over 20 million new users and streaming over 8 million movies, television programs, movie trailers, and advertisements each month (Littleton, 2009). Still smaller rivals like Truveo (www.truveo.com), blinkx (www.blinkx.com), and Clicker (www.clicker.com) are carving out places for themselves in the video marketplace by guaranteeing access to professional content and improving search recommendations in an attempt to make the viewing experience smoother (Helft, 2009). Combine the unique users of every online video site, and you'll find that more than 85 percent of all connected Americans watch online videos, totaling almost 31 billion views each month. That's an astounding monthly average of 182 online videos per user (Lipsman, 2010). Add the ever-expanding number of mobile Internet users accessing video content—over 6 million Americans watch online videos from their cell phones each month—and the impact of video content is only going to grow over time (Steele, 2008).

Understanding that video content resonates, marketers are investing in complex visual advertising programs that are capturing online attention. When bottled water company Evian wanted to put the brakes on its rapidly declining sales, they turned to a French advertising company, who promptly created a one-minute clip of roller-skating babies (http://snipurl.com/evianbabies) that was viewed 45 million times in its first six months, making it one of the most watched online commercials of all time (Sage, 2009). And when Zappos—a successful online shoe company catering to the young and trendy—wanted to make a digital splash and draw attention to its new line of clothing, they turned to a streaking nudist running through the streets of New York City wearing nothing more than sneakers and a "strategically positioned frontward fanny pack" (Newman, 2009). The videos—posted first on YouTube (http://snipurl.com/zapposad)—have been viewed tens of thousands of times, drawing the attention of major media outlets like CNN and the *Huffington Post* (Newman, 2009).

Blendtec—a company selling high-end blenders—has gotten into the visual influence game as well, designing a series of surprising videos starring an intentionally geeky presenter using the company's signature line of products to destroy items ranging from iPhones and two-by-fours to glow sticks and video cameras. These videos have increased sales by 20 percent (Li & Bernoff, 2008). Even ultra-conservative companies like Lands' End and L. L. Bean are pushing away from an overreliance on traditional print marketing programs. In an attempt to be seen as more hip—and to attract younger consumers who rarely shop from catalogs—both companies are creating video shorts designed to advertise new lines of clothing that are being posted on store-dedicated YouTube channels. "It's a different step forward for us, but one that makes sense for where this customer shops," recognizes Lands' End president Nick Coe (Smith, 2009).

Gaming, which is just as influential as online videos, is consuming more and more recreational time; and contrary to popular belief, gamers span almost every demographic category. Sixty-five percent of American households own game systems. The average gamer is thirty-five years old and has been playing for thirteen years. Twenty-five percent of people over the age of fifty are gamers, too. Almost 300 million new systems are sold every year, and by 2012, 80 percent of all gaming households will use units connected to the Internet, making collaborative play possible. Like online video, mobile devices are having a direct impact on gaming practices: 36 percent of the heads of American households now play games on their cell phones and PDAs—perhaps explaining the 63 percent of parents who believe that video games play a positive role in the lives of their children (GRABstats, 2008).

Not only are Internet users consuming amazing amounts of visual content, they are also creating amazing amounts of visual content—uploading images and video to the Web at almost unbelievable rates. In mature digital markets like the United States, almost 80 million user-generated pictures and 25 million user-generated videos are uploaded to the Web each month. A full 50 percent of U.S. Internet users share pictures on the Web, and almost 20 percent share their own videos (eMarketer, 2009). The popular photo-sharing website Flickr (www.flickr.com) saw its 4 billionth image uploaded in October of 2009 (Champ, 2009). "By the time Net Generation kids reach their twenties," writes Don Tapscott, author of *Grown Up Digital*, "the typical Net Gener has spent over 20,000 hours on the Internet and over 10,000 hours playing video games of some kind" (2009, Kindle location 1980–1984).

The impact that high levels of exposure to visual content has had on teen minds has been nothing short of profound. Heavy gamers, for example, notice more—both within and outside their primary field of vision. Unlike the brains of nongamers—trained to use neurological mechanisms to tune out unimportant peripheral information—the brains of gamers are *drawn* to additional content that might otherwise have been ignored. What's more, gamers process visual information at a faster clip than nongamers—and even short periods of increased interaction with video content can train one's brain to process visual information faster. As Tapscott writes:

> People who play a lot of video games can track more objects at one time than people who don't. Second, they are better at monitoring in a cluttered world; they can more quickly identify a target briefly presented in a field of clutter. And third, experienced game players are better at processing a rapid stream of visual information. (2009, Kindle location 2015–2019)

Often described as "screenagers," iGeners are drawn to visuals when interacting with content. Taught from an early age that images and icons serve unique purposes online, today's students read differently—looking first to find meaning from graphics. iGeners, who perform far better in classrooms that work to communicate key ideas through images, almost universally ignore text-heavy directions. In a visual world, size and color matter, because they add emphasis and importance to information and ideas, and speed is second nature—a lesson learned every time an iGener watches television. Where their parents are overwhelmed by the multiple streams of information enabled by our visual world, iGeners are bored by the slow-moving messages of yesterday (Tapscott, 2009).

The Internet has even changed how people remember the most traditional content: news stories. The beginning-to-end broadcast models that newspapers, magazines, and radio and television programs have relied on for centuries are woefully ineffective at communicating information to the iGeneration. Instead, content that is remembered is interactive, providing users with opportunities to see streaming video or to independently explore related content (Tapscott, 2009). Responding to this reality, traditional media outlets invested early and often in video content—an action that paid off: almost 40 percent of adult Internet users watch news videos online (Madden, 2007).

The lesson to be learned: influence in the new media ecology is dependent on more than creating sticky stories. Instead, influence in the new media ecology is dependent on the ability to create sticky stories communicated through powerful digital images and videos.

Initial Attempts at Visual Influence

Thankfully, the same kinds of characteristics that define traditionally influential stories—simplicity, concreteness, unexpectedness, credibility, and emotion—also define the most memorable images and videos. Evian, Zappos, and Blendtec—the three companies recognized earlier for their innovative video advertisements—created short, simple bits that played on the unexpected. Roller-skating babies, confident nudists, and exceptionally destructive blenders aren't everyday occurrences for most people, after all. Each video was set in a familiar location, however, and stars intentionally ordinary characters that viewers can relate to, lending an element of concreteness to the advertisements. Finally, it's almost impossible to watch any of these videos without laughing out loud, and humor as an emotion is almost always memorable to viewers (Cashmore, 2009).

For classes studying global poverty, telling powerful stories through images and videos is a natural fit. The consequences of global poverty are often unexpected to viewers—especially students in the developed world. While most are aware that our world has rich and poor nations, few have specific details to draw from. For instance, they may not realize that the majority of the world lives on less than ten dollars per day, that twenty-five thousand children die each day due to extreme poverty, and that nearly a billion people entered the 21st century unable to read a book (Shah, 2009). What's more, the consequences of global poverty are inherently tangible. Viewers confronted with images detailing life in developing nations can make concrete comparisons to their own lives and be unquestionably challenged by the visible differences. Finally, the consequences of global poverty can be intensely emotional, forcing viewers to wrestle with morality: Is it fair that children in other countries are starving? How should I feel when I see families living in squalor? Do I have a responsibility to people who aren't as fortunate as I am?

Structuring digital storytelling and visual influence projects focused on any contentious issue—including global poverty—should begin by crafting messages built around still images. While video can be more captivating, it requires a set of technical skills that most teachers and students new to digital projects will struggle with. Using familiar applications like PowerPoint to create single slides is a far more approachable task. Not only are most teachers and students comfortable with the basic steps involved in creating slideshows, but they are also comfortable with a variety of forums for sharing finished projects. PowerPoint slides can become a part of classroom presentations, can be shown with simple technology on school televisions, and can be printed in color on quality paper and posted around a building. This ability to instantly create motivating final products that target local audiences builds momentum for any attempt to introduce students to the skills of visual influence.

But don't be fooled. While most of the students in your classroom are likely to be comfortable with—even bored by—the basic features of PowerPoint, few will have had any formal instruction in the careful composition of quality slides. Instead, after years of creating presentations with little guidance, most students create slides that are hard to follow, poorly organized, and filled with distractions. They'll choose background colors and font styles that are difficult to read and inappropriate for the intended audience. They'll overuse transitions between slides and bullet points, convinced that moving text is engaging. They'll include too much text, too many clip art images, and too many sounds. Their final products are rarely professional.

Breaking these habits begins by sharing several samples of quality PowerPoint slides with your classes. They must learn to strip away the frills that are typically found in student-created slides and to focus on the kinds of simple, unexpected, concrete, credible, and emotional messages that Chip and Dan Heath argue are the most influential. Memorable PowerPoint slides do the following:

- **Use powerful images as backgrounds**—As we learned earlier, digital photography has become increasingly popular and accessible in the past decade, and people willingly share their images with the world. With a bit of searching, students are likely to find beautiful pictures that can become the centerpiece of their PowerPoint slides. Stressing the important role that the right visual can play in changing people's minds can almost instantly improve the quality of the messages that your students are creating.

- **Include memorable catchphrases**—Can you complete the following sentences? "Help Woodsy spread the word. Never be a _____ ." "Oscar Mayer has a way with _____ ." "Have a Coke and a _____ ." Birds, bologna, and smiles have never been the same, have they? They're paired forever with short, memorable catchphrases that were used in clever marketing campaigns. The most influential messages follow the same course of action, relying on a handful of carefully crafted words instead of overwhelming amounts of text-based evidence.

- **Are visually appealing**—While colors, icons, and text shapes, sizes, and layouts have been used to catch the attention of viewers since the invention of the television, few students make careful decisions in these areas when creating their own visuals. Instead, they're drawn to shocking colors and Word Art. Teachers must show students how colors, contrasts, and placement decisions can be used to make individual words and messages stand out without turning slides into sloppy creations that turn viewers off.

The activity at the end of this chapter, "The Characteristics of Memorable Images" (pages 99–101), can be used to introduce your students to the characteristics of the best PowerPoint slides. It asks students to answer a series of questions, based on the work of Chip and Dan Heath, about two different images designed to influence thinking on global poverty. After working through this activity, students should have a better sense of the elements of persuasive images. Then students should be ready to create their own influential digital images and can use the handout "Checklist for Creating Influential Visual Images" (pages 102–103) to structure their efforts. Finally, students can use the "Public Service Announcement: PowerPoint Slide Scoring Rubric" (pages 104–105) and the "Scoring Influential Visual Images" rubric (pages 106–107) to provide one another with feedback on the quality of the finished products they create.

A Word About Creative Commons

One of the best lessons that can be taught in projects built from visual content is that images, music tracks, and videos all carry the same kinds of copyright protections as text. While students generally understand that lifting content from a book, article, or encyclopedia without citing the original source is bad practice, they are far less careful when creating multimedia products. The results are presentations filled with content quickly drawn from Google searches. Visual influence assignments are natural opportunities to introduce your students to the concept of digital authorship and attribution.

The first step in preparing your students to use multimedia content responsibly is to introduce Creative Commons. Drawn from the open-source movement, in which software developers make their code openly available and allow others to freely change what was once considered proprietary content, Creative Commons is a nonprofit corporation founded in 2001 with the intent of making it easier for digital authors to share their final products. In the first eight years of its existence, over 130 million works—including one full length album by the major-label band Nine Inch Nails—were licensed under Creative Commons (Creative Commons, n.d.a).

When a digital author creates a piece of content and decides to freely share it with others, he or she has six different Creative Commons licenses to choose from. Like traditional citations, every Creative Commons license requires attribution: anyone using Creative Commons content must give credit to the original creator of the piece he or she has chosen to use. In addition, digital authors can set the following conditions on the use of their content (Creative Commons, n.d.b):

- **Attribution Share Alike**—This license gives users permission to use and change a digital author's original content however they like—including for commercial purposes. By using this license, digital authors guarantee that their original content will always remain open for use by others. They also promote Creative Commons by requiring that new versions of their original works remain free and open to others as well.

- **Attribution No Derivatives**—This license gives users permission to share and publish a piece of content created by a digital author as long as the original work remains unchanged and proper credit is given.

- **Attribution Non-Commercial**—This license gives users permission to use and change a digital author's original content however they like as long as any new pieces created are being used for noncommercial purposes. Using the Attribution Non-Commercial license ensures digital authors that others are not making money off of their original works.

- **Attribution Non-Commercial Share Alike**—Similar to the Attribution Non-Commercial license, this license gives users permission to use and change a digital author's original content however they like as long as the new pieces are being used for noncommercial purposes and remain free for others to use in the same way. Not only do digital authors that select the Attribution Non-Commercial Share Alike license ensure that no one makes money off of their original works, but they also actively promote continued contributions to Creative Commons.

Creative Commons content is generally pretty easy to find on the Internet. Pieces licensed under Creative Commons will usually be clearly identified with statements and/or icons found in headers, footers, and sidebars. Using the advanced options of popular search engines like Google, users can also sort images, videos, and music results by license. Finally, there are several online Creative Commons warehouses that researchers can turn to when looking for content for multimedia projects. Some of the best include:

- **Wikimedia Commons** (http://commons.wikimedia.org)—While educators have often turned their noses up at Wikipedia, encouraging students to find alternative research sources created by easy-to-identify experts, Wikipedia users are some of the most open content creators in the world. The Wikimedia website contains a collection of images and videos posted in Wikipedia that are often copyright free.

- **MorgueFile** (www.morguefile.com)—Like Wikimedia, morgueFile is designed as a warehouse of images that are copyright free and available to any user for any project with little restriction. The photographers who share their images in morgueFile are working to create a set of reference images on common topics for the world to use. They take great satisfaction in lowering the barrier to incorporating high-quality photography into school-related projects and often only request an image citation or an email for a picture to be used.

- **Flickr Creative Commons** (www.flickr.com/creativecommons)—Flickr is another website that has earned its share of grumbles from teachers and district technology leaders. While there are legitimate reasons for concern with Flickr—users can definitely find inappropriate content posted by others—Flickr also has an absolutely incredible collection of images that photographers have made available under Creative Commons licenses. While students in elementary and middle school should never be encouraged to explore Flickr alone, this is a resource that any teacher designing visual influence projects is going to want to explore.

- **GarageBand** (www.garageband.com)—Like their parents and grandparents, music continues to play a prominent role in the lives of our students, which makes the selection of background tracks one of the most exciting parts of any visual influence project. Providing access to the work of independent artists in nearly every genre, GarageBand is the best source for music licensed under Creative Commons.

- **ccMixter** (http://ccmixter.org)—ccMixter is another great source of background music for students working on visual influence projects. What makes ccMixter interesting, however, is that it actively encourages users to remix tracks created by others, giving students an inside look into what Creative Commons content is all about. ccMixter provides access to a range of different sound effects and ambient noises that can be used in digital projects as well.

Introducing your students to content licensed by Creative Commons is an important first step toward encouraging digital responsibility. By making use of Creative Commons content, your students will begin to see those who produce non-text-based content as authors with ideas worth protecting too—an important lesson for anyone interested in visual influence.

Digital Storytelling

Once students have honed their skills creating influential still images, they are ready to begin experimenting with digital storytelling. Digital stories use images, music, narrative, and voice to bring characters, situations, and ideas to life. The best digital stories are often structured similar to traditional stories—with a sense of tension and conflict developed through a clear beginning, middle, and ending. Like any influential idea, the best digital stories play on senses and emotions to make abstract concepts, experiences, and beliefs tangible and concrete.

For students, learning to create influential multimedia expressions is not only essential, it's exciting because it resembles the kinds of storytelling that they are surrounded by every day—and this excitement pays dividends for classroom teachers willing to experiment with video. Digital storytelling requires students to interact with content at a much deeper level than more conventional forms of storytelling. Communicating through text is a relatively straightforward process for traditional authors, who use only words to engage with audiences. Digital storytellers, however, need to consider how images and music—combined with lighting, camera angles, transitions, and colors—can be used to emphasize key points and move audiences to act. Learning to use these tools together to craft a unified message requires a nuanced understanding of a concept.

Your first digital storytelling projects should begin in the same digital photography warehouses that your students used when creating influential still images, rather than with video cameras. By eliminating video footage from your earliest digital storytelling projects, you simplify an editing process that can be overwhelming for both you and your students. Instead, focus attention on the content necessary to create influential messages and scaffold a new media learning experience that can range in complexity from incredibly simple to incredibly sophisticated (Davidson, 2004). While your students may be convinced that they are ready to script and stage their own scenes complete with voice-over narration and sound effects from day one, they stand a better chance at gaining influence if their early attempts require nothing more than selecting and arranging a series of digital images into a convincing narrative and then adding a background track to generate interest and emotion.

This scaffolding process, argues nationally recognized multimedia expert Hall Davidson, should start with teachers putting together digital kits for their classes that contain all of the pieces necessary for creating influential videos:

> What replaces the camcorder in the classroom is a folder of curriculum-based images, sounds, and narratives. They sit together in a kit like a jigsaw puzzle, ready to be assembled by students. . . . Building videos means assembling video, audio, and story elements—including writing. With digital video, all of these elements can be prefabricated for final student assembly. The notion of scaffolding is the idea [that] the teacher supplies elements for use during the early stages of a project. (2004)

Creating digital kits for your classes—which are typically posted online in wikis, uploaded to shared folders on district networks, or organized onto CDs or jump drives by topic—can also speed up the process of video creation, a primary concern of teachers working with new tools or in schools with limited access to digital resources. Students can practice creating influential visual messages without investing hundreds of hours independently creating—or digging through—source material. Better yet, complete digital kits mean that students need less direct supervision from their teachers to create videos—an important consideration in classes with twenty-five to thirty students. As Hall Davidson writes:

> When the construction kit is simple and complete, assembling an impressive looking digital video is much easier than in the days of in-camera editing. The margin for error is also smaller when all the necessary parts are already there. No matter how simple the assembly, students will learning [sic] the basic editing skills they will need as they move to more sophisticated and original projects. (2004)

To preserve student choice, however, and to better measure levels of student mastery in your room, consider filling each digital kit with a wide range of content to choose from. Along with high-quality items, select images and music that are deeply powerful but communicate the wrong emotions. Find content that is incredibly tactile as well as content that fails to appeal to any senses. Include detailed voice-over narration clips or text-based graphics that might look convincing, but that fail to focus on a few key points. Doing so will result in a range of interesting final projects and can help you better assess what your students know and can do.

Once you've designed a digital kit that can be used to create a powerful story on the topic you are studying in class, it's time to introduce students to a few key organizing points that they should consider when assembling their videos. These organizing points—which are detailed along with other important considerations for creating influential videos in the "Public Service Announcement Scripting Template" found on pages 108–113—include the following actions:

- **Cluster slides.** Even when students are relying heavily on images for the body of their videos, a central organizing strategy is necessary. Students should be sure to cluster related facts, images, and graphics by category when assembling their final products. Viewers will then see the logical progression of the content.

- **Use catchphrases as transitions.** Remember that simple phrases highlighting key points can serve as cornerstones for influential ideas. Students can be taught to craft and then use these simple phrases throughout their videos as transitions that emphasize main ideas repeatedly throughout a presentation. The best place to use catchphrases is at the end of each cluster of slides. That way, viewers will know when images or facts on a new subcategory are about to appear.

- **Establish a "content rhythm."** Having a clear pattern in the way that content is presented in a video makes communicating a main idea much easier. When viewers can predict what is going to come next, they spend more time focused on ideas and less time focused on presentation details. Some content-rhythm patterns that may work for student presentations built from digital kits include: Fact—Fact—Catchphrase—Image; Image—Fact—Fact—Image—Catchphrase; or Image—Image—Fact—Image—Image—Fact.

Convincing students that clustering, catchphrases, and content rhythms matter can often be a challenge in and of itself. While the best videos all include some form of organization and structure, these elements are rarely transparent and obvious to viewers. To tackle this challenge, consider using the "Examining a Video" activity found on page 114, which asks students to reflect on a video focused on global poverty titled *Poverty Matters* (http://blip.tv/file/2606998) that was created by middle schoolers using a digital kit.

After students are comfortable with their video scripts and the content they have collected, it is time to introduce an editing application that can be used to publish videos. While there are several different applications—both software and Web based—that can be used to arrange and publish videos, most share the following features in common:

- **The ability to import content from external sources**—The first step that students will have to take when assembling their final videos is to point their editing application to any content—images, graphics, audio files—they are planning to use in their final product. Most applications enable users to create folders for each new project.

- **The ability to "storyboard" video content**—Storyboards are graphic organizers that are used to sequence content in developing video projects. In editing applications, these graphic organizers generally allow users to click and drag any visual content—still images, videos, PowerPoint slides, graphics—into place. They also tend to allow users to easily insert transitions between clips in a developing presentation.

- **The ability to add background music tracks**—Typically, audio tracks are found directly beneath the visual media in a video editing storyboard. Adding a song or a sound effect to a developing presentation usually involves nothing more than dragging a file from a project folder to this audio track.

- **The ability to record voice narration**—While many students use mp3 players or other external devices to record narration for their video projects, and while teachers may include narrated clips in their digital kits, most video editing applications also allow users to record narration as well. This narration is often added only after images and background tracks have been organized, and it is automatically inserted into the appropriate section of the developing storyboard.

- **The ability to publish final copies in multiple formats**—Once a user has selected and organized the images, audio files, and transitions they would like to include in their videos, most editing applications will publish final copies in any number of formats. Guided by a series of simple questions that help determine the right format for the intended purpose of the project, students can ask editing applications to render videos appropriate for playing online, on full-sized computers, or on handheld devices like BlackBerries or iPods.

When your students are ready to begin publishing their own scripted videos, several handouts and screencast tutorials available only in the online resource collection for this book **(go.solution-tree**

.com/technology) may be worth exploring. The online-only handout "Assembling Your Public Service Announcement" is a step-by-step guide for using one of the most popular free video-editing applications available, Windows Movie Maker (http://download.live.com/moviemaker), to assemble and produce a video similar to the *Poverty Matters* sample shared earlier. You can also find an overview of several other video editing applications in the online-only handout "Video Editing Applications." Finally, a checklist to help you prepare for digital video projects ("Teacher Digital Video Checklist," pages 115–118) and a scoring rubric for video-based influence projects ("Public Service Announcement: Video Scoring Rubric," pages 119–120) are included at the end of this chapter.

When students have completed their influential videos, the final step is to share their finished products with the wider world—a process that has gotten easier as more and more video warehouses become available. While YouTube will always remain a popular forum for posting videos with students who are most motivated by communicating with friends, there are other sites that may be more appropriate for school-related content. Two of the best are TeacherTube and blip.tv.

TeacherTube (www.teachertube.com)—an education-friendly version of YouTube—is a great place to post school-related content because the primary audiences for TeacherTube videos are other teachers and students. For students crafting influential messages, posting videos on TeacherTube helps spread ideas to a generation of people who have the potential to drive real change in their lifetimes. For teachers, TeacherTube provides a free, permanent, and safe digital home for the content that their classes create.

One of the newest video sharing websites is blip.tv (www.blip.tv). Started in 2005 as a competitor to YouTube, blip.tv has one main advantage over its bigger and better known cousin: blip.tv hasn't been blocked by school networks yet! That means classes who are trying to view your students' work at school won't have any troubles. The site hasn't taken off yet, though—so your videos won't reach as many people as they would on YouTube—and while hosting videos on blip.tv was free as of the fall of 2009, it may not be free forever.

Outside of cost and the availability of age-appropriate content, the primary criterion to consider when selecting a service to host school-based videos is whether or not viewers can leave comments on the content that your students have created. Comments from viewers—like those discussed in chapter 2 on blogging—can serve to motivate student authors and become a valuable source of real-world feedback. When parents and peers make suggestions or celebrate successes, students are far more likely to listen. It is equally important, however, to teach students crafting influential visual messages that comment sections can become forums for conversations—and conversations can be used to convince. While sharing videos on sites that don't allow comments may raise awareness, static content is rarely enough to drive viewers to action. Influence happens best only after attention has been captured and conversations have begun (Li & Bernoff, 2008).

Finally, remind your students that their final products can be shared in more than one forum. Creating accounts and monitoring comments posted in several different services may seem like a lot of work at first, but doing so ensures that influential ideas stand in front of as many different audiences as possible. It's important to remember, though, that new services are always being added and old services are dying away in our fluid digital world. While your students may have chosen the appropriate forums for their content today, there might be better options tomorrow. The most influential content creators are always on the lookout for new ways to share what they are making.

Final Thoughts

When he started teaching language arts to middle grades students six years ago, George Mayo of Silver Springs, Maryland, had no real intentions of becoming a leading expert in using video in teaching and learning. He just knew that a part of his curriculum required that he introduce students to the elements of good stories—conflicts, characters, mood, tone—and that another part of his curriculum required that he introduce students to the elements of persuasion. Most importantly, though, George knew that the key to teaching his students these very traditional skills rested in a new medium for communication. "Students love video," he argues. "Student motivation and interest go up when you give them the chance to create video-based projects. They also love to use technology. When set up correctly, video-based projects promote higher order thinking skills" (G. Mayo, personal communication, January 2, 2010).

For George, setting up multimedia projects correctly begins with providing real structure for students, who are often tackling new tasks for the first time. The best projects depend on objectives and guidelines that clearly define the ideas and concepts to be included in final products. Students also need to know exactly what kind of finished piece they must create—an influential still image, a video built from a digital kit, a public service announcement—and have access to samples that can be used as models. "Make sure you give students plenty of time at the beginning of the project to brainstorm," George writes. "If students invest time and effort coming up with a solid plan, they are more vested in the final product. The groups that do not adequately plan at the start tend to have the hardest time getting to the finish line" (G. Mayo, personal communication, January 2, 2010).

Correctly setting up multimedia projects built from still images or video also depends on efficient and effective procedures for handling new classroom tools. Teachers should think through how equipment is going to be passed out and collected in an orderly way—and should find ways to enlist students in this process. By holding students accountable for managing and maintaining the cameras and computers necessary for producing visual products, teachers build an army of responsible allies and make their own work far more manageable (G. Mayo, personal communication, January 2, 2010).

Finally, successful multimedia projects may just depend on teachers' willingness to find additional time to support their students. It's not always possible for classes to master new skills inside the typical fifty-minute period—especially when those skills require sophisticated interactions with content and tools. Offering to work with students before school, during lunch periods, and after school can ensure that groups who are struggling experience success, too. Sometimes, the best strategy is to start with a small handful of motivated students—a group needing differentiation, an after-school club, or a digital lunch bunch—who can help work the kinks out of new digital projects before they are widely introduced across classes, teams, or grade levels (G. Mayo, personal communication, January 2, 2010).

While structuring successful multimedia projects may seem like an intimidating proposition at first, for George, the benefits are well worth it:

> Challenging projects help to build a strong classroom community. . . . Students inevitably end up supporting each other as the project progresses and tech "experts" start to stand out and offer their help to groups who need it. We always share our work as a class when we're finished, and the students love seeing what others have created. There's a real sense of accomplishment when we complete our digital stories, and that's fun to see! (G. Mayo, personal communication, January 2, 2010)

In the end, we simply can no longer ignore images and video as a medium for communication. While our schools remain text-driven institutions, our students are surrounded by visual messages the moment they walk out of our classrooms. Learning to be creators rather than simply consumers of this engaging content is an essential first step toward gaining influence in the 21st century.

The Characteristics of Memorable Images

One of the first steps toward creating powerful visual messages is to examine images created by others. In this activity, students are asked to use the criteria outlined in *Made to Stick* (Heath & Heath, 2007) to evaluate two separate images designed to provoke thinking around the issue of global poverty.

Image One

Adapted from "Homeless in Sugamo 1" by james-fischer. Creative Commons 2006.

(A larger, color version of image one can be found online by visiting http://snipurl.com/image1)

Image Two

Adapted from "Save Our Children" by rachdian. Creative Commons 2009.

(A larger, color version of image two can be found online by visiting http://snipurl.com/image2)

Questions for Consideration

1. Like any content, both of these images have strengths and weaknesses. Begin by listing everything that you like about image one. What is most impressive to you? Least impressive? What are your initial reactions to image one? If you were to change anything about image one, what would it be?

   Then, answer the same questions about image two.

2. The most influential messages are simple. They are stripped down, sharing only core principles and key ideas with audiences. Which of these images does a better job at sharing a small handful of core principles with viewers? How are those core principles

page 1 of 3

communicated with the audience? What would you do to make the more complicated image simpler?

3. The most influential messages are unexpected, either communicating with audiences in a nontraditional way or sharing ideas that are startling. Is there anything surprising about either of these images? What impact does that have on you as a viewer? How does that surprise impact the message that the creator is trying to communicate?

4. The most influential messages are concrete. Instead of sharing complicated language, they appeal to the basic senses of the audience. Which of these two images does a better job appealing to your senses? What senses—touch, taste, sight, sound, smell—does the author tap into? How? Does this change the way you feel about the message they are trying to share? How?

5. The most influential messages are credible. The ideas shared must be believable to viewers. Something about the message has to resonate with an audience's experiences. Which of these two images can you relate to better? Which seems more believable? Why?

6. The most influential messages are emotional, making viewers feel instead of simply think. Influential people know that when they can tap into powerful emotions like joy, anger, hilarity, shame, fear, or pain, their ideas are more likely to be remembered. Which of these images does a better job of making you feel instead of just think? What emotions does it evoke? Why?

7. When crafting visual messages, the layout, size, and color of all fonts and images are incredibly important. The best visual images appear balanced and clean to viewers, rather than distracting. How do you think the authors of these two slides did at creating balanced, clean images? Are there any glaring mistakes that either author made that could be easily fixed? What do you like the best about the layouts and font selections in these two slides?

8. Which of these two images looks the most similar to the visuals you've been creating during your school career? Which looks the most similar to the visuals created by your teachers? Is this something that you can be proud of? Why?

9. What changes do you plan to make to the visuals you create in the future? Why do these changes make sense? Do you think that your viewers will be surprised by your decisions? Is that good?

Resource

Heath, C., & Heath, D. (2007). *Made to stick: Why some ideas survive and others die.* New York: Random House.

Checklist for Creating Influential Visual Images

Creating influential visual images requires careful attention to the key elements of memorable ideas. Use this checklist to help think through the visual image that you are required to create on the topic we are studying in class.

Questions to Consider

1. Describe your intended audience for this visual. Who is likely to see the work that you create? What are they likely to know already about the topic we are studying? What experiences will they have already had with the topic? How are they likely to feel about the topic?

2. How do you want your audience to feel about the topic? What do you want them to know or do after they finish seeing your visual?

3. What information can you share about the topic that is likely to be the most convincing to your audience? What information is likely to be the most surprising? Are there any bits of evidence that you think your audience will find convincing *and* surprising?

4. If you had to summarize your own feelings about the topic in one sentence or less, what would your summary look like? What would you first say to people when trying to convince them to care about the topic? Can you craft this one-sentence summary into a memorable catchphrase for your visual?

5. Have you visited a Creative Commons warehouse (listed at the end of this checklist) and selected several potential images to use in your visual? Have you copied and pasted the source for your image into a Works Cited page?

6. Which image carries the strongest emotions? How does the image make you feel? Have you checked with several of your peers to see if the image makes them feel the same way? Are the emotions shared in your image the emotions that you are trying to share about the topic?

7. What senses—touch, taste, sight, sound, smell—are conveyed the best in your image? How are those senses communicated? Will viewers be able to feel what the characters in the picture are feeling? Why?

page 1 of 2

8. Have you chosen an image that will carry some familiarity for your viewers? What about the circumstances portrayed will they be able to relate to? Is there something about the characters that will seem familiar? The setting? The situation? Why is this image a good choice for your audience?

9. Where are you going to place the text in your visual? Do you have enough room for all of your text to appear and be seen easily from a distance? Are you planning on using colors and text sizes to draw attention to individual words or ideas? Which ones? Have you selected a font that won't be distracting?

Warehouses for Creative Commons Images

Photographers who share their work in the following image warehouses allow others to use their content in digital projects as long as they are given credit. Photographers often specify how they'd like to be cited. Some request that links to the original content be included in new products created. Others prefer to be emailed directly before content is used.

Wikimedia

Chances are that most of your teachers have grumbled about Wikipedia once or twice. "It's unreliable!" they cry. "You can't trust the content that you find there." And while some of those arguments may be true, Wikipedia users are some of the most open content creators in the world. Wikimedia (http://commons.wikimedia.org) connects to a collection of images and videos posted in Wikipedia that are often copyright free—or are free for use in most situations with nothing more than a citation of the original source.

MorgueFile

Like Wikimedia, morgueFile (www.morguefile.com) is designed as a warehouse of images that are copyright free and available to any user for any project with little restriction. The photographers who share their images in morgueFile are working to create a set of reference images on common topics for the world to use. They take great satisfaction in providing high-quality photography for school-related projects and often only request an image citation or an email request for a picture to be used.

Flickr Creative Commons

Flickr is another one of those websites that many teachers and parents grumble about. Chances are that it is blocked on your school's computers. And while students should never explore Flickr without a parent or teacher's permission, they can also find an absolutely incredible collection of images that photographers have made available to the public. Images found in Flickr's Creative Commons gallery (www.flickr.com/creativecommons) can literally be used for almost any project that is related to education with nothing more than a credit to the original photographer.

Public Service Announcement: PowerPoint Slide Scoring Rubric

When rating a public service announcement built from a PowerPoint slide, three categories are important to consider: the content included, the production enhancements that make the PowerPoint slide more engaging, and the overall appearance of the final product. The following rubric will help you determine the quality of your public service announcement PowerPoint slide. *Content* refers to the statistics, facts, statements, and quotations used to introduce the issue to viewers. *Production* and *enhancements* refer to the fonts, colors, and images used to evoke emotions and to polish a presentation. *Overall appearance* refers to the general sense communicated by the PowerPoint slide as a whole.

Basic	Intermediate	Advanced
Content		
Content is often inaccurate. Facts must be checked again. The language used to deliver content is inappropriate for this audience. Audiences will struggle to make sense of the issue being presented because of inaccurate or insufficient content. Audiences are unlikely to be interested in this issue after viewing this slide.	Content is accurate, but not especially engaging. Better fact selection would have improved the value of the final product. Content is delivered in language that is appropriate for the intended audience. Audiences are left with unanswered questions about why this issue matters. Audiences may enjoy this presentation, but are unlikely to be moved to action.	Content included is accurate and engaging. Content paints a moving picture of the issue being presented. Content is delivered in language that is appropriate for the intended audience. Audiences are drawn into this issue and moved to action by the content.
Production/Enhancements		
The image chosen may seem unrelated to the issue being studied. Source for the image chosen has not been included. Little has been done to use fonts, colors, text sizes, or images to enhance this PowerPoint slide.	The fonts, colors, and text sizes chosen make learning from the PowerPoint slide possible. Source for the image has been included, but may not be free from copyright protections. The fonts, colors, text sizes, and image selected for this PowerPoint slide are interesting, but may not always communicate the appropriate emotions.	Fonts, colors, and text sizes have been used to emphasize critical ideas in this PowerPoint slide. Source for the image has been included, is publicly available, and is licensed for use under Creative Commons. Image has been carefully selected to evoke an emotional response from viewers.

page 1 of 2

Basic	Intermediate	Advanced
PowerPoint slide comes across as careless and amateurish to audience.	PowerPoint slide is a strong student product, but few would describe it as professional.	PowerPoint slide has a professional look and feel that engages viewers. Viewers will easily remember this slide.
Overall Appearance		
Slide includes too much text, text that is poorly sized, or fonts that are unreadable when shared with an audience. Quality of the image is poor. Image is poorly sized, distorted, too dark, or too light. There appears to be no logical layout to the slide. Content and images appear to be scattered, making the message hard to follow. The use of Word Art and clip art is unprofessional, distracting viewers from the intended message of the slide.	Slide includes an appropriate amount of text that is clearly visible and easy to read when shared with an audience. The quality of the image shared is average. While the image is generally undistorted, it may distract viewers and/or be inappropriate for the intended message of the slide. There is a clear organization to the slide, but the organization may be ineffective, causing the viewer to work in order to understand the intended message of the slide. If Word Art or clip art have been used, it has been done appropriately and does not distract viewers.	Text has been carefully chosen, communicating important ideas in as few words as possible. As a result, the slide is clearly visible, easy to read when shared with an audience, and very informative. The image shared is extraordinary. Not only is it undistorted and appropriate for the intended message of the slide, but it is also powerful and engaging. The organizational strategy for the slide is effective. Important content stands out without confusion. Word Art and clip art have *not* been used. Instead, the intended message is communicated through powerful words, clean fonts, and an interesting image.

Scoring Influential Visual Images

When rating an influential message built from an image, three categories are important to consider: the content included, the production enhancements that make the image more engaging, and the overall appearance of the final product. This rubric is designed to help teachers and students rate visual images. Consider circling the individual statements that best describe the efforts of the student you are responsible for giving feedback to.

Above Average
Your visual caught my attention right from the beginning because you've chosen an image that evokes so much emotion. It definitely makes me feel instead of simply think, and it appeals to so many of my senses that I can almost imagine myself in the same situation as the people in the photograph.

I'm also glad that you didn't cover such a powerful picture with tons of words because the image is influential on its own. What's even better is that the words you did include are catchy and memorable. While they are simple, they leave me curious, wanting to learn more about the topic we're studying, and they communicate a few key ideas really well.

You've also done all of the simple things right. You've chosen an image from a Creative Commons warehouse and included a reference to the source that is large enough to be read. You've selected fonts that are appropriate for your audience and that blend nicely with your image, and you've been creative with sizes and colors, drawing the viewer's attention to important words and ideas without being distracting.

Overall, this image is memorable and amazing. It makes me want to take action—and anyone who can create an image that can move someone to action is going to be influential! |

Average
I really like the image that you've chosen for your visual. It is colorful and interesting, and it looks like it was taken by a professional. The hitch is that I'm not really moved by your picture. The emotions expressed aren't very strong—or they're not appropriate for the message that you're sending. While I enjoyed looking at this picture, it doesn't draw me in.

I think you've done a great job with the text in your visual, though. Your catchphrase is easy to remember, and I like where you've placed it. You've also avoided the common student visuals mistake: adding too much text to a slide! I'm definitely not distracted by anything that you've written, and I know what key ideas you're trying to share.

You could make a few simple changes to improve your slide. I'm not sure whether or not you've chosen an image from a Creative Commons warehouse because I couldn't find/read the reference to the source for your picture. The colors and sizes of the fonts that you have chosen also make parts of your slide hard to read. I had to work in some places to understand what you were saying, and making your viewers work isn't a good thing.

Overall, this image is a good start. I definitely enjoyed looking at it, but I'm not sure that I'll remember it. It makes me think, but it hasn't made me feel—and the key to being influential is making viewers feel. |

Needs Improvement

I hate to say it, but I'm struggling with your visual. Perhaps most disappointing is the image that you've chosen. It just doesn't make me think or feel anything about the topic we're studying in class. I'm not sure what emotion you were trying to communicate, and your choice doesn't touch any of the major senses. All of that is disappointing to me as a viewer.

I also think you've made a common mistake: you've included so much text on your slide that it's hard for me to figure out what is really important. You would have been better off to strip away as much content as possible and only include a few key ideas instead of a ton of information that's difficult to read and remember.

And while your slide is certainly bold, it also seems careless and distracting. The fonts, colors, designs, and clip art images of the slide became more important than the message that you were trying to send.

Overall, this image needs work. It was hard to follow at best and downright frustrating at worst. While I'm likely to remember the layout choices that you've made, I'm not sure that I learned anything new or meaningful about the topic.

Questions for Reflection

1. What features of this image were the strongest to you? What was it about those features that caught your attention? What impact do you think those features will have on an audience?

2. If you were to make one concrete change to this visual, what would it be? Why would it make sense to tackle this change first? What impact would your change have on an audience?

3. Are there any specific technical tips or tricks that you can suggest to the creator of this visual?

Public Service Announcement Scripting Template

You can use this scripting template to plan a public service announcement (PSA) similar to the *Poverty Matters* presentation posted online at www.blip.tv/file/2606998.

Creating an Outline

Title of your PSA:

Consider giving your PSA a clever title that will make it memorable to viewers. Like the titles of books or movies, PSA titles are important for engaging viewers. An engaging title can even bring viewers to your presentation by itself!

Topic of your PSA:

Subcategories of your topic:

1.   2.

3.   4.

When planning your PSA, organizing the categories of facts, statistics, statements, and opinions that you collect on your primary issue into subcategories lends structure to your final piece. For example, if your primary issue is poverty, the content you collect might be organized into categories related to poverty in Asia, Africa, South America, and the United States. Your content might also be organized into categories by different indicators of poverty such as average salaries, levels of education, access to technology, or number of hours worked.

In one sentence, summarize the main idea you're hoping to communicate in your PSA:

Thinking through the primary purpose for your PSA early will help you make important decisions about the facts, fonts, images, and music to include in your final product. Examples: *"After watching my PSA, I want my audience to know that life is very different in developed countries than it is in developing countries."*

Emotion you're trying to communicate:

Why this emotion makes sense for your PSA:

Every PSA is designed to persuade viewers to take action on an issue of importance. As a result, every PSA must attempt to make viewers feel specific emotions. Thinking through how you want your viewers to feel early in the planning process will help you make better choices as you develop your final product.

Gathering Content

The most critical elements in any public service announcement are the facts, statistics, opinions, and quotations that you choose to share with viewers. Without convincing content, you'll never be able to convince viewers to feel the same way that you do about your topic.

Use the following table to begin collecting content for your public service announcement. Remember to find content from each of the subcategories that you identified earlier.

Types of Content	Your Content
When collecting **facts and statistics**, consider crafting comparisons or cause-and-effect statements. Remember to record the source for all statistics that you gather so your viewers can check your presentation for accuracy. Facts and statistics will make up the majority of good persuasive presentations. Example: *While 95 percent of the people in the United States can read and write, 21 percent of the people in Burkina Faso can read and write.* (comparison)	Sources used:
All public service announcements are designed to be persuasive. Persuasion requires content creators to share their **opinions**. Be sure to use words and phrases connected to the emotion that you're hoping to communicate! Example: *Poverty is devastating countries, destroying families, and leaving children to fail.*	Sources used:
Quotations from recognized experts, international superstars, or the people closest to your issue can be particularly persuasive. Example: *"My greatest wish is just to have a chance."* —Maresh, age 5	Sources used:

Planning Your Catchphrase

One of the ways that producers of persuasive videos influence readers is by repeating short, memorable catchphrases throughout their presentations. Influential catchphrases will reinforce the main idea and the emotion that the video is hoping to convey. Catchphrases can also be used to provide structure and organization for the video by separating sections related to different subtopics. Finally, catchphrases can be used to convince viewers to take action. Be sure to draft a few catchphrase options and then select the best.

Use the following table to craft a catchphrase for your presentation.

Main Idea	Emotions to Convey	Catchphrase Options
Poverty is an issue we should all care about.	Sadness, shock, amazement	Are *you* okay with that? Poverty's real. You can help. Someone's starving.
Your main idea:	Your emotions:	Your catchphrase planning:

Selecting Images

Because public service announcements share a ton of information in a short period of time (two to three minutes), you should include images that communicate powerful emotions and ideas. Quality images can catch a viewer's attention and tell a story all at once.

Selecting images is *not*, however, a quick and easy process. Just like music files and written text, photos are often protected by copyright. To ensure that you are not breaking copyright laws, you must select images from Creative Commons photo libraries and include links back to the original images found online. The most popular Creative Commons photo libraries are:

- **Flickr Creative Commons**—www.flickr.com/creativecommons/
- **Wikimedia Commons**—http://commons.wikimedia.org/wiki/Main_Page
- **MorgueFile**—www.morguefile.com

Use the following table to select four to five images to use in your presentation; copy and paste the image's URL into the final column.

Title	Short Description	URL
A lady with an umbrella	A picture of a very old Japanese homeless woman with a grooved face	www.flickr.com/photos/ sukanto_debnath/508956163/

Title	Short Description	URL

Organizing Content

Now that you've collected the source material for your public service announcement, you are ready to begin organizing your content and your images into an influential final product. Remember that persuasive videos often include short groupings of similar facts or images followed by catchphrases that are repeated throughout the video.

Use the following table to begin organizing the content for your video. In the first column, list the facts, statistics, opinions, quotations, or images that you plan to use in your presentation. In the second column, list any special effects you'd like to use, such as transitions between slides, different font colors, or capitalization for emphasis. Be aware that a two-minute video will require about twenty total scenes.

Scene	Special Actions and Effects
The average American makes $42,000 per year.	Make *$42,000* larger than other fonts. Use yellow for *$42,000* and white for all other words. Use "fade out" transition at the end of slide.
The average Zimbabwean makes $200 per year.	Make *$200* larger than other fonts. Use yellow for *$200* and white for all other words. Use "fade out" transition at the end of slide.
Are you okay with that?	Use catchphrase to end the section on salaries. Capitalize *you*. Use yellow for *you* and white for all other words. Use "fade out" transition at the end of slide.

Teaching the iGeneration © 2010 Solution Tree Press • solution-tree.com
Visit **go.solution-tree.com/technology** to download this page.

Scene	Special Actions and Effects

Selecting Background Music

Like images, the music that you choose to include in your public service announcement can communicate powerful emotions and ideas to your viewers. If you carefully select a quality background track, you can reinforce the main idea of your presentation and engage your audience at the same time.

Just like photographs and written text, though, photos are often protected by copyright. To ensure that you are not breaking copyright laws, you must select audio files from Creative Commons audio libraries and include links back to the original files found online. The most popular Creative Commons audio library is GarageBand (www.garageband.com), a website on which up-and-coming artists in every musical genre freely share their music with audiences.

While not all songs on GarageBand are available for use in your presentation—bands can decide what they'd like to share and what they'd like to protect—you're sure to find something interesting that you can use in your video. You'll know that a song is available for use if you see the following icon posted on the song's homepage:

DOWNLOAD MP3

Use the following table to identify two or three songs that may work for your final presentation. Copy and paste the URL into the final column.

Song Title	Short Description	Name of Band and URL of Song
"Stand Alone"	A heavy metal song that has a gloomy feel to it. Lyrics talk about standing alone to fight challenges. Good for video persuading people to help fight poverty.	Band: SevenPercentSolution www.garageband.com/song?|pe1|S8LTM0LdsaSgZVixYW4

Song Title	Short Description	Name of Band and URL of Song

Now that you've finished planning your public service announcement, it's time to begin assembling your final copy. To do so, follow the directions on the tip sheet "Assembling Your Public Service Announcement" (see **go.solution-tree.com/technology**).

Examining a Video

One of the first steps that you should take before creating your own influential video is to carefully examine a digital story created by other students. Spend a few minutes answering the following questions while watching *Poverty Matters* (http://blip.tv/file/2606998), a video created by middle schoolers and designed to introduce viewers to global poverty.

Questions to Consider

1. Begin by watching the *Poverty Matters* video from beginning to end. What emotion does the video attempt to convey? How do you think the digital authors feel about global poverty? How are they trying to make you feel about global poverty?

2. Now, watch *Poverty Matters* a second time. What kinds of content have the authors used to try to influence their audience? How has that content been organized?

3. Are there any logical categories or segments in the video? Are there any patterns in the way content is presented that viewers can pick up on?

4. In a written piece, authors use transitions between paragraphs in order to signal to readers that ideas and arguments are changing. How do the digital authors of *Poverty Matters* indicate that ideas are changing? What impact does this decision have on viewers?

5. Videos require digital authors to use more than just images to communicate messages. Text sizes, colors, and digital effects like transitions can also help set the mood and lend structure to a piece. How have the digital authors of *Poverty Matters* used these kinds of visual elements?

6. It would be hard to watch *Poverty Matters* without being drawn to the music, wouldn't it? It's an in-your-face kind of track. But does it support the general message of the video? Are the words and beat appropriate? Why? Does the rhythm add emotion to the piece, or lend a sense of beginning, middle, and ending?

7. What lessons can you learn about effective digital messages from *Poverty Matters*? Are there any strategies that you'll try to replicate in your own work? What will you remember the most about *Poverty Matters*? Do you think that was the message the digital authors wanted you to remember the most?

Teacher Digital Video Checklist

While teacher- and student-created video projects are rapidly becoming a part of today's classrooms, they require careful planning and structure. This checklist can help you think through the kinds of technical and pedagogical questions that you'll need to answer before video projects are successful in your classroom. Answer the questions to help you determine whether or not you are prepared to facilitate digital video projects in your classroom. Then, list the actions you need to take, and consider including the names and contact information of anyone who can help you with completing the action step. Also include the date for when the action step will be completed.

Technical and Procedural Preparations

1. Have you checked with your school or district's technology services specialists to ensure that your classroom and/or school's computers can handle the demands of video editing and publishing?

   Your Response/Next Steps:

2. Have you checked with your school or district's technology services specialists to see which video editing applications are already installed on your classroom computers?

   Your Response/Next Steps:

3. If you are planning on using an online video editing application, have you made sure that the program you have chosen is on your district's approved software list? Is it available behind your school's firewall?

   Your Response/Next Steps:

4. If you are planning on using an online video editing application, have you thought through how students will sign in to the program? Will they need individual user accounts? Will you create one account for your classes to share?

   Your Response/Next Steps:

5. Have you experimented with the key features of the video editing application that you are planning to use? Can you import content, arrange videos, and add transitions, background tracks, and narration? Can you publish a final copy?

   Your Response/Next Steps:

6. Will your students be able to accomplish each of these video editing tasks without troubles? If not, are you planning on training a small handful of students to serve as technology helpers during your classroom video project?

    Your Response/Next Steps:

7. If you are planning on allowing students to create more sophisticated presentations with video-based source material, have you acquired enough video cameras for several groups to work at once? Have you practiced getting source material off of your video cameras and onto your computer?

    Your Response/Next Steps:

8. If you are planning on allowing students to take their own still images for your digital video project, have you acquired enough digital cameras for several student groups to work at once?

    Your Response/Next Steps:

9. If you are planning on allowing students to use source material—images and/or video— that they generate, are you aware of your district's photo and video release policies? Have you thought through the ways that these policies will change the content that your students can collect?

    Your Response/Next Steps:

10. Have you developed a plan for sharing the final products that your students create? Will your videos be posted online? If so, have you chosen a video warehouse that can be accessed behind your school's firewall? Have you created an account and practiced uploading video to this warehouse?

    Your Response/Next Steps:

Pedagogical Preparations

1. Are you comfortable with the characteristics of influential ideas? Have you introduced these characteristics to your students?

    Your Response/Next Steps:

2. Are you planning on introducing several sample videos for your students to explore that demonstrate the characteristics of influential ideas in action? Where will you find these videos?

   Your Response/Next Steps:

3. Have you thought through the natural connections between your video project and other required outcomes in your curriculum? Are you going to be able to integrate this assignment into the work that you are already doing? How?

   Your Response/Next Steps:

4. Are your students aware of and comfortable with using catchphrases, content rhythms, and slide clusters to add structure to their videos?

   Your Response/Next Steps:

5. Are you planning on creating a digital kit for your students that includes images, graphics, music tracks, and voice-over narration connected to your topic? Will these digital kits include a wide range of content, allowing for student choice and providing you with better opportunities to assess student mastery of visual influence?

   Your Response/Next Steps:

6. Will your digital kit include graphics—charts, graphs, statistics—connected to your topic? If so, have you collected these graphics? Do you know how to use tools like PowerPoint to save content as image files that can be used in digital videos?

   Your Response/Next Steps:

7. Are you planning on allowing your students to assemble their own digital kits for your video project? If so, are they well-versed enough in the topic that you are studying to be able to identify a wide range of potential content types to acquire?

   Your Response/Next Steps:

8. If you are planning on allowing students to assemble their own digital kits, have you introduced Creative Commons and the responsible use of digital content? Have you identified potential sources where students can easily find images and video licensed under Creative Commons?

Your Response/Next Steps:

9. Have you thought through where your digital kits will be stored? If you're going to post all content online or in a folder on your school's shared network, have you taught students how to access those source folders? Can students access your digital kits from home if necessary?

Your Response/Next Steps:

10. Will your students work through a careful scripting process before beginning to assemble their digital videos? If so, have you created or copied scripting templates to structure this work? Are students aware of the elements that you expect to be included in their digital stories?

Your Response/Next Steps:

Public Service Announcement: Video Scoring Rubric

When rating a public service announcement built from a video, three categories are important to consider: the content that has been included, the delivery and sequencing of the presentation, and the digital enhancements that make the visual production more engaging. The following rubric will help you determine the quality of your final product. *Content* refers to the statistics, facts, and quotations used to introduce the issue to viewers. *Delivery* and *sequencing* refer to the structure used to introduce content to viewers. *Production* and *enhancements* refer to the fonts, colors, images, transitions, and background music used to evoke emotions and to polish a presentation.

Basic	Intermediate	Advanced
Content		
Content is often inaccurate. Facts must be checked again. The language used to deliver content is inappropriate for this audience. Sources for content are not shared, are out of date, or are unreliable. Audiences will struggle to make sense of the issue being presented because of inaccurate or insufficient content. Audiences are unlikely to be interested in this issue after viewing the presentation.	Content is accurate, but limited. More detail would have improved the value of the final product. Content is delivered in language that is appropriate for the intended audience. Some of the sources for content are not entirely clear or reliable. Audiences are left with unanswered questions about why this issue matters. Audiences may enjoy this presentation, but are unlikely to be moved to action.	Content included is accurate and engaging. Content paints a thorough and complete picture of the issue being introduced. Sources for content are reliable, current, and shared with the audience. Content is delivered in language that is appropriate for the intended audience. Audiences are drawn into this issue and moved to action by content.
Delivery/Sequencing		
There does not appear to be a logical pattern for sequencing content, leaving viewers confused. While all content presented is connected to the same issue, statistics, facts, statements, and quotations appear to haphazardly wander across a range of subtopics and categories.	A logical plan for delivery and an effective sequencing of content are clear to viewers. Most content has been broken into obvious subtopics and categories that are evident to audiences. A few statistics, facts, statements, or quotations seem misplaced, potentially confusing audiences.	Delivery and sequencing of content are carefully focused and structured, making it highly likely that viewers can learn new content easily from this presentation. Content has been broken into obvious subtopics and categories that are clearly evident to audiences.

page 1 of 2

Basic	Intermediate	Advanced
Presentation may seem incredibly short or painfully long to the audience. Audiences will struggle to learn from this presentation and will find viewing a chore.	Presentation is an appropriate length and will hold the attention of the audience. Audiences could learn from this presentation without challenge.	Audience is so engaged by the content, delivery, and sequencing that they are disappointed when the presentation ends.
Production/Enhancements		
Little has been done to use fonts, colors, text sizes, background music, or images to enhance this presentation. Transitions may be overused or inappropriate for a professional finished product. Instead of moving viewers through a presentation, they become distractions. Presentation comes across as careless and amateurish to viewers.	The fonts, colors, and text sizes used make learning from the presentation possible. The background music and images selected for this presentation are interesting, but may not always communicate the appropriate emotions. Transitions move viewers through the presentation without distraction. The presentation is a strong student product, but few would describe it as professional.	Fonts, colors, and text sizes have been used to emphasize critical ideas in this presentation. Background music lends a sense of clear and appropriate emotion to the issue being studied. Images have been carefully selected and organized to evoke emotional responses. Transitions are carefully selected and engaging, visually moving the audience through the presentation without causing distractions. Presentation has a professional look and feel.

CHAPTER FOUR

Studying Challenging Topics Together

Working at CERN—a physics laboratory in Geneva, Switzerland, employing thousands of people from around the world—in the late 1980s and early 1990s, Tim Berners-Lee had an all-too-common 21st century desire: to be able to effectively interact with coworkers regardless of their location, the types of computers they were using, or the format of files they were creating. Efficient interaction, Berners-Lee figured, would make everyone smarter because they would have access to shared information and could develop a collective intelligence based on what they knew together. Efficient interactions were impossible at that point in time, however, because there was no single standard for communication between computers and no easy way to meet with everyone individually. Determined to build a system that would enable connections to both information and individuals regardless of the devices that they were using, Berners-Lee created the World Wide Web (Gillies & Cailliau, 2000).

At first, Berners-Lee didn't have global intentions for his invention. His initial goal was simply to create a solution for the communication challenge that he was facing in the workplace. "There was never a feeling of 'Heh, heh, heh, we can change the world,'" he said in a 2005 interview with the *Telegraph*, a British newspaper. "It was, 'This is exciting, it would be nice if this happened,' combined with a constant fear that it would not work out" ("Three Loud Cheers," 2005). It didn't take long for Berners-Lee to become convinced, however, that the World Wide Web had potential that could change the world in far more meaningful ways. "I'd like to see it building links between families in different countries . . . to allow us to browse people's websites in different languages so you can see how they live in different countries" ("Three Loud Cheers," 2005).

While Berners-Lee hasn't yet seen the World Wide Web being used to completely break down global barriers between countries, teens—who have always been driven to communicate—have wholeheartedly embraced the new opportunities to connect facilitated by the Web. Berners-Lee's vision of the Web was always a place in which people could "read and write," and today's teens are finally taking advantage of this vision. In fact, as of 2007, more than half of all online Americans between the ages of twelve and seventeen had created accounts on social networking services like MySpace and Facebook. Most check their digital profiles at least once—and many multiple times—each day, connecting both with friends that they see frequently and those that they only see once in a while (Lenhart & Madden, 2007).

Contrary to popular belief, though, few teens use social networking websites to flirt or find new friends. Instead, they're managing existing relationships by making plans, sharing thoughts, touching base, sending public and private messages, commenting on one another's blogs, and posting on each other's profiles (Lenhart & Madden, 2007). They form groups around causes, and they give and take surveys. They build diverse core networks that they rely on for guidance and advice (Hampton, Sessions, Her, & Rainie, 2009). "By providing tools for mediated interactions," writes danah boyd, "social media allow teens to extend their interactions beyond physical boundaries. Conversations and interactions that begin in person do not end when friends are separated" (boyd, 2010, p. 80).

Heavy skepticism surrounds social networking websites, however. Rather than seeing MySpace and Facebook as highly motivating destinations for communication—a fundamental building block for learning—most parents and teachers see them as nothing more than forums for hurtful behaviors like gossiping and cyber-bullying. We worry about time spent staring at digital profiles, convinced that our students are losing the social skills necessary for interacting in face-to-face environments. Worse yet, popular programs like NBC's *To Catch a Predator* (www.msnbc.msn.com/id/10912603) and PBS's *Growing Up Online* (www.pbs.org/wgbh/pages/frontline/kidsonline/) leave us questioning how safe our students really are while living online.

The consequence of this skepticism, argues social learning consultant Steve Hargadon, is that digital opportunities for communication have been almost completely pushed aside in the 21st century classroom. He writes:

> Social networking sites, at their core, are just aggregations of a set of Web 2.0 building blocks—forums, directories, "friending," chat, etc. Just as you can build either a casino or a school with basic construction materials, the materials are not the issue. It's the end use for which they are assembled and fitted. The first sites that were constructed using Web 2.0 building blocks were, as often as not, "casino-like," leading to the impression that social networking was a time waster at best, and an unsafe place to be at worst. But there's no reason why the same building blocks that built those social networking "casinos" can't be used to create schools, libraries, meeting halls, teachers' lounges—which is exactly what we're starting to see happening today. It's even arguable that these building blocks are more effective as educational tools than as social ones. (Hargadon, 2009, p. 2)

This chapter is designed to help teachers find ways to use social tools for communication in order to create the kinds of meaningful educational experiences that Hargadon describes. We begin with a careful look at how the four unique traits of digital conversations—persistence, searchability, replicability, and invisible audiences—are changing teen communication patterns. We also study the impact that carefully structured digital conversations can have on the social status of marginalized students and the characteristics of learning experiences that are the most motivating to today's teens.

Then we explore how Socratic circles, a centuries-old instructional practice, can bridge the gap between what students are currently doing and what we'd like to see them doing online. We also introduce the differences between collaborative and competitive dialogue—communication styles that accomplished teachers systematically teach to their students whether or not they are connected—and share handouts for structuring productive synchronous and asynchronous conversations. Teachers who work through these materials will be better prepared to create electronic forums in which their students can join together with local and international peers to have Socratic-style conversations around contentious topics.

New Media Environments Are Changing Today's Teens

While new tools for facilitating conversations are playing an increasingly prominent role in the lives of our students, few have spent as much time studying the unique characteristics of digital communication as danah boyd, a social media researcher at Microsoft Research New England. boyd, whose professional interest has always been the impact that social media is having on teens and identity, demonstrates early and often in her chapter of *Hanging Out, Messing Around, and Geeking Out* (2010) that today's teens value opportunities to connect online. "While these teens may see one another at school, in formal or unstructured activities, or at one another's houses," she writes, "they use social media to keep in touch with their friends, classmates, and peers when getting together is not possible . . . For many contemporary teenagers, losing access to social media is tantamount to losing their social world" (boyd, 2010, p. 79).

Perhaps the greatest challenge facing the digitally connected teen, though, is that they are *always* plugged in. Paired with widespread access to high speed and wireless Internet connections, their mobile phones, iPods, and gaming devices extend communication in ways that were once impossible—and while most teens thrive on this newfound ability to talk at any time, there are social implications for unchecked connectivity. Online profiles must be diligently maintained or students run the risk of losing status among their peers. Messages must be returned immediately or students run the risk of offending friends. Public expressions of friendship must be at once significant and sincere or students run the risk of quickly becoming embroiled in social drama at school (boyd, 2010).

Complicating matters is that all of this interaction takes place in rapidly changing digital forums defined by four unique characteristics (boyd, 2007):

1. **Persistence**—Most electronic communication is permanent. Comments added to threaded discussions can be viewed days, weeks, or months later. Participants unable to be present at

the time of a conversation can still see what others had to say. No one is left out of a digital conversation, and opinions expressed—whether good or bad—hang around.

2. **Searchability**—When digital conversations are recorded and names are attached to content, the thoughts and ideas of any individual become instantly searchable. With little effort, users of digital communication tools can profile peers, accessing information publicly posted over long periods of time.

3. **Replicability**—Content added to digital conversations can also be copied and pasted easily. Ideas and opinions shared spontaneously can be taken out of context and spread quickly through email, texts, and instant messaging services, carrying long-term unintended consequences.

4. **Invisible audiences**—When communicating with traditional audiences, speakers have a good sense of who is listening and can tailor messages accordingly. Digital audiences, however, are difficult if not impossible to define. The invisible members of digital audiences—those who inadvertently stumble across public expressions—may interpret ideas differently than they were originally intended.

The persistent, searchable, and replicable nature of digital conversations held publicly in front of invisible audiences means that social gaffes can be especially costly for today's teens. Pictures and videos of inappropriate or irresponsible behavior are reposted across the Internet. Slurs and insults made in moments of frustration become public knowledge immediately. Rumors spread uncontrolled, leaving victims unprotected and socially destroyed. The structural boundaries that limit communication in traditional environments—Who is present? What did they see or hear? What can they remember? Who will they tell? What evidence do they have to share?—are nonexistent in digital forums, amplifying the consequences of communication mistakes in the 21st century (boyd, 2007).

But the same four characteristics of digital forums—persistence, searchability, replicability, and invisible audiences—can have a positive impact on students when electronic conversations become a regular part of classroom instruction. First, the transparent nature of electronic conversations provides an equalizing opportunity for students who are typically disenfranchised. Students who are socially or economically isolated, who often have academic difficulty and lack status among their classmates, are frequently stereotyped as nonlearners by peers and judged as uninterested by teachers. Students in these groups, however, tend to participate in electronic conversations at higher rates than they participate in traditional classroom conversations, earning intellectual recognition for perhaps the first time (Ferriter, 2005).

Students who face social pressures to conform also engage in electronic conversations at higher rates than they participate in traditional classroom conversations. The potentially anonymous nature of digital dialogue serves as a "safety blanket" for students afraid of ridicule. Because joining in electronic conversations can be done anywhere, there is little risk of being embarrassed by poorly polished comments. Thoughts added to electronic conversations can be carefully crafted before they are posted. These assurances encourage participation from students who would have sat on the sidelines in the classroom, hypersensitive to the potential negative reactions of classmates and friends (Ferriter, 2005).

Finally, electronic conversations can challenge thinking. Students who participate in digital dialogue are forced to clarify their preexisting notions as they consider alternative positions. This process of mental justification is a higher-level thinking skill, and one of the strongest benefits of electronic conversations (Ferriter, 2005). What's more, students can tailor their participation in electronic conversations, following strands or individuals that are the most motivating. This ability to tailor the experience provides a level of intellectual differentiation that is hard to find in traditionally structured classrooms. Better yet, the permanence of electronic conversations means that they never lose their instructional value. Students can wrestle with new concepts or return to reflect on their initial positions whenever it is developmentally appropriate to do so.

Knowing that their students are already gathering with local peers in digital forums for communicating, accomplished teachers are working to craft school-based conversations that catch the attention of teens, who have traditionally turned away from online activities that seemed too academic. The key, not surprisingly, is building forums around interesting content. Students don't automatically reject online conversations with learning-related outcomes and higher levels of adult participation. They do, however, draw clear lines between opportunities to interact informally with peers and opportunities to study topics of deep personal interest. As the researchers behind the MacArthur Foundation's Digital Youth Project concluded, "Friendship-driven and interest-driven online participation have very different kinds of social connotations . . . friendship-driven activities center on peer culture, adult participation is more welcome in the latter, more 'geeky,' forms of learning" (Ito et al., 2008, p. 2).

Digital teens are also drawn to learning experiences that allow the following:

- **Self-directed exploration**—In new media environments, students are surrounded by opportunities to experiment, to explore without predetermined outcomes or goals in mind, and to receive immediate feedback from diverse audiences.

- **Peers to demonstrate authority and expertise**—In new media environments, students regularly learn from one another, whether they are showing friends how to defeat a shared video game or are being shown tips and tricks for working with new tools. These opportunities have fundamentally changed how teens view authority and expertise.

- **Students to wrestle with meaningful issues**—Schools have traditionally been charged with preparing students for meaningful careers. As a result, instruction emphasizes the mastery of skills seen as essential for success in the workplace. In new media environments, however, students are often exposed to concepts that are far more complex and morally pressing.

Preparing to play an active role in public conversations around these issues resonates with students. (Ito et al., 2008)

The implications that the rapidly changing communication practices of tweens and teens hold for educators are clear. First, our students are more connected to their local peers—friends from church, teammates, neighbors—than ever before. While social media allow for communication across geographic boundaries, most teens remain primarily interested in communicating with people they already know (Ito et al., 2008), which means motivation levels for school-based conversations should be high. What's more, the persistent, searchable, and replicable nature of digital conversations can create opportunities for marginalized students to gain social status in front of their peers (Ferriter, 2005). But in order to guarantee participation, school-based conversations must revolve around meaningful content, allow students self-directed opportunities for exploration, and respect the expertise and authority of all participants.

The challenge, however, is that one side effect of the standards and accountability push in education during the past decade has been a tendency to push self-directed learning and exploration aside in today's classroom as a response to external pressures. Communities convinced that end-of-grade exam scores are reliable indicators of the success or failure of students and schools have taken steps to systematically script instruction, crafting sets of lessons that teachers are required to implement without variation (Perlstein, 2007). While higher passing rates on standardized exams show the kinds of positive trends that leave policymakers and district leaders convinced that our schools are succeeding, we end up with classrooms defined by instructional practices that are poorly aligned with the learning environments our students are creating for themselves, using new media, beyond school. In fact, because of the social tools available to our students outside of school we could even be creating a learning divide in which some students view school learning as a teacher-directed activity and true learning as a self-directed activity.

Collaborative Versus Competitive Dialogue

The solution is surprisingly simple and thousands of years old: it's time for teachers to reintroduce their students to Socratic circles. Based on the thinking of the ancient Greek philosopher and teacher Socrates, Socratic circles give students the opportunity to interact with one another in conversations around shared texts connected to provocative issues. There are no predetermined outcomes or learning goals attached to Socratic circles—and the best conversations are student-led. "Socratic circles turn partial classroom control, classroom direction, and classroom governance over to students by creating a truly equitable learning community in which the weight and value of student voices and teacher voices are indistinguishable," writes high school English teacher Matt Copeland, author of *Socratic Circles: Fostering Critical and Creative Thinking in Middle and High School* (2005, p. 3).

If you were to watch a traditional Socratic seminar in action, you'd see a classroom divided into two groups: an inner circle of participants wrestling directly with the content being studied and an outer circle of silent observers tracking provocative ideas and conversation behaviors. Members of the inner circle—having read and annotated a shared text ahead of time—would work first to create meaning. Questions would be asked, ideas would be challenged, and conclusions would be drawn. Their peers in the outer circle would then provide constructive feedback on the interactions that took place between classmates before moving into the inner circle and continuing the conversation themselves. "It is the interaction between the inner and outer circles that enables students to control the direction and process of the dialogue taking place," writes Copeland (2005, p. 9).

Throughout the seminar, the classroom teacher would be managing logistics: keeping time, allowing both groups to play the participant and observer roles, tracking patterns of interaction, summarizing key ideas, and facilitating a final discussion about both the content and the conversational strengths and weaknesses of the class. While teachers may begin inner circle conversations with focused questions and redirect student groups when discussions stall, their primary responsibility is to turn control of the dialogue over to their students. "Of course, the teacher is still nearby to take those reins back if the horses begin to run wild and out of control," writes Copeland (2005, p. 62).

Successful Socratic circles depend on teaching students the differences between collaborative and competitive dialogue. Competitive dialogue—frequently rewarded by our world—is predicated on the belief that there are winners and losers in every conversation. Companies fighting for market share, politicians fighting for votes, and celebrities fighting for attention are all modeling competitive dialogue. In competitive dialogue, everyone is an opponent instead of an ally (Copeland, 2005).

Collaborative dialogue, on the other hand, depends on a mutual desire to create shared knowledge. "One of the most prevalent misconceptions students have about Socratic circles is that they are a form of competitive debate in which participants argue to win," writes Copeland. "This can be destructive to the quality of classroom dialogue, because dialogue represents the collaborative quest to construct knowledge" (2005, p. 46). Participants in collaborative dialogue assume that everyone has good intentions, changing the way that they respond to one another. Open-minded questions are asked, and emphasis is placed on drawing new conclusions instead of on deciding whose initial positions were correct. Challenges are seen as pathways to new learning, and participants look for strengths in the positions of others as opposed to pointing out perceived weaknesses (Copeland, 2005).

Promoting the kind of dialogue that leads to the collaborative construction of knowledge depends on introducing students to a set of specific conversation behaviors. These behaviors include working to engage silent students, to make conversations safe for every participant, to ask good questions, to correct inaccurate thinking, and working through disagreements.

Working to Engage Silent Students

In many classroom conversations, there will be students who sit silently and watch the conversation go by. To the casual observer, these students may appear uninterested at best and unintelligent at worst. Silent participants, however, are often actively listening and mentally engaged. They're simply intimidated by assertive peers and unwilling to elbow their way into spirited conversations.

Recognizing that multiple perspectives strengthen shared understandings, students in the most successful collaborative discussions see silent peers as missed opportunities and systematically use targeted questions to draw them into the conversation. To reinforce the importance of engaging everyone in a collaborative dialogue, teachers publicly highlight examples of successful efforts to include students who would have otherwise remained silent. They also stress that silent students have a responsibility to lend their voices to shared conversations, painting inaction as a behavior that carries intellectual costs for everyone.

Working to Make Conversations Safe for Every Participant

In many classroom conversations, a small handful of students end up—often unintentionally—dominating the course of a discussion. Making frequent comments focused on areas of personal interest, they ignore the contributions of others and jump in anytime there is a moment of free space that no one else is filling. To the casual observer, it seems like these students are talking to themselves!

Changing this behavior starts with careful conversation tracking by both teachers and students. Assertive students must be able to visually see that their involvement limits the opportunities for others to get involved. Assertive students should also be taught to ask open-ended questions, to elicit thinking from other peers, and to build on strands of conversation that have already been started. Teachers should highlight places where the work of an otherwise dominant participant brought new ideas to the collective table.

Working to Ask Good Questions

The collaborative construction of shared knowledge depends on one key ingredient: good questions. Good questions hook participants, encouraging them to share. Good questions challenge peers to think differently, lead conversations in new directions, and leave room for other participants. Sometimes good questions are asked of the entire group. Sometimes good questions are asked of individual members. Regardless, good conversations cannot happen without someone who is willing to ask the kinds of questions that make other people think.

Encouraging students to question begins and ends with spotlighting the most provocative and challenging ideas added to each conversation. Celebrating questions reminds students that effective contributions to ongoing conversations aren't always statements of opinions or facts. While working in the outer circle of a Socratic seminar, teachers can ask students to record motivating questions and extend strands of thinking when they become members of the inner circle. Good questions can also be revisited during follow-up conversations, posted in classroom collections, or become the focus of new studies.

Working to Correct Inaccurate Thinking

Regardless of how carefully students have studied a topic, inaccurate information is bound to be shared during the course of any collaborative conversation. Students who share inaccurate information are not intentionally trying to confuse their peers, they just don't know as much about the conversation subject as they think they do. Seeing correction as a form of disrespect, however, most students allow inaccuracies shared during Socratic circles to go unchallenged.

Working to change this behavior depends on helping students understand that correcting peers isn't inherently disrespectful. Instead, when handled with careful language and in the context of a collaborative effort to build shared understanding, it can be an intentional attempt to help someone grow as a learner. Challenging inaccuracies is best done by presenting direct evidence—the text being studied, previous lessons, independent learning experiences—of competing perspectives. Doing so encourages students making inaccurate statements to mentally wrestle with ideas that they once held to be true.

Working Through Disagreements

Good conversations are bound to have moments of open disagreement between participants. In fact, conversations *without* disagreement are typically evidence of poorly selected topics or poorly prepared students. Conversations in which everyone agrees also tend to be the least motivating to today's students who want to wrestle with provocative ideas together. The challenge with competing viewpoints in Socratic circles, however, is that students are taught from an early age that polite participation in classroom activities means avoiding disagreements.

For collaborative conversations to result in new learning, students need to be encouraged to embrace intellectual discord as an opportunity to polish and refine collective thinking. Reaching the point where an open-minded approach to disagreement is possible depends on teaching students to trust the intentions of their peers. When thinkers in a Socratic circle believe that everyone is working toward the same end goal—to learn together—it is possible to disagree with an idea instead of an individual. Students should also be taught to use specific words or phrases when expressing disagreement and to publicly share times when their thinking has been changed by peers. Making the successful outcomes of disagreement transparent lends a sense of safety to collaborative conversations around controversial topics.

■ ■ ■ ■ ■ ■ ■ ■ ■ ■ ■ ■ ■ ■ ■ ■ ■ ■ ■

Accomplished teachers recognize that the content outcomes of collaborative conversations are only possible when students are skilled communicators. As a result, they design frequent opportunities for their students to reflect on positive dialogue behaviors over the course of an entire school year. Role-playing—which allows students to fine-tune a set of responses to the kinds of situations they are likely to experience during the course of collaborative discussions—is one of the most effective forms of practice. A series of potential role-plays that you can use to introduce your students to these collaborative conversation behaviors can be found in the handout "Learning About Conversation Behaviors" (pages 139–144). Then use the handout "Targeting Conversation Behaviors" (pages 145–146) to begin a class dialogue about the role-play activity.

Creating Digital Opportunities to Connect

Socratic circles resonate with today's students primarily because they align so well with the characteristics of the digital worlds that our children inhabit beyond school. Questions from peers provide the most significant challenge in the best Socratic circles, because emphasis is placed on learning together. Authority and control over the direction of inquiry rest in the hands of participants. Socratic circles are defined by collective exploration and collaboration around meaningful problems, which are characteristics of the learning situations that iGeneration students are most passionate about (Tapscott, 2009).

The best news is that translating Socratic practices to the kinds of online conversations that our students are already having is easy using new media tools for communication. Software applications such as Ning (www.ning.com) and Blackboard (www.blackboard.com) allow teachers to create ongoing, asynchronous digital forums focused on topics being studied in class. Synchronous discussions are being held using applications such as Skype (www.skype.com) and Dimdim (www.dimdim.com). Some teachers are even using instant messaging and microblogging applications such as Chatzy (www.chatzy.com) and Twitter (www.twitter.com) to extend classroom conversations around interesting content.

Classrooms across the country are even finding ways to enhance their in-school Socratic circles with synchronous and asynchronous learning tools. Chat applications allow students in the outer circle to instantly interact around the information being shared by the inner circle. Facilitators can encourage students in the outer circle to use the Web to search for and confirm the information being shared in the inner circle. This process allows all students to be engaged in the learning process and provides opportunities for collaborative dialogue that builds meaning.

For students, access to digital conversations around school-based content—whether they take place at home or in school—is unexpectedly motivating. Evidence of that motivation can be found in the following quotes, collected from a 2008 survey of sixth-grade students who used VoiceThread (http://voicethread.com), a free tool for facilitating asynchronous conversations, over the course of an entire year to extend Socratic circles started in their language arts and social studies classrooms:

> VoiceThread allows me to hear the thoughts of many other students just like me! I can think differently about the same topic, and people really do challenge my mind. I also like to respond to people and challenge their thinking and share the way I think with them.

> Commenting, arguing, discussing, and agreeing on many different topics . . . is very fun. Although, sharing your views about things and having people respond is the best thing about VoiceThread!

> I really enjoy VoiceThread because it's a cool way to have a digi-conversation with people from your class . . . Several new ideas that I wouldn't have thought of bounce around my head after I visit VoiceThread. It's something new every day.

> The reason why I like our VoiceThread . . . is because it gives you a chance to communicate with people online and also you get to see their opinion . . . Personally I hate ending

conversations because you never know if something is going to pop into your mind. (as cited in Ferriter, 2008)

While synchronous and asynchronous opportunities to connect are equally motivating to students and provide similar opportunities for practicing collaborative dialogue, each requires teachers to take a unique set of instructional steps.

Structuring Asynchronous Conversations

Instructionally, structuring the kinds of asynchronous conversations that can motivate your classes depends on the careful selection of content for students to respond to and interact around. The best asynchronous forums are often extensions of traditional Socratic circles. Along with introductory comments sharing simple conversation reminders and directions, post the quotes, questions, and ideas that sparked animated thinking in your inner and outer circles before opening digital discussions to your students. When you're ready to introduce your digital discussion to your classes, encourage students to carefully preview the developing conversation. Asking students to use the "Previewing an Asynchronous Conversation" tool (page 147) to track their initial thinking before adding posts to your digital seminar can help ensure that all contributions are meaningful and interesting.

Remember that your role in asynchronous forums should mirror the role that teachers play in traditional Socratic circles. You are there to support students, not to control conversations. Ask provocative questions to stimulate stalled conversations, model proper discussion language, spotlight particularly original thoughts in class, use selected contributions as extensions in lessons, and help students identify motivating strands of conversation to join. For the duration of an asynchronous conversation—which is typically focused on one topic and has clear starting and ending dates— create a borderless learning experience in which the thinking done online spurs discussions in your classroom, and the thinking done in class spurs productive contributions to the intellectual collaboration taking place online.

In classes struggling with the kinds of behaviors that support collaborative dialogue, it can be helpful to introduce students to a series of specific comment types and templates that encourage healthy contributions to asynchronous discussions. These comment types—described for students in the handout "Commenting in an Asynchronous Conversation" (pages 148–149)—can include the following:

■ **Starter comments**—Sometimes students will add new content such as questions, statistics, images, videos, and quotes to an asynchronous conversation. Each new piece of content added must be paired with a starter comment that focuses the thinking of other participants. Starter comments can introduce the source for new content, the connections between new content and the existing conversation, and/or a position statement explaining how a student feels about the new content that they've brought to a digital conversation.

- **Kicker comments**—Sometimes students will be the first to add thoughts to a thread started by another participant. These types of comments are called kicker comments because they "kick off" a strand of conversation. Students making kicker comments should begin by responding to questions asked by the user who posted the original content. Students making kicker comments should then explain their own thinking—backing assertions with evidence, connecting to ideas shared in class, supporting or disagreeing with the ideas of others. Finally, students making kicker comments should finish with interesting, open-ended questions that encourage others to speak up.

- **Pushback comments**—Sometimes students will want to respond to something that another participant has said in an asynchronous conversation. They may agree and want to add more elaboration to support a central point, or they may disagree and want to challenge the thinking of peers. These kinds of comments in a collaborative conversation are called pushbacks. Pushback comments must begin with a quote from the thinking to be supported or challenged and must include enough elaboration to allow others to easily follow the direction of the conversation.

- **Answering comments**—Sometimes students will want to answer a question leveled directly at them or asked of the entire group that has been added to an asynchronous conversation. In many ways, responding to questions is the lifeblood of collaborative dialogue, because such responses let participants know that their ideas are valuable and interesting to others. Thoughtfully responding to questions encourages participation and keeps digital conversations moving forward and interesting. Students answering comments should begin their post with the question that was asked, include a thorough answer, and ask follow-up questions whenever possible.

It can also be helpful to share sample strands of discussion with students when structuring asynchronous learning opportunities. Sample strands serve as de facto role-plays of digital conversations, allowing students to explore the characteristics of positive interactions, to see the language of digital dialogue modeled, and to pinpoint the kinds of behaviors that cripple online conversations. While the most effective sample strands of conversation will always be those drawn from the work done in your own classroom, an initial reflection sheet, "What Can Digital Conversations Look Like?" can be found on pages 150–151. Finally, developing effective asynchronous conversation skills depends on providing students with meaningful feedback. After completing an online conversation, ask students to use the "Scoring Student Participation in Asynchronous Conversations" rubric (pages 152–153) to rate the contributions of one of their peers and the "Reflecting on an Asynchronous Conversation" (page 154) to guide reflection. Doing so will create a classroom environment in which effective digital communication is an expectation that students are willing to hold one another accountable for.

Technically, structuring the kinds of asynchronous conversations that can motivate your classes starts by selecting a service for hosting digital discussions. While there will always be dozens of services to choose from, the basic features that you should consider before making a final decision will always remain the same:

- **Simultaneous strands of conversation**—The best digital conversations allow students to target their participation, focusing on the ideas that are the most individually motivating. As a result, good forums for digital communication allow users to create and maintain several different strands of conversation related to the same topic at the same time.

- **Control of conversation privacy settings**—In the most progressive classrooms, conversations around controversial topics are open for public viewing and participation, which provides an audience for student ideas and a source for new challenges to the fundamental beliefs developed during the course of digital discussions. Sometimes, however, district policies prohibit this kind of transparent work online, requiring classroom conversations to be closed to public viewing. Any application that you choose for digital conversations must allow you to tailor privacy settings appropriate for your students and school.

- **Interaction around a wide range of content types**—Today's students are increasingly motivated by interactive learning opportunities driven by multimedia content. Most early asynchronous conversations are text-based, which can be inherently dissatisfying to teens used to websites that regularly incorporate streaming audio and video. Selecting applications that allow students to both consume and produce video and audio content in asynchronous conversations can help ensure that motivation levels in your classroom remain high.

- **The ability to search and archive any conversation**—As your students become more adept at interacting with one another in digital forums, you'll not only find that the conversations they engage in will become powerful examples of collaborative thought, but also that the content generated can be used to promote continued reflection long after a conversation ends. Ensuring that each conversation becomes a long-term learning tool depends on selecting a service that allows users to search within conversations as well as archive them once they end.

One of the best free tools available to teachers interested in asynchronous conversations is VoiceThread (http://voicethread.com). Known as a "group audio blog," VoiceThread allows users to interact around a wide range of content types. Video clips, images, documents, charts, graphs, and PowerPoint presentations can all be uploaded and used to start individual strands of conversation. What's more, text, audio, and video comments can be added to VoiceThread conversations, lending a sense of interactivity and personality that is often missing in asynchronous conversations.

Teachers interested in encouraging students to practice articulating thoughts in writing can require students to add text-only comments to VoiceThread conversations, while teachers working with struggling writers or students who need to practice public speaking skills can require students to add audio or video comments to VoiceThread conversations. This ability to tailor both the content and the comments in asynchronous conversations to the unique needs of any classroom is what makes VoiceThread one of the best starting points for any teacher interested in creating a digital home for collaborative dialogue. To see what VoiceThread conversations can look like in action, explore the samples introduced in the "VoiceThread in Action" handout found on pages 155–156.

After selecting a service to host your asynchronous conversations, you'll need to think through a wide range of other technical considerations. You'll need to consult with your school or district's technology services department to make sure that you are following any procedures and protocols that have already been established for asynchronous conversations. You'll need to make careful choices about the privacy settings for your digital discussions, ensuring that your students are safe while working online. You'll need to experiment with the asynchronous application that you have chosen to be sure that it is accessible behind your district's firewall and that it functions well on the computers that your students have access to. The "Asynchronous Conversation Checklist" (pages 157–159) can help you effectively prepare for successful asynchronous conversations.

Structuring Synchronous Conversations

Structuring asynchronous discussions between peers who know one another offline neatly aligns with the ways in which new media environments are already being used by your students, making the integration of school-based conversations more approachable for everyone. However, limiting digital conversations to local peers overlooks the very real potential to develop the kinds of cross-border relationships and understandings that Tim Berners-Lee imagined when first designing the Internet. The most accomplished 21st century teachers are using synchronous conversations to break down the walls of their classrooms and connect their students to classes in other countries, because they recognize that exposure to international peers means exposure to multiple perspectives on the kinds of critical issues—poverty, global warming, drought, wars, deforestation, immigration—that pose challenges worldwide.

These experiences, argues Don Tapscott (2009) in *Grown Up Digital*, are essential to developing the kinds of globally aware and active citizens that our world needs in order to survive:

> Will their civic activity around the world become a new kind of activism? Will they rise to the challenges of deepening problems that my generation is handing them? Never has there been a time of greater promise or peril. The challenge of achieving that promise and in so doing saving our fragile planet will rest with the Net Generation. Our responsibility to them is to give them the tools and the opportunity to fulfill their destiny. (Kindle location 851–855)

Giving your students the tools to fulfill Tapscott's vision of global activism begins by selecting an application for hosting synchronous conversations. In most cases, this decision begins by having a conversation with your school or district's technology services specialists. Unlike the Web-based tools used for asynchronous conversations, which generally place few demands on a school's digital resources, tools for synchronous conversations can stretch a network's capability to capacity. As a result, many districts carefully monitor the synchronous communication in their schools, defining specific procedures that must be followed when connecting with classes in real time and supporting specific services for conducting these kinds of conversations. Also, many school districts have built familiar social media tools into their learning management systems in order to ensure that all communications can be monitored. Working carefully with your technology services department can guarantee that you aren't confronted with any digital surprises during synchronous conversations.

Once you've been given permission to conduct synchronous conversations, the following three questions can help you select the right application:

- **Are you planning informal conversations between individuals and/or small groups?** Often, the most engaging cross-border conversations occur between individuals and/or small groups, giving students intimate opportunities to interact with peers from other countries around controversial issues. These kinds of synchronous conversations require nothing more than simple applications like Skype (www.skype.com) that allow users to see one another through webcams while talking.

- **Would you like to see students making more formal, large group presentations to one another?** As classes study controversial issues at a deeper level, there may come a time when opportunities for large group presentations—complete with PowerPoints, desktop sharing, and interactive Web browsing—become desirable. These kinds of complex synchronous conversations require more sophisticated, feature-rich webinar applications like Dimdim (www.dimdim.com) that allow presenters to create online meeting rooms and share information in a variety of formats with audiences at predetermined times.

- **Is ease-of-use your primary concern?** For many teachers, the primary concern with any attempt at integrating new technology is finding tools that are approachable. Doing so removes digital barriers and increases the likelihood that new instructional opportunities stick. If ease-of-use is your primary concern, consider synchronous applications like tinychat (www.tinychat.com) or TodaysMeet (http://todaysmeet.com), which will allow you to quickly create enhanced chat rooms in which students can interact with one another through text and video-based conversations.

After selecting an application for hosting your synchronous conversations, you'll need to think through a wide range of additional technical questions. Will your students need individual accounts to use the service that you've selected? If so, how will those accounts be created? Are you planning to record and archive each synchronous conversation? If so, where will the archived recordings be posted? Does your school have a quiet room that can be set aside for classroom videoconferencing? If so, how can you make sure that students working with international peers are uninterrupted during the course of their conversations? Each of these questions—along with eleven others—can be found on the "Teacher Videoconferencing Checklist" (pages 160–163). Working through this checklist will make certain that you're prepared to conduct synchronous conversations in your classroom.

Giving students the opportunity to fulfill Tapscott's vision of global activism also depends on finding classes to partner with—perhaps the most intimidating challenge for teachers new to digital learning experiences. The good news is that you're not the only teacher interested in pairing your classes with peers abroad. The rise of the Internet has left thousands of classes connected and looking for conversations. Companies like ePals (www.epals.com) have been connecting classrooms globally for years and have expanded to provide social media tools to enhance communication.

By exploring the following libraries of teachers and classes willing to use digital tools to communicate, you're likely to find a potential match in no time. Be prepared to be persistent, however. Like any digital resource, some of the contact information that you find in these warehouses may be out-of-date or inaccurate:

- **Skype in Schools wiki** (http://skypeinschools.pbworks.com)—The Skype in Schools wiki may be the single best resource available for teachers interested in making connections with classrooms beyond their own schools. Not only can you find comprehensive directories listing the usernames, grade levels, and content areas of teachers who are interested in using Skype with their students, you can also post "Want Ads" advertising particular projects that you are hoping to establish connections around.

- **Skype other classrooms** (http://snipurl.com/sfapo)—With thousands of followers, Sue Waters—who writes at the Edublogger—is a respected voice on the role that emerging technologies can play in today's classrooms. In December of 2008, Sue compiled a list of classrooms interested in making connections through Skype that is sorted by country, continent, and time zone. Including places like Ecuador and Algeria, Sue's list may give your students the chance to collect interesting perspectives from places in the world that they've never heard of!

- **Find classes for joint online projects** (http://snipurl.com/sfatm)—Widely recognized as the master of educational resources, Larry Ferlazzo created this list in the spring of 2009, detailing the best ways to find classes for joint online projects. An ESL teacher from Sacramento, California, Larry includes a wide range of online resources, suggestions, and strategies for taking the first steps toward starting joint online projects with classrooms around the world. While the sources that he references aren't directly connected to using synchronous conversations in the classroom, all will be invaluable in thinking through the kinds of connections that are possible when working beyond the walls of your school.

As you work to select classes that you want to connect with, place the topic of the conversation that you are planning at the front of your mind. If you are studying global poverty, for example, look for classes in the developing world that can provide first-hand accounts of life in poor nations, or for classes in social welfare states that take completely different national approaches to wealth and social justice. Finding potential synchronous conversation partners with competing viewpoints and experiences will add the mental tension and intellectual discord that drive motivating discussions and real learning. Poor choices at this stage—selecting partners in nations whose approaches and perspectives mirror those in your own country—will limit the learning outcomes of the digital conversations that you are working so hard to structure.

Preparing students for synchronous conversations around controversial issues like global poverty requires more than simply making good choices when selecting sister schools, however. Much like the skills necessary for effective participation in Socratic circles and asynchronous conversations, students engaged in real-time discussions with classes in other countries must be ready to have their own thinking challenged—and to challenge the thinking of their global peers. They must recognize that controversial issues like global poverty have no simple answers and must see synchronous videoconferences as an opportunity to think together. Finally, they must be willing to approach every synchronous conversation with an open mind and a willingness to change their preconceived notions about the topic being studied based on information collected from international peers.

The "Tracking Your Videoconference" handout—found on pages 164–166 and designed to walk students through a set of structured pre-, during-, and post-videoconference questions—can help your classes make the most of synchronous conversations. Also included at the end of this chapter are a "Student Videoconferencing Preparation Checklist" (pages 167–168) that can be used to plan and prepare for synchronous conversations, a set of simple directions for using Skype ("Skype Skills to Master," pages 169–170) to conduct synchronous conversations, a reflection sheet ("Reflecting on Digital Conversations," page 171) students can use to consider the overall value of synchronous conversations, and a list of additional resources ("Additional Sources for Studying Videoconferencing and Skype," pages 172–173) that teachers can use to explore how innovative classes are using synchronous conversations in their classrooms. All of these materials lend the kinds of structure that successful videoconferences rely on. Visit **go.solution-tree.com/technology** to download interactive versions of these pages.

Final Thoughts

For twelve-year-old Tommy, science was the best class of the school day because it never seemed to end. Not only did he have hands-on experiences with light, sound, and heat to look forward to, but he also had ongoing asynchronous conversations to engage in each day once he'd gotten home. Together with his classmates, he was involved in a never-ending cycle of scientific thought that started during second period and ended just before bedtime. In animated conversations before class, during lunch, around their lockers, and online, Tommy and his like-minded peers spent time designing original experiments, testing hypotheses, sharing observations, drawing conclusions, and asking new questions. "I love educational subjects," said Tommy, "and now that I had a message board with science as its topic, I had the message board that I liked. It was very fun to talk to other people online and discuss the subjects we were studying in class" (T. Pendleton, personal communication, May 27, 2004).

Tommy, a quiet boy who'd moved to the United States in the middle of the school year and initially had troubles fitting in, quickly became a digital star. The questions he asked made others think differently and kept them coming back for more. His creativity made others imagine. Dozens of new experiments—conducted both at home and in the classroom—were born from strands started by Tommy in asynchronous conversations. For Tommy, the digital opportunities to communicate created by his teacher encouraged students to spend more time thinking about school. "They go to school, they do their homework, and then log on—so they spend more time learning than if they just went to school and then did their homework," he argued (T. Pendleton, personal communication, May 27, 2004).

Through it all, Tommy and his peers felt in charge, studying interesting questions simply because they could. Like the best Socratic circles, their digital conversations were defined by independence and action, essential keys to learning described by noted philosopher and educator Mortimer Adler. "All genuine learning is active, not passive," wrote Adler in *The Paideia Proposal*. "It involves the use of the mind, not just the memory. It is a process of discovery, in which the student is the main agent, not the teacher" (1998, p. 50).

The same sense of student-driven discovery can become a part of the intellectual life of your classroom if you are willing to create opportunities—both online and in school—for collaborative dialogue between peers.

Learning About Conversation Behaviors

One of the keys to any successful classroom conversation is encouraging students to practice working through a set of scenarios demonstrating common conversation behaviors. By doing so, teachers provide students with opportunities to develop strategies for facilitating ongoing dialogue regardless of the circumstances of a particular conversation.

The scenario cards on the following pages are designed to serve as role-play models. Assign each scenario to a student group. Then, allow groups to practice and deliver performances based on their scenario cards to their classmates. As each group performs, have students fill out the "Targeting Conversation Behaviors" handout (pages 145–146).

Follow each performance with a conversation spotlighting successful and unsuccessful interactions between participants.

Scenario 1: Don't Forget About Silent Suki

In many classroom conversations, you will find students who sit silently and watch the conversation go by. On the outside, they may seem lazy and uninterested, but on the inside, they're often the most active participants. They really are listening—and if you can draw them into the conversation, you might just learn something remarkable that you hadn't considered. Silent Sukis aren't unintelligent. They're just not the kind of people who are going to elbow their way into an active conversation.

Your job is to craft a short (three- to five-minute) role-play that warns our class not to forget about Silent Sukis in conversations.

Potential Characters

Teacher—The teacher's job is to start a conversation on the topic of school uniforms. Consider asking a question like, "If our school considered a school uniform policy, how would you feel?"

Rashad—Rashad is a confident character who feels strongly that school uniforms are a bad idea because they take away a student's right to express his or her personality. He speaks often, asks tons of great questions, and makes good points that other students agree with.

Rebecca—Rebecca agrees with Rashad that school uniforms are a bad idea. She often extends on something that Rashad says or answers one of Rashad's questions, giving more details that he hadn't considered. Together, she and Rashad make a convincing case that school uniforms are a bad idea.

Suki—Suki sits silent for most of the conversation, but if you watch her body language, you can tell that she is interested in the conversation. She follows speakers with her eyes, sits forward, looks thoughtful, and may even try to speak every now and then, only to be cut off by Rashad and Rebecca's excitement.

Ira and Diego—Ira and Diego represent the average students in this conversation. You can tell by their body language that they're engaged, and both make solid contributions whenever they have the chance to speak. Rashad and Rebecca seem to know this about Ira and Diego. As a result, they seem really interested in what both have to say. They ask Ira and Diego more questions than they ask Suki, and they build off of their contributions.

Key Point

Remember that you're trying to remind your peers that silent students often have information that is worth sharing in a conversation. That means Suki has to do something unexpected and remarkable in your presentation.

Perhaps at the end of your role-play, Suki finally gets a chance to speak, making an incredibly thoughtful statement about why school uniforms make sense—something like "but wouldn't school uniforms make everyone—especially poor students—feel a little less threatened by school because they know they wouldn't have to compete over clothes?"

The other students—including Rashad and Rebecca—become animated, obviously wanting the conversation to continue, but the teacher steps in, moving the group on to a new activity.

Your ideas:

Remember that the ideas on this scenario card are just suggestions. Your role-play can take an entirely different direction as long as it emphasizes the importance of engaging quiet group members in conversations.

page 2 of 6

Scenario 2: When Ridiculous Rashad Just Can't Keep His Mouth Closed

In many classroom conversations, you will find students who end up completely dominating the course of a discussion. They make rambling comments, ignore the contributions of others, and jump in any time there is a moment of free space. When you watch one of these conversations from the outside, it seems like these Ridiculous Rashads are talking to themselves!

Your job is to craft a short (three- to five-minute) role-play that warns our class about the dangers of Ridiculous Rashads in conversations.

Potential Characters

Teacher—The teacher's job is to start a conversation on the topic of school uniforms. Consider asking a question like, "If our school were to consider a school uniform policy, how would you feel?"

Rashad—Rashad is a loud and borderline obnoxious character who is the first to jump into the classroom conversation about school uniforms. His comments are longwinded and filled with twelve-dollar words that may or may not be used appropriately. As soon as other students finish a comment, Rashad jumps right in—even if it means talking over his peers. Often, Rashad completely ignores what other students have said, starting new strands of conversation on his own.

Rebecca—Rebecca is a really bright young lady who really wants to listen and learn from Rashad at the beginning of the conversation. She concentrates on what he's saying, no matter how long his comment rambles on. Then, she tries to respond—only to have Rashad jump back into the conversation and talk over her. Eventually, she gets frustrated by his refusal to listen and his tendency to talk all the time.

Ira and Suki—Ira and Suki represent the average participants in this conversation. Neither says very much, but both seem to be interested and listening as the conversation begins. When they do make contributions, their thoughts are appropriate and focused on the topic. Over time, though, Rashad's speeches bore Ira and Suki. As the conversation progresses, you can tell by their body language that both have completely lost interest.

Diego—Like Rebecca, Diego shows great patience with—and interest in—Rashad at the beginning of the scenario. He, too, gets frustrated with Rashad's willingness to talk over his peers, though. The difference between Diego and the other participants, though, is that by the end of the conversation, he is working actively against Rashad. He interrupts Rashad's ramblings abruptly, asking other group mates questions that are completely unrelated to the points that Rashad is trying to make. Rashad eventually grows to believe that Diego is rude.

Key Point

Remember that you're trying to remind your peers that students who talk too much and don't take time to listen end up turning off their peers. That means Rashad's group mates have to show that they eventually grow tired of him. Perhaps they start rolling their eyes whenever he starts to speak. Perhaps they start talking between themselves quietly, ignoring him completely. Perhaps they sigh or groan each time that he talks over them.

Either way, they look incredibly happy when the teacher steps in and moves their group to a new activity!

Your ideas:

Remember that the ideas on this scenario card are just suggestions. Your role-play can take an entirely different direction as long as it emphasizes the damage that can be done by talking too much in conversations.

Scenario 3: The Power of Remarkable Rebecca's Good Questions

Good conversations depend on one key ingredient: good questions! Good questions hook participants and encourage them to share. Good questions challenge participants to think differently about topics. Good questions lead conversations in new directions and leave room for other people to participate. Sometimes good questions are asked of the entire group. Sometimes they are asked of individual members. Regardless, good conversations cannot happen without someone who is willing to ask the kinds of questions that make other people think.

Your job is to craft a short (three- to five-minute) role-play that shows our class how good questions can improve the quality of conversations.

Potential Characters

Teacher—The teacher's job is to start a conversation on the topic of school uniforms. Consider asking a question like, "If our school were to consider a school uniform policy, how would you feel?"

Ira and Rashad—Ira and Rashad represent the average participants in this conversation. From their body language, you can tell that both are interested in the topic and engaged by the thinking of their peers. However, neither ask very many questions. Instead, their comments tend to be statements. They're all connected to the topic, they may share interesting facts or different points of view, but they don't automatically encourage other students to respond.

Rebecca—Rebecca is the star of this conversation. Her body language sends the message that she's motivated and involved, but it is the quality of her questions that really makes her stand out from her peers. She asks questions of the group that force them to look at the topic of school uniforms from a new point of view. She asks questions of her peers that force them to clarify their statements. In fact, almost every contribution that Rebecca makes comes in the form of a question that leads to new conversations: "Diego, I really liked your point about the cost of school uniforms, but don't you think parents would save money by not buying the trendy, brand name clothes we all wear right now?"

Suki—To the audience, Suki and Rebecca seem like best friends. That's because Suki is incredibly motivated by the questions that Rebecca is asking. She works hard to answer Rebecca, proving to be an incredibly intelligent and thoughtful participant in the conversation. Together, Rebecca and Suki make a powerful team: Rebecca asks remarkable questions that Suki answers in a way that forces her peers to think differently about school uniforms.

Diego—Diego is also involved in this conversation from the beginning: listening, building on the thoughts of his peers, sharing concrete details from research. Like Ira and Rashad, though, he doesn't ask many questions—and the questions that he does ask either raise points that have already been made in the conversation or have obvious answers that don't really stimulate conversation: "Do you think school uniforms are good?" "Should we have school uniforms?"

Key Point

Remember that you're trying to remind your peers that questions make for great conversations. To make this point clear, three characters are really important: Diego, whose questions are not very sophisticated and do little to make the conversation move forward, Rebecca, who asks the kinds of questions that get everyone talking, and Suki, who always seems to give thoughtful responses to Rebecca's questions. That means Rebecca is going to have to do a good job listening to the group and asking questions connected to the ideas being shared. Rebecca's group mates are going to have to seem animated and excited to answer the great questions she's asking.

Your ideas:

Remember that the ideas on this scenario card are just suggestions. Your role-play can take an entirely different direction as long as it emphasizes the idea that good questions make for great conversations.

Scenario 4: What if Inaccurate Ira Is Just Plain Wrong?

In many classroom conversations, you will find students who end up sharing information that is inaccurate. They might argue that bullfighting is okay because there are plenty of bulls in the deserts of Spain or that exploring Saturn would be easy because it's right next door to Earth. They're always well-intentioned—they just don't know as much about the topic as they think they do!

Your job is to craft a short (three- to five-minute) role-play that shows our class how to politely correct Inaccurate Iras when they are just plain wrong!

Potential Characters

Teacher—The teacher's job is to start a conversation on the topic of school uniforms. Consider asking a question like, "If our school were to consider a school uniform policy, how would you feel?" The teacher should also remind students to use the notes that they've taken on school uniform policies when making their arguments in the class conversation.

Ira—Ira is a really motivated participant in the conversation. You can tell from his body language that he's interested and involved. He shares a few good ideas with the group and builds on the comments of his peers. At some point in the conversation, though, Ira makes a statement that is wildly inaccurate such as, "You know, parents are going to have to buy more allergy medicine if we go to school uniforms, because so many kids are allergic to clothes."

Rashad—Like Ira, Rashad is an active participant in the conversation, making good comments and adding on to the thoughts of his peers. He asks good questions, listens appropriately, and works to get even the quiet members of his group involved. His weakness, though, is that he doesn't want to disagree with anyone—so when Ira makes inaccurate statements, Rashad always agrees: "You're right, Ira, I hadn't thought of that."

Suki—Suki is the star of this conversation. She's involved from the beginning, listening, building on the thoughts of her peers, asking good questions, and getting everyone involved. She seems to know just the right time to speak, and she never talks over anyone. The difference between Suki and Rashad, though, is that Suki is unwilling to let Ira's inaccurate statements go unchallenged. Instead, she *politely* pushes back against Ira's thinking: "Ira, where did you find that information in our research? Can you give us some examples of clothes that students are allergic to?"

Rebecca and Diego—Rebecca and Diego represent the average participants in this conversation. They get involved when the opportunity seems right, adding comments and making statements that are accurate and connected to the ideas being discussed. Their body language also makes it clear that they're surprised by the inaccurate comments being made by Ira. Every time that he says something strange, they send puzzled looks to one another. They may also smile, chuckle, or laugh quietly together. They never bother to correct Ira, though. Instead, they just let the conversation move forward without comment.

Key Point

In many ways, your role-play is the most important for our class to see because peers are rarely willing to challenge the thinking of their classmates even when it is wrong!

To make this point clear, Rashad, Suki, and Ira have to play their parts perfectly: Ira's inaccurate statements have to be obviously wrong—almost to the point of being comical—but he has to appear to genuinely believe that what he is saying is true. Rashad shouldn't bat an eye at Ira's inaccuracies. Instead, he should agree no matter how strange Ira's assertions are. And Suki must challenge Ira without being challenging. She must show that she isn't critical of Ira. Instead, she just wants to help him learn.

Your ideas:

Remember that the ideas on this scenario card are just suggestions. Your role-play can take an entirely different direction as long as it emphasizes the idea that it is okay to challenge classmates who bring inaccurate information to the conversation.

Scenario 5: Disagree Without Being Disagreeable, Diego

Good conversations are bound to have moments where you disagree with the thoughts and ideas of other participants. In fact, if a conversation doesn't have any disagreement, it's probably pretty boring. There are two sides to every story, after all. While it is completely appropriate to express differing points of view in group conversations, it is also important to learn to disagree without being disagreeable.

Your job is to craft a short (three- to five-minute) role-play that shows our class how to act when disagreements arise in conversation.

Potential Characters

Teacher—The teacher's job is to start a conversation on the topic of school uniforms. Consider asking a question like, "If our school were to consider a school uniform policy, how would you feel?" The teacher should also remind students to use the notes that they've taken on school uniform policies when making their arguments in the class conversation.

Diego—Diego is super motivated to participate in this conversation. He's brought the notes that he made while researching, and he has a strong opinion about school uniform policies: he hates them. You can almost hear the scorn in Diego's voice when he talks about school uniforms; he barely listens when Rebecca—who believes that uniforms are a good idea—tries to make a case that doesn't line up with his point of view.

Rebecca—Rebecca is equally motivated to participate in this conversation, but she doesn't think that school uniforms are a bad idea at all. As a result, she's at odds with Diego from the beginning of the conversation. She tries asking him questions and sharing facts from her research, but Diego sees her as an enemy and won't listen to a thing that she says. Eventually, she stops trying to interact with Diego and instead ends up having a really good conversation with Rashad.

Rashad—Rashad and Rebecca end up being the co-stars of this conversation. Like Diego, Rashad tends to think that school uniforms are a bad idea. Unlike Diego, Rashad is willing to consider other points of view. As a result, he and Rebecca have a great conversation. Instead of competing with one another and trying to be right all the time—the mistake that Diego makes—Rashad and Rebecca ask one another great questions, challenge the evidence presented by their partners, and see one another as co-learners who are thinking about a topic together.

Ira and Suki—Ira and Suki represent the average participants in this conversation. Both are engaged and interested, and both make positive contributions whenever they have the opportunity. You can also tell through their body language, though, that they are turned off by Diego's aggressiveness. Neither is willing to correct him, however. Instead, they generally ignore and avoid him, choosing instead to interact with Rebecca and Rashad.

Key Point

Remember that you're trying to remind your peers that everyone involved in a conversation is a partner rather than an adversary. To make this point clear, Diego has to come across as the most difficult guy you've ever worked with in class. To Diego, this conversation isn't about learning—it's about winning. By making Diego super disagreeable, the interactions between Rashad and Rebecca—who disagree with one another about the central issue but enjoy wrestling with ideas together—will look positive.

Your thoughts:

Remember that the ideas on this scenario card are just suggestions. Your role-play can take an entirely different direction as long as it emphasizes the importance of disagreeing without being disagreeable.

Targeting Conversation Behaviors

To track what you are learning about cooperation in classroom dialogue, complete the following handout while watching each of the groups in class role-play common conversation behaviors.

Scenario 1: Don't Forget About Silent Suki

Whose behavior stands out in this scenario? What is it about his or her behavior that is extraordinary?

Have you ever seen this kind of behavior in a conversation before? Did it help or hurt the work of the group? Why?

What strategies do you think group members can use to either encourage or discourage this kind of behavior?

Scenario 2: When Ridiculous Rashad Just Can't Keep His Mouth Closed

Whose behavior stands out in this scenario? What is it about his or her behavior that is extraordinary?

Have you ever seen this kind of behavior in a conversation before? Did it help or hurt the work of the group? Why?

What strategies do you think group members can use to either encourage or discourage this kind of behavior?

Scenario 3: The Power of Remarkable Rebecca's Good Questions

Whose behavior stands out in this scenario? What is it about his or her behavior that is extraordinary?

Have you ever seen this kind of behavior in a conversation before? Did it help or hurt the work of the group? Why?

What strategies do you think group members can use to either encourage or discourage this kind of behavior?

Scenario 4: What if Inaccurate Ira Is Just Plain Wrong?

Whose behavior stands out in this scenario? What is it about his or her behavior that is extraordinary?

Have you ever seen this kind of behavior in a conversation before? Did it help or hurt the work of the group? Why?

What strategies do you think group members can use to either encourage or discourage this kind of behavior?

Scenario 5: Disagree Without Being Disagreeable, Diego

Whose behavior stands out in this scenario? What is it about his or her behavior that is extraordinary?

Have you ever seen this kind of behavior in a conversation before? Did it help or hurt the work of the group? Why?

What strategies do you think group members can use to either encourage or discourage this kind of behavior?

Your Final Thoughts

Which conversation behaviors do you think are the most common in conversations between students at our grade level? Why?

Which conversation behaviors do you think are the least common in conversations between students at our grade level? Why?

Which conversation behaviors do you think you will personally have the most trouble mastering? The least trouble? Why?

Previewing an Asynchronous Conversation

Title of Presentation:

While previewing this asynchronous conversation, track your thinking on this handout. Remember that good participants in digital conversations are always asking questions, making connections, forming opinions, and gathering facts. Be sure to note specific places where you'd like to add comments or respond to other viewers. Consider starting your comments with phrases like: *I notice, I wonder, I realized, You can relate this to, Although it seems, This reminds me of, I'm not sure that,* and *If I were _____, I would _____.*

Thread Title:

Content Description
What key points are expressed in the content of this thread? In the comments added by your peers?

Your Initial Thoughts
What ideas do you agree with here? Disagree with? What new directions would you like to take this conversation in?

Possible Comments
Write a draft of a potential comment here. Remember to use the computer to polish any text comments that you add to our conversation.

Questions for Reflection

1. Do you agree with the general direction that this conversation is heading in? Why or why not? What key points are being left out that you intend to bring to the digital table?

2. What connections can you make between this conversation and content that you've studied in other places and at other times? How can you integrate those connections into this conversation?

3. Which strand of conversation is the most motivating to you? Why? When will you return to see how that strand of conversation is developing?

Commenting in an Asynchronous Conversation

Title of Presentation:

Over the next several days, we'll continue the conversation that we started in our last Socratic circle online. Use this handout to script any comments that you plan to add to our digital discussion. Remember that scripting comments will help you post ideas that are easy to understand. Also remember that if you plan to add text comments, you should proofread for spelling and grammar errors.

Starter Comments

Sometimes you will add new content (threads, images, quotes, video) to an asynchronous conversation. When you do, it is important to include a starter comment to focus the thinking of other participants.

The following sentence stems will help you structure starter comments for new content that you add to our asynchronous conversation.

What do you notice about this   titled
and showing   ?

Kicker Comments

Sometimes, you'll find that you are the first person to add comments to content added by someone else in our asynchronous conversation—or you might have a completely original idea that no one else has brought up yet. These types of comments are called kicker comments because they "kick off" a new strand of conversation. When making a kicker comment, it is important to remember to respond to any questions asked by the user who posted the original content. It is also important to finish kicker comments with interesting questions that will encourage other viewers to speak up.

The following sentence stems will help you structure interesting kicker comments.

I noticed   .

This was interesting to me because   .

Pushback Comments

Sometimes, you'll want to respond to something that another participant said in our asynchronous conversation. You may agree and want to add more elaboration. You may disagree and want to challenge their thinking. These kinds of comments are called pushbacks. In a pushback comment, it is important to quote the person you are responding to so that other participants will know what caught your attention. It is also important to elaborate on your point of view and to disagree agreeably! Impolite people are never influential.

The following sentence stems will help you structure interesting pushback comments:

                                        said   .

I (agree/disagree) with (him/her) because   .

I think that   .

I am wondering if   .

Answering Comments

Sometimes, you'll want to answer a question that another commenter asked in an asynchronous conversation. Their question may have been directed right to you, or may have been asked to the group as a whole. Responding to questions is incredibly important because it lets others know that their ideas are valuable and interesting. Responding to questions helps keep asynchronous conversations moving forward and interesting.

The following sentence stems will help you structure interesting answering comments:

                asked   . This is a really interesting question,   .

I think   .

I also think   .

Do you agree with me? Looking forward to your reply!

What Can Digital Conversations Look Like?

A group of middle school students using pseudonyms recently extended a Socratic circle on hatred by having an asynchronous conversation together on Voicethread (http://ed.voicethread .com/share/88781/). Use this handout to study one strand from that conversation, in which students reflected on a quote from their original seminar.

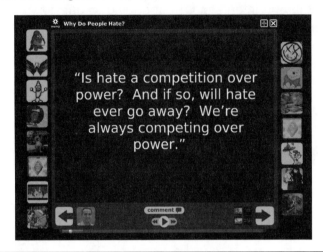

Student Conversation
Darth Tater: Here's an interesting quote on hatred that came from a seminar on hatred in my classroom. What do you think the connections are between hatred and power? Do hatred and and a quest for power go hand in hand?
Evil Barney: I think that the quest for power just sets the stage for hatred to occur. Whenever I play the game Risk, I notice that I become frustrated with other players that stop my conquest. I bet when people are trying to gain power on a large scale in real life, that frustration builds up like lava in a volcano and comes out as violence and hate all at once.   I don't think power is completely to blame for hatred, but it definitely helps hatred come along. What else do you think power does for hatred?
Mearan: Hate, most of the time, is competing over power. For example, you are nominated for president. Then, another candidate wins the election. You aren't going to be very happy are you? You will end up generating hate to that person, even if it is only a small bit.   Now, hate cannot be stopped, for it is a natural human emotion. As I have said before "we could create the illusion of it disappearing, but it will never be true." Saying that, we could lessen people's will to be in a higher power. It could lessen the hate, but it would never go away. Is there anyway to eliminate the humans need to be at the top of power?
The Happy Man: Mearan said: Is there anyway to eliminate the humans need to be at the top of power?   My answer is that there really isn't. The only thing we can do is to either get rid of that power, or to make power a little less glamorous. Most likely neither of those things is going to happen. The most anyone can do is wait for something to happen that does eliminate that need.   But in the grand scheme of things is there really any need for one person to have all that power?

page 1 of 2

Student Conversation

Pooh Bear: Evil Barney said: "I think that the quest for power just sets the stage for hatred to occur."

This really grabs my attention. Everyone keeps on saying that hate is expressed because of power. But what Evil Barney says is that power is kind of a step up to get to hatred. It leads to hatred . . .

When you feel power or the more you want it, it forces your hate to come out even stronger. A lot of the time in life, for some reason, people want to be powerful. I don't understand. What is the significance of this? Why is control such an exciting word to people?

It's kind of like and evil scientist or somebody in a movie. You might gain something so great, and so wanted by other people that it can get out of hand. By people wanting that thing (power) so much, you feel hate against them because they want the power that you have and you don't want to be taken away.

So I guess my overall question is: Why do people love the feeling of power and control?

Mearan: Evil Barney said: "I think that the quest for power just sets the stage for hatred to occur," and Pooh Bear said: "Power is kind of a step up to get to hatred. It leads to hatred."

I somewhat agree with this. However, I see power as more of a fuel. Let's think of hate as fire. The more the quest for power occurs, the more fuel you will have. So, if you have lots of fuel and then light the flames hatred, the flame will be big. Depending on the amount of fuel you had at the start, the flames of hatred will last longer, or it will be bigger.

So a quick clap for your new way of thinking. Anyone else see this from a different viewpoint?

Questions for Reflection

1. What types of conversation comments (starter, kicker, pushback, answering) can you find in this sample strand of collaborative dialogue?

2. If you were to rank these comments in order from the most important to the least important, what would your rankings look like? Why?

3. If you were to improve one of these comments, which would you choose? What revisions would you make?

4. If you were to join this conversation, what type of comment would you add? Where would you place it?

5. Which participant do you think made the most significant contributions to this sample strand of comments? Which made the least significant contributions? Explain your thinking.

Scoring Student Participation in Asynchronous Conversations

Like any new skill, students need to get regular feedback in order to become stronger participants in asynchronous conversations. This rubric is designed to help teachers and students rate participation in the asynchronous conversations that we have in class. Consider circling the individual statements that best describe the efforts of the student you are giving feedback to.

Above Average

The comments that you've added to our asynchronous conversation are all clearly connected to the topic we are studying. Because you knew so much about our topic, you raised points that no one else had considered. Almost everything that you wrote made me want to learn more.

What's even better is that you started some of the most active strands in our conversation—and your comments always made me want to respond! I found myself arguing with your points of view, answering your questions, and thinking harder each time I came across one of your comments.

The best part about your comments, though, is that you always seemed to find a way to respond to others. I liked that you asked and answered questions and pushed back against the thinking of others. I felt like you wanted to learn as much as you wanted to teach in our conversation, and that you respected the viewpoints that others brought to the table. All of that shows me that you were a good listener—and good listening makes or breaks conversations.

I'm really glad that you were participating in our conversation because I learned so much from you—and from the people who were responding to you!

Average

The comments that you've added to our asynchronous conversation are all clearly connected to the topic that we are studying, but in many places they seem simple. While one or two of your ideas made me think about our topic in new ways, most of the time it seemed like you weren't adding anything new to our conversation. I almost always looked at the comments that you added because I knew they would have potential, but I often ended up disappointed because there weren't enough details to leave me jazzed.

I'm also not sure that you've done a good job encouraging other people to participate in our conversation. I liked that you were asking questions, but the questions that you asked could all be answered easily and they rarely started new strands of thinking. I'm also not sure that I saw you answer any questions in our conversation—even when others asked you something directly! Finally, many of your comments repeated ideas that had already been shared by others. All of this makes me wonder whether or not you were listening to the rest of us.

I can't wait to watch you participate in our next conversation because you are right on the edge of being a star. With a bit more effort to share original thoughts and to get others involved, your comments will change minds!

Needs Improvement

The comments that you added to our conversation were disappointing. Most of the time, they seemed unconnected to the topic that we were studying, which interrupted some great strands of thinking. I'm not sure that you put much effort into sharing knowledge or bringing new ideas to our discussion—and that's surprising because you've got good ideas to share.

The worst part, though, is that I didn't see any attempts from you to join a conversation. You posted your own thinking time and again, but never responded to anyone. You didn't push against the ideas of your classmates, you didn't ask questions, and you didn't start any new strands for us to consider. In short, you did a lot of talking but you didn't do any listening!

I hate to say it, but your posts always seemed to distract me, and that was discouraging.

Reflecting on an Asynchronous Conversation

After a digital conversation has run its course, it is important for you to think back on what you've learned. The following four questions can serve both as a reflection guide and as evidence that you have engaged in a meaningful way with the topic we're studying together.

Questions for Reflection

1. Highlight a comment from our recent conversation that closely matches your own thinking. Why does this comment resonate with—or make sense to—you?

2. Highlight a comment from our recent conversation that you respectfully disagree with. If you were to engage in a conversation with the commenter, what evidence or argument would you use to persuade them to change their point of view?

3. Highlight a comment from our recent conversation that challenged your thinking in a good way or made you rethink one of your original ideas. What about the new comment was challenging? What are you going to do now that your original belief was challenged? Will you change your mind? Do more researching, thinking, or talking with others?

4. Highlight the strand of conversation from our recent conversation that was the most interesting or motivating to you. Which ideas would you like to have more time to talk about? Why? What new topics does this conversation make you want to study next?

VoiceThread in Action

One of the most popular tools for asynchronous conversations is VoiceThread, a group audio blog that allows users to add text, audio, and video comments to slides containing a wide range of multimedia content. To see what VoiceThread can look like in action, spend a few minutes exploring the following conversations, which were all created by a sixth-grade language arts teacher extending traditional Socratic circles beyond the classroom.

Genocide in Darfur

http://ed.voicethread.com/share/62276/

In the spring of 2007, a group of middle grades students in Massachusetts, Maryland, Virginia, and North Carolina joined together to raise attention about the genocide occurring in Darfur—a region of the African nation of Sudan. Along with blog entries and wikis designed to explain genocide to their peers, these students wrestled with the world's responsibility to help challenged nations in this VoiceThread discussion, which used political cartoons to start provocative strands of conversation.

Why Do People Hate?

http://ed.voicethread.com/share/88781/

In the fall of 2008, two language arts teachers—one working with sixth graders and the other working with eighth graders—brought their students together for a Socratic circle focused on the concept of hate. For the sixth graders, this conversation was an extension of their study of the Holocaust. For the eighth graders, this conversation was an extension of their studies around the theme of justice and injustice. This VoiceThread gave both groups of students the opportunity to interact with one another before and after the traditional Socratic circle was held at school.

Learning About Adaptation and Mutation

http://ed.voicethread.com/share/518424/

In the spring of 2009, a sixth-grade science teacher had his students use Flip Video camcorders to create short papercraft videos designed to introduce the concepts of natural selection, adaptation, and mutation to their peers. Then, he uploaded each group's final product to VoiceThread and asked classmates to provide one another with feedback about the overall quality of the videos produced. Doing so gave students the opportunity to practice giving and receiving constructive criticism.

Questions for Reflection

1. Is there evidence of meaningful conversation between students in these VoiceThread samples? What was surprising about the conversations that developed here? Were you impressed by anything that you saw, or is this the kind of work that you would expect from students engaged in asynchronous conversations around school-based topics?

2. What weaknesses do you see in the conversations that developed between students in these VoiceThread samples? What conversation skills are these groups of students still

struggling to master? How would you go about strengthening those weaknesses in your classroom?

3. Could your students pull off this kind of conversation with one another? What do you think it would take to get them to translate their classroom conversations into online forums? What skills would they need to learn first? When will you start teaching those skills?

4. What ideas will you steal from these VoiceThread samples to use in your own work with students? Do the format and content of any of these conversations resonate with you or meet elements of your required curriculum? Which conversation would your students be drawn to? How would you change one of these conversations to make it more appropriate, interesting, or motivating for the students in your classroom?

Asynchronous Conversation Checklist

Asynchronous conversations provide teachers with approachable ways to extend Socratic circles and provide students with opportunities to engage around classroom content beyond the school day. This preparation checklist will help you structure successful asynchronous learning experiences for your students. Use the following questions to help determine whether or not you are prepared to facilitate asynchronous conversations in your classroom. Also, in the last column, consider including the names and contact information of anyone who can help you with your action steps as well as the date when the action step will be completed.

Technical and Procedural Preparations

1. Have you checked with your school or district's technology services specialists to ensure that your school's Internet connection can successfully handle the demands of asynchronous conversations?

    Your Response/Next Steps:

2. Have you checked with your school or district's technology services specialists to see if there are any asynchronous conversation services that they suggest or support?

    Your Response/Next Steps:

3. Have you checked with your school or district's technology specialists to see if they have any specific policies or procedures regarding student participation in asynchronous conversations?

    Your Response/Next Steps:

4. Have you experimented with the asynchronous conversation service that you are planning to use to see if it is accessible at school? Are you certain that it will run effectively on the computers that your students have access to?

    Your Response/Next Steps:

5. Have you thought through the privacy settings that you plan to use for your asynchronous conversations? If you intend to make your conversations public, are you sure that you are following the Internet safety protocols required by your school or district?

    Your Response/Next Steps:

6. Have you mastered the basic skills necessary to add content and comments to conversations in the asynchronous application that you plan to use with your students? Will you be able to introduce these skills to your students?

   Your Response/Next Steps:

7. Have you created user accounts and passwords for your students? If not, how will your classes add comments to your developing conversations?

   Your Response/Next Steps:

8. When will your students add new content or comments to your asynchronous conversations? Are you expecting them to work primarily from home on this project? Will your students need access to external devices—microphones, video cameras—to add comments to your conversations? If so, how will they access these devices?

   Your Response/Next Steps:

9. Have you set aside time to introduce students to the basic features of the digital application that you've chosen to use for asynchronous conversations? Will you train students to serve as digital mentors for their peers?

   Your Response/Next Steps:

Pedagogical Preparations

1. Are you planning on using asynchronous conversations to extend Socratic circles started in your classroom? If so, when will these Socratic circles take place? How will you choose content for the online conversation once your Socratic circle ends?

   Your Response/Next Steps:

2. Do your students understand the kinds of discussion behaviors found in collaborative conversations? Have they had a chance to engage in collaborative conversations in class? Which behaviors do they struggle with?

   Your Response/Next Steps:

Teaching the iGeneration © 2010 Solution Tree Press • solution-tree.com
Visit **go.solution-tree.com/technology** to download this page.

3. Are your students comfortable with the language of collaborative dialogue? If not, will you introduce several sample strands of conversation for students to explore? Is it important to introduce your students to the types of comments that users add to collaborative conversations?

Your Response/Next Steps:

4. Do your students have enough background knowledge to be effective participants in your asynchronous conversation? How will you support their continued exploration of the topic you are studying?

Your Response/Next Steps:

5. Have you worked out a system for spotlighting the work being done in your digital conversations? Will you spend a few minutes each day highlighting individual contributions and interactions? Will students use rubrics to rate the work being done by their peers?

Your Response/Next Steps:

6. Have you created handouts to structure student thinking before, during, and after your asynchronous conversation?

Your Response/Next Steps:

7. Have your students worked through a series of role-plays that present a complete range of conversation scenarios—open disagreements, passive participants, off-task behavior, inaccurate statements?

Your Response/Next Steps:

8. Will you continue to use the conversations that your students engage in as tools for learning even after they have ended? How? Will archived conversations be available for students to study? Will provocative concepts raised in your conversations become topics for continued study in class? Who will make these decisions and/or set new directions based on the outcomes of your asynchronous conversations?

Your Response/Next Steps:

Teacher Videoconferencing Checklist

Skype (www.skype.com) has rapidly become one of the easiest ways for students to interact with the world beyond their classroom walls. With a bit of digital moxie, any teacher can facilitate real-time connections between classes on different continents or bring recognized experts into their rooms.

While Skype is a free tool that is easy to use, this preparation checklist will help you structure successful experiences for your students. Use the following questions to determine whether or not you are prepared to facilitate Skype conversations in your classroom. Also, consider including the names and contact information of anyone who can help you with your action step as well as the date when the action will be completed.

Technical and Procedural Preparations

1. Have you checked with your school or district's technology services specialists to ensure that your school's Internet connection can successfully handle the demands of a synchronous videoconference?

    Your Response/Next Steps:

2. If you are planning on bringing a digital guest speaker into your classroom, have you checked with your principal and followed your school or district's policies for using guest speakers in lessons?

    Your Response/Next Steps:

3. Have you created a Skype user account?

    Your Response/Next Steps:

4. Have you downloaded the Skype application onto the computer that you plan to use for videoconferencing?

    Your Response/Next Steps:

5. Have you installed a webcam on the computer that you plan to use for videoconferencing and then tested your webcam for audio and video quality?

    Your Response/Next Steps:

6. Have you added your digital guests to your Skype contact list and run a short test call with them to ensure that your Skype connection will be clean?

Your Response/Next Steps:

7. If you are planning on presenting to your entire class, have you reserved a data projector so that your students will be able to easily see your digital guests?

Your Response/Next Steps:

8. If you are planning on allowing groups of students to conference with peers or experts, have you found a quiet location with an Internet connection for Skype conversations to take place?

Your Response/Next Steps:

9. Are you planning on recording this videoconference? If so, have you sought guidance and support from your school or district's technology services experts?

Your Response/Next Steps:

Pedagogical Preparations

1. Have you checked with your school or district's technology services specialists to see if they have any specific policies or procedures regarding student participation in classroom videoconferences?

Your Response/Next Steps:

2. If your students are working in small groups to conference with peers or experts, have you introduced them to the Skype application?

Your Response/Next Steps:

3. If your students are working in small groups to conference with peers or experts, do your students have enough technical skill to deal with potential digital disasters—webcams dying, connections dropping, audio feeds failing?

Your Response/Next Steps:

Teaching the iGeneration © 2010 Solution Tree Press • solution-tree.com
Visit **go.solution-tree.com/technology** to download this page.

4. If your students are working in small groups to conference with peers or experts, have you worked out a schedule for individual conferences?

   Your Response/Next Steps:

5. Have you modeled the steps involved in using Skype for videoconferencing—and in troubleshooting common digital disasters—for your students?

   Your Response/Next Steps:

6. Have you considered training a small cadre of student technology leaders to facilitate Skype videoconferences for their peers?

   Your Response/Next Steps:

7. Do your students have enough background knowledge on the topic of your videoconference to be effective participants?

   Your Response/Next Steps:

8. Are the purpose and the desired outcome of your videoconference clear to your students?

   Your Response/Next Steps:

9. Have you created handouts to structure student thinking before, during, and after your classroom videoconference?

   Your Response/Next Steps:

10. Have you developed a plan for allowing students to debrief and process what they've learned once your videoconference has ended?

    Your Response/Next Steps:

11. Will your students share their new learnings with the digital peers or guest experts that they videoconference with?

    Your Response/Next Steps:

12. Do your students have the kinds of discussion skills necessary to participate in collaborative conversations?

Your Response/Next Steps:

13. Have you given students the opportunity to practice engaging in collaborative conversations with one another?

Your Response/Next Steps:

14. Have your students worked through a series of role-plays that present a complete range of conversation scenarios—open disagreements, passive participants, off-task behavior, inaccurate statements?

Your Response/Next Steps:

Teaching the iGeneration © 2010 Solution Tree Press • solution-tree.com
Visit **go.solution-tree.com/technology** to download this page.

Tracking Your Videoconference

While using a digital tool like Skype to host a videoconference is exciting in and of itself, it is important to remember that videoconferences aren't about using neat tools. Instead, they are about using neat tools to learn something valuable or to gather new ideas about the topics we're studying in class! Use the following handout to guide your thinking before, during, and after your upcoming videoconference in order to be sure that connecting with digital guests is a meaningful learning experience that we can be proud of.

Note that good thinkers always enter conversations with an idea of what it is they expect to learn. Use the first set of questions to prepare your thinking before your videoconference even begins. During your conference, remember that good thinkers are always working mentally; they look for new ideas, challenge inaccurate statements, find areas for agreement, and make new discoveries. Use the second set of questions to guide your thinking during the course of your videoconference. After your conference, remember that the potential for learning from a videoconference doesn't end as soon as you disconnect from the Internet. In fact, some of the best learning happens only after you have the chance to sit and think for a while. Use the final set of questions to debrief after your videoconference is over.

Before Your Conference

1. List everything that you already know about your digital guests—their age, their experiences with our topic of study, the conditions in their state or country, ideas that they have already shared about our topic of study, etc.

2. Based on what you know about your digital guests, how do you think they are likely to feel about our topic of study? What about their experiences—age, conditions in their state or country, ideas already shared—is likely to shape their opinions on our topic of study?

3. Do you think you are likely to agree with your digital guests during your videoconference? What thoughts, ideas, and opinions are you likely to share?

4. Are you expecting there to be any sources of disagreement between your thinking and the thinking of your digital guests on the topic we are studying? What are they? Why are you likely to disagree?

5. What points do you really want to get across in the course of your digital conversation? What ideas connected to our topic of study are the most important for participants to wrestle with?

Teaching the iGeneration © 2010 Solution Tree Press • solution-tree.com
Visit **go.solution-tree.com/technology** to download this page.

During Your Conference

1. What comments have your digital guests made that resonate with your own thinking about our topic of study? What is it about these comments that rings true for you?

2. Can you expand on the thoughts that you and your digital guests share in common? Do you have any additional facts or opinions that connect to the key ideas that you agree on? How can you add new ideas to conversation threads that have already started?

3. Have your digital guests made any comments that you don't agree with? What are they? Why don't you agree with them? Can you provide any facts or opinions to challenge the thinking shared by your digital guests?

4. What important ideas haven't been raised in your videoconference yet? Would raising these ideas add to the current conversation or would it end up interrupting the good thinking that is already happening?

After Your Conference

1. How has your thinking about the topic that we are studying in class changed now that you've had the chance to speak to your digital guests? Are there any new ideas that you're dying to explore? Do you doubt any ideas that you once believed were true? Are there any ideas that you are more convinced than ever are important for understanding the issue that we've been studying?

2. What caught you off guard or left you wondering during your conversation with your digital guests—either about the topic that we've been studying or the people that you were speaking to?

3. How would you explain any of the similarities between your thinking and the thinking of your digital guests? Why would they think the same way that you do about the topic that we've been studying?

4. How would you explain any of the differences between your thinking and the thinking of your digital guests? What is it about their circumstances or experiences that led them to draw different conclusions about our topic of study than you?

5. Who would you like to speak to next about the topic that we've been studying? Why would this be an interesting person or group to speak to? What questions would you try to answer in that conversation?

Student Videoconferencing Preparation Checklist

To gather new points of view about the topics we've been studying in class, you are going to use Skype (www.skype.com) to connect with and interview someone beyond our classroom. You might be interviewing a recognized expert—businessman, college professor, researcher—in the field we are studying, or you might be interviewing a group of students from classrooms in different corners of the world.

Regardless of who we are interviewing, use the following checklist to prepare for your videoconference.

Questions to Consider

1. Have you practiced role-playing the typical conversation behaviors that you are likely to experience in your videoconference?

   Your Response/Next Steps:

2. Have you completed the "Before Your Conference" section of the "Tracking Your Videoconference" handout (page 164)?

   Your Response/Next Steps:

3. Have you arranged a time for your videoconference that works well for all participants?

   Your Response/Next Steps:

4. Have you confirmed that nothing has changed in the schedule of your digital guests that will prevent them from attending your videoconference?

   Your Response/Next Steps:

5. Have you arranged for a quiet place to hold your videoconference?

   Your Response/Next Steps:

6. Have you worked through the "Skype Skills to Master" handout (pages 169–170)?

   Your Response/Next Steps:

Teaching the iGeneration © 2010 Solution Tree Press • solution-tree.com
Visit **go.solution-tree.com/technology** to download this page.

7. Do you have the username and password for the Skype account that you will be using during your videoconference?

   Your Response/Next Steps:

8. Do you know the Skype username for the digital guest that you will be calling?

   Your Response/Next Steps:

9. Have you tested your Internet connection and webcam to be sure that you won't have any major technical problems?

   Your Response/Next Steps:

10. Do you have a plan if major technical problems occur during your videoconference?

    Your Response/Next Steps:

11. Have you decided on a group member to make introductory comments that explain what your group's goals are for this videoconference?

    Your Response/Next Steps:

12. Have you decided on a group member to serve as your recorder or note taker?

    Your Response/Next Steps:

13. Have you decided on a group member whose primary responsibility is to push back against the statements of your digital guest?

    Your Response/Next Steps:

14. Have you developed a set of good questions about your topic that you hope to ask during the course of your videoconference?

    Your Response/Next Steps:

Teaching the iGeneration © 2010 Solution Tree Press • solution-tree.com
Visit **go.solution-tree.com/technology** to download this page.

Skype Skills to Master

Before you can conduct an effective videoconference using Skype (www.skype.com), you'll need to know how to master several basic Skype skills. Work with a partner and a computer with Skype installed to explore each of the following skills.

Opening Skype

On many computers, Skype will open automatically once the computer is turned on. If this is true for your computer, you will find an orange icon in the computer's system tray—the collection of icons found in the bottom right-hand corner of your computer.

If Skype doesn't open automatically on the computer you are using, you can launch it from the **Skype folder** found under **Programs** in your computer's Start menu—or the **Applications** menu in the **Finder** window on a Mac. (You'll need a Skype username and password, though.)

Checking Audio Settings

To be sure that your microphone and speaker volumes are loud enough for a successful Skype conversation, select **Options** found under the **Tools** menu at the top of your Skype window. Then, select **Audio Settings** from the menu on the left-hand side of the **Options** window that appears.

Check to see that the **Automatically Adjust Microphone Settings** and **Automatically Adjust Speaker Settings** options are selected.

Testing Your Webcam

It is also important that you test your webcam before making a Skype call. Doing so will ensure that your webcam is working and that your digital guests will be able to see you.

To check your webcam, select **Options** found under the **Tools** menu at the top of your Skype window. Then, select **Video Settings** from the menu on the left-hand side of the **Options** window that appears. Your webcam should automatically start. Check the image that appears for quality. Does anything in the background—pictures, windows, chalkboards—make it difficult to see you? If so, consider moving to a new location.

Also, check to see that **Only From People in My Contact List** is selected from the **Automatically Receive Video From** menu and that **People in My Contact List** is selected from the **Show That I Have Video** menu.

Making a Skype Call

Begin by finding the person that you are trying to call under the **Contacts** tab found on the left-hand side of your Skype window. (You will know that they are online and ready for your call if the icon next to their screen name is green.) After selecting the contact that you are trying to call, select the **Video Call** button found at the top of the contact window that appears on the right-hand side of your computer screen.

Your computer will automatically dial your contact. When they answer, you will see their video appear in the center of your screen. Your video will appear in a small box in the bottom left-hand corner of your screen. Be sure to pay attention to your video so that you can adjust your camera during the course of the conversation if needed.

Planning for Disaster

While Skype is a great service that will work without a hitch most of the time, disasters—losing audio or video, having the Internet crash—are always possible when working online with a free tool. Having a plan for disasters will make these unexpected moments less stressful.

The first step to take when planning for disaster is deciding at the beginning of a videoconference who will take action when something goes wrong as well as what that action will be. Perhaps you will work to call your digital guest back. Perhaps he or she will call you back.

You can also communicate through instant messages. To send an instant message, type your thoughts in the **Instant Message** box found at the bottom of your contact window and then click the blue **Send Message** button.

Reflecting on Digital Conversations

Now that you've worked through your first videoconference, it's time to do a bit of reflection about the strengths and weaknesses of digital conversations. Spend a few minutes answering the following questions with the members of your videoconferencing group.

Questions for Reflection

1. If you were to rate the value of videoconferencing as a way to gather new ideas on topics we are studying on a scale of one to five—with one representing "completely useless" and five representing "the best thing ever"—what would your rating be? Why?

2. What would you say is the greatest strength of videoconferencing as a way to gather new ideas on our topics?

3. What would you say is the greatest weakness of videoconferencing as a way to gather new ideas on our topics?

4. Did you have any trouble with technology during your videoconference? If so, how did you solve the problems?

5. What will you do differently the next time you videoconference in class? If you were to give one tip to the next group conducting a videoconference in class, what would it be? Why?

6. What can your teacher do differently to make sure that student groups have successful experiences with videoconferencing in class? Were there any areas in which you felt unprepared for your videoconference? What would have helped you feel more competent or comfortable?

Additional Sources for Studying Videoconferencing and Skype

Most teachers who are new to videoconferencing have a million questions: Will guest experts really be willing to come into my classroom? Can I record the conversations that my students have in Skype? What kinds of things are other classes doing with videoconferences?

The following resources may just answer some of those kinds of questions for you. Use the "Additional Notes/Reminders" column to list ideas in the resources you've explored that caught your attention. Do these ideas raise any additional questions or present interesting new directions for your work?

Name of Resource	Additional Notes/Reminders
Videoconferencing Out on a Lim (http://vcoutonalim.org) Janine Lim could have the single most exciting job in the world: she coordinates videoconferencing experiences for eighteen school districts in southwest Michigan. Luckily for you, she also writes extensively about her work on her blog, Videoconferencing Out on a Lim. Spend some time with Janine's resource-rich site and you'll find examples of projects that students across the K–12 continuum are engaged in, links to presentations about the power of videoconferencing in the classroom, connections to other bloggers who write extensively about videoconferencing, and research that supports the important role videoconferencing can play in student achievement.	
Met Any Good Authors Lately? (http://snipurl .com/sfboh) One of the best things about being a K–12 classroom teacher is that everyone—sports stars, university professors, business experts, published authors—likes helping kids learn a little bit more about their work, especially when helping is as easy as firing up a computer and connecting with classrooms via videoconference! This 2009 article from the *School Library Journal* details a set of authors at almost every grade level who are willing to conference with your kids for free. How's that for a good deal?	

Name of Resource	Additional Notes/Reminders
50 Awesome Ways to Use Skype in the Classroom (http://snipurl.com/sfc0q) Often the biggest challenge for teachers new to videoconferencing is imagining projects that fit into their current work. This 2009 post from the Teaching Degree.org blog should open your mind to what is possible with Skype. It includes an annotated description of fifty websites on which teachers detail projects, share resources, provide tip sheets, and engage parents using Skype, which is an amazing digital destination for anyone just beginning to consider the potential that videoconferencing holds for his or her kids and classes.	

CHAPTER **FIVE**

Collaborating to Solve Problems

Second-year elementary teacher Amanda Summers looks over her math curriculum and decides that she wants her fourth- and fifth-grade students to understand geometry through a lens outside of the textbook. Before she teaches a lesson to the students, she poses a problem in the form of a task: work on a team, as architects and builders, to design a futuristic house that is aesthetically appealing because of its geometrical design. After posing the question, Mrs. Summers designs a series of formative assessments to ensure that her students understand the fundamental principles of geometry. Then, she engages her classes in lessons on design and home building (A. Summers, personal communication, January 13, 2010).

As part of the unit, she decides to invite an architect to share real-world examples of interesting designs and a foreman from a construction company to discuss home building. Armed with these examples and experiences, her students form teams and begin to work on their plans, which must be approved by the "governing board of builders" before model construction can begin. Mrs. Summers knows that this project will take longer than she usually spends on the textbook unit, but she is looking forward to the final presentations of student designs. She also realizes that solving open-ended problems without clearly defined solutions can be inherently motivating to her students (A. Summers, personal communication, January 13, 2010).

How often do these kinds of student-driven, problem-centered learning experiences happen in your classrooms? If you work in traditional brick-and-mortar schools, your answer is likely to be discouraging. Current models of standards-based instruction don't always lend themselves to a problem-based approach to learning, which is inherently time consuming and messy. Many creative teachers, however, have been designing instruction this way for years with amazing success. While it is not enough to simply design problems and turn students loose—mastery depends on teachers who can help students understand the content connected to the initial challenge, the steps necessary to solve problems, and the skills necessary to collaborate—it is possible to make your classroom a place in which creativity and innovation around meaningful questions play central roles in mastering the required curriculum.

This chapter begins with a review of what research says about the three levels of problems. Then, we examine the important role that collaboration can play in developing collectively intelligent solutions. Finally, we explore how businesses are using wikis to pair employees in collaborative efforts and present a set of tips and tricks for structuring wiki-driven problem-solving projects in classrooms. The chapter ends with a series of handouts that can be used to teach students to tackle defined problems without clear solutions and to introduce wikis as a tool for knowledge creation.

In a World Full of Problems

The American philosopher and educational reformer John Dewey described the process of problem solving in five logical steps: (1) a difficulty is felt; (2) the difficulty is located and defined; (3) possible solutions are considered; (4) consequences of these solutions are weighed; and (5) one of the solutions is accepted, tested, and evaluated (Dewey, 1910). While students may not work through each step individually or sequentially—especially if they join a team working on a predetermined problem—there is a logical flow involved in developing the most effective solutions.

Jacob Getzels, a professor of education at the University of Chicago and noted expert on creativity and problem solving, worked with Mihaly Csikszentmihalyi to take Dewey's thinking one step further, identifying three distinct types of problems (Getzels & Csikszentmihalyi, 1967, 1976):

- **Type 1 problems**—Type 1 problems are generally the easiest to solve. The problem is clear to both the presenter and the solver, and both are aware of one method for generating the right solution. Type 1 problems involve little more than working systematically to apply a predefined process to discover one "correct answer." Simple mathematics problems—$2 + 2$, 5×4—are examples of Type 1 problems.

- **Type 2 problems**—Type 2 problems are also clearly defined for both the presenter and the solver, and while a straightforward method for generating one correct answer exists, neither the method nor the answer are immediately apparent to the solver. Solving Type 2 problems depends first on identifying the right process and then applying that process to generate a solution. Mathematics word problems—If Johnny has eight slices of pizza and he sells each for two dollars, how much money will he raise?—are straightforward examples of Type 2 problems.

- **Type 3 problems**—The problem, the method for working toward resolution, and the complete range of potential outcomes are ambiguous and poorly defined to both the presenter and the solver in Type 3 problems. Solving Type 3 problems begins by defining the exact nature of the challenge: What is being asked? Are there solutions for this problem? Is this a problem worth solving? Then, solvers identify and evaluate potential solutions, selecting the one most likely to resolve the original challenge.

Unlike Type 1 and 2 problems, Type 3 problems have no clear correct answers. In fact, presenters and solvers often interpret the problem and develop solutions differently based on their background or experiences. The problem that opened this chapter—Can you design a futuristic house that is aesthetically pleasing because of its geometric design?—is a good example of a Type 3 problem.

Solving challenging problems is a higher-order task requiring students to marshal intellectual resources and develop cognitive strategies. Complex problems must be broken down into manageable chunks. Background experiences—particularly those connected to similar problems—must be consulted. New information must be collected, plans of action must be crafted, and potential solutions must be tested and evaluated. The best problem solvers are persistent, unwilling to surrender, and unafraid of failure. They also possess a measure of confidence in their own abilities, providing the assurance necessary to move forward in the face of ambiguity (Kirkley, 2003).

To complicate matters for classroom teachers, simply teaching students specific processes for tackling complex challenges does little to develop problem-solving skills. While working systematically lends important structure to student attempts at problem solving, context knowledge is far more important. As Jamie Kirkley of Indiana University writes:

> In fact, researchers concluded that knowledge of context was the most critical feature of skill in problem solving. Thus, current research supports problem solving as a situational and context-bound process that depends on the deep structures of knowledge and experience (Palumbo, 1990). When teaching problem solving, authentic problems in realistic contexts are essential. (2003, p. 7)

Solving Type 3 problems effectively—including the kinds of complex, cross-border challenges (global warming, poverty, deforestation, drought) that have been at the center of the projects spotlighted in each chapter—depends on building problem-specific content knowledge. Solvers who have carefully explored the reasons a problem exists, the impacts of the problem, the emotions evoked by the problem, and the solutions that have already been applied are more likely to develop new and innovative approaches with potential.

Building Collective Intelligence

Successfully solving Type 3 problems is also a task best left to collaborative groups. In fact, as James Surowiecki argues in *The Wisdom of Crowds* (2004), individual expertise is almost impossible to develop in areas as broad and intangible as problem solving. "Auto repair, piloting, skiing, perhaps even management: these are skills that yield to application, hard work, and native talent," writes Surowiecki. "But forecasting an uncertain future and deciding the best course of action in the face of that future are much less likely to do so" (2004, Kindle location 648–653). Individual experts working to solve complex problems are consistently outperformed by groups, draw conclusions contradictory to those held by other experts in the same field, and overestimate the reliability of their own conclusions (Surowiecki, 2004).

In a culture that has a long history of venerating experts, this conclusion can be hard to swallow. Simple proof can be found in one of the most unlikely places: *Who Wants to be a Millionaire*, the once-popular game show hosted by Regis Philbin pitting ordinary Americans against a series of fifteen increasingly complex questions. Answer all fifteen questions correctly, the show promised contestants, and walk away a millionaire; stumble, however, and walk away with nothing. The show's real attention-grabber was pairing each contestant with three unique lifelines. When stumped by difficult questions, they could delete two multiple-choice options, call a friend who they believed was worth consulting, or conduct an instant survey of the studio audience.

For the average viewer watching from home, lifelines—particularly phoning a friend and polling the audience—were the highlight of every episode. And with thousands of dollars at stake, advice drawn from individual expertise or the collective intelligence of a randomly assembled crowd of people could either change a contestant's life or leave them empty-handed. With the benefit of hindsight, most contestants would have turned to the random crowd instead of their hand-picked experts every time: over the course of the show's history, studio audiences picked the right answer 91 percent of the time (Surowiecki, 2004).

Nothing in Surowiecki's study of the wisdom of crowds—including the results of popular game shows—suggests that individual expertise doesn't exist. As Surowiecki explains:

> It does mean that however well-informed and sophisticated an expert is, his advice and predictions should be pooled with others to get the most out of him . . . the group's decision will consistently be better decision after decision, while the performance of human experts will vary dramatically depending on the problem they're asked to solve. (2004, Kindle location 681–690)

According to Surowiecki, however, groups must be cognitively diverse, independent, and decentralized in order to solve problems effectively. Groups that are cognitively diverse—which can be easy to create in classrooms—include individuals with a range of aptitudes, ideas, and personal interests. When groups are cognitively diverse, they are more likely to consider a range of potential solutions to shared problems simply because members draw from unique sets of background experiences. In every field dependent on innovation, most of the early solutions proposed in group projects will fail or be abandoned, but having access to multiple perspectives increases the likelihood that the best solutions will be uncovered and polished (Surowiecki, 2004).

The members of collectively intelligent groups also exhibit a high degree of independence from one another. In the context of conversations around group dynamics, independence refers to the ability of members to act as individuals free from the influence of their peers. While team members in any group situation will work to shape the thinking of their peers, the strongest groups see diverse thoughts as sources for potential solutions (Surowiecki, 2004). Independent thinking can be difficult for elementary, middle, and high school students, however, who would rather protect relationships than push contrary positions. As a result, teachers must consistently celebrate groups that embrace independence.

Surowiecki's final condition for group intelligence is a certain level of decentralization. Decentralization—the flexibility to make autonomous decisions and set independent directions—encourages motivation and promotes innovation. Decentralized groups are highly invested in their work, resulting in final products that are carefully polished (Surowiecki, 2004). The challenge for elementary, middle, and high school teachers is that classroom groups often benefit from a certain amount of structure early in their development. Without any guidance, support, or coordination—characteristics of completely decentralized projects—students are likely to become frustrated and work without a clear direction. Too much guidance, support, and coordination, however, stifle the natural creativity necessary to generate novel solutions for knotty problems.

The first step, then, for teachers interested in giving students opportunities to collectively develop solutions for complex international problems is to ensure that all groups, whether they are self-selected or teacher assigned, are cognitively diverse. Next, teachers must emphasize the important role that independent thought plays in developing effective solutions. Students must feel comfortable voicing disagreement within groups, a skill introduced in chapter 4; otherwise, ideas with potential are likely to be stifled.

Finally, teachers must delicately balance the benefits of decentralization with the need for structure. Several handouts provided at the end of this chapter can help with this task. The first—"Understanding the Problem" (pages 191–192)—is designed to lead students through a meticulous study of any issue. The second—"Evaluating Potential Solutions" (page 193)—forces students to think carefully about the strengths and weaknesses of their preferred solution for a global challenge. Both can help groups develop the problem-specific content knowledge that good solutions depend on.

The last—"Rating Potential Solutions" (page 194)—is designed to encourage independence in groups, providing students with a safe way to express disagreement with their peers while evaluating the solutions being explored. When groups are ready to articulate their potential solutions, they can use the "Problem-Solution Introductions" (pages 195–197), "Writing Solution Paragraphs" (pages 198–200), and "Rating Problem-Solution Pieces" (pages 201–202) handouts to craft effective final products.

Wikis in the Workplace

For businesses in increasingly competitive marketplaces, every day brings new Type 3 problems to solve: Which products are the most likely to catch fire in the next six months? How can we convince consumers to invest in our products even as disposable income becomes a smaller line item in personal budgets? What services can we offer to improve the shopping experience in our stores? Where can we save money? Businesses, therefore, are perfect case studies for teachers interested in learning more about collaborative problem solving in action.

In many companies, these types of questions are answered by small handfuls of executives working at the top of complex hierarchies. Senior management teams establish vision, make important decisions, and give directions. While channels for communication make it theoretically possible for entry-level employees to suggest improvements that can impact the entire organization, the process is poorly defined and slow. Expertise, rather than collective intelligence, demonstrated by years of experience and formal titles drives corporate problem solving in most traditional organizations (Tapscott & Williams, 2006).

The consumer electronics giant Best Buy, however, realized early on that important insight rested in the hearts and minds of its employees—including those working on the sales floors in their two thousand stores. Even with detailed statistical reports tracking every purchase made from the multibillion dollar corporation, senior executives working from the company headquarters in Richfield, Minnesota, understood that they couldn't possibly tell store managers or associates in rural Kansas or the Atlanta suburbs which products and services their customers would be drawn to. They lacked a nuanced understanding of local context—and in an industry competing over the smallest margins, local context could mean the difference between success and failure. Recognizing this, Best Buy set out to tap into the wisdom of its very own crowd (Tapscott & Williams, 2006).

Ask any senior manager over the age of fifty, and they'd likely tell you that tapping into the wisdom of 155,000 employees spread out over fifty states and five countries is an impossible task not worth pursuing. Robert Stephens, the thirty-seven-year-old founder of Best Buy's innovative Geek Squad tech services team realized, however, that his digitally savvy employees were already using new media tools to share problem-specific content knowledge with one another. Specifically, anywhere from twenty to four hundred employees from across the globe had been joining together in spirited synchronous sessions of *Battlefield 2*—an online, multiplayer war game—building relationships and informally sharing solutions to common problems at the same time. "They're talking and they're hanging out," says Stephens, "and often, they're talking shop and swapping tips" (Tapscott & Williams, 2006, Kindle location 4324–4329).

Best Buy's next steps were prescient: under the leadership of Stephens, then-CEO Brad Anderson, and Senior Manager for Social Technology Gary Koelling, the company rolled out an entire collection of digital tools bundled in a private network called Blue Shirt Nation designed to systematically capture and organize the shared knowledge of their organization. Particularly important to these efforts was a corporate wiki on which employees created an unbelievable amount of shared content. Projects were managed, products were developed, and troubleshooting guides were posted and polished by fifteen thousand voluntary contributors. Sales associates finally had access to the tips and tricks of their peers, and senior managers finally had access to the minds of their most invested employees—a cognitively diverse, independent, and decentralized group (Tapscott & Williams, 2006).

When compared to the millions of entries in Wikipedia—the free global encyclopedia with articles written in 240 languages—the content being created in Blue Shirt Nation pales in comparison, but both projects are tangible examples of peer-production, and both share three traits that can be instructive to teachers interested in using wikis to structure collaborative problem-solving projects (Tapscott & Williams, 2006):

1. **The final product of collaboration is information.** Wikipedia and Blue Shirt Nation are successful wiki-based collaborative problem-solving projects because users are coproducing knowledge—and coproducing knowledge requires little from participants outside of time, intelligence, and an Internet connection. Collaboration around more tangible products or problems, on the other hand, requires a greater investment on the part of participants—communication has to be precise, materials have to be acquired, face-to-face meetings have to be organized—discouraging ongoing contributions.

2. **Work can be broken down into independent chunks.** Collaborating around problems on Wikipedia or Blue Shirt Nation requires little systematic coordination. Geographically dispersed participants can tackle tasks asynchronously, contributing to the development of a solid final product without relying on anyone else. Not only does this lend a sense of independence and decentralization to both projects—two of Surowiecki's (2004) criteria for creating collectively intelligent groups—it also lowers the costs of participation.

3. **The actual costs for creating final products are low.** Nothing about the work being done on Wikipedia or Blue Shirt Nation carries hidden costs. Because the content created is self-selected, there is little investment in corporate planning and direction setting. What's more, because wikis are a simple text-dependent technology, training is unnecessary and finding space to store final products is easy.

The question most often asked by those considering wikis as a tool for learning from the wisdom of crowds, though, is why do people participate? After all, the thousands of volunteers actively creating Blue Shirt Nation—and the millions creating Wikipedia—are not being rewarded in the traditional sense for their contributions. According to Jimmy Wales—the founder of Wikipedia—three factors motivate people to voluntarily coproduce content:

1. **Opportunities to interact with other people**—As we learned in chapter 4, humans are naturally driven to connect. While the connections between individuals coproducing content on Wikipedia and Blue Shirt Nation are primarily digital, any opportunity to work together on a shared task can be engaging. "Why do people play softball?" asks Wales. "It's fun, it's a social activity" (Tapscott & Williams, 2006, Kindle location 1315–1322).

2. **Opportunities to interact with motivating content**—The Best Buy Geek Squad takes real pride in their role as technology savants. While they're unlikely to spend any time documenting the seasons of the past ten Super Bowl Champions, turn them loose to design a better jump drive—an actual task that Best Buy asked of the Geek Squad—and you'll get hundreds of polished sketches and interesting designs. Collaborative problem solving, then, depends on content that motivates participants.

3. **Opportunities to work toward a meaningful shared outcome**—Jimmy Wales isn't surprised that millions of pages of content have been created on Wikipedia by volunteers. "We are gathering together to build this resource that will be made available to all of the people

of the world," argues Wales. "That's a goal that people can get behind" (as cited in Tapscott & Williams, 2006, Kindle location 1322–1328). Voluntary coproduction projects are more likely to be successful when they share a significant and meaningful outcome (Tapscott & Williams, 2006).

What lessons can teachers learn from Wikipedia and Best Buy about using wikis as tools for organizing collaborative problem-solving projects? Perhaps most importantly, the characteristics of successful corporate coproduction efforts mirror the characteristics of engaging learning experiences. Our best lessons have always included opportunities for students to interact with one another around motivating content. What's more, the work done in our classrooms is knowledge-driven, and successful group projects are broken down into manageable chunks. To put it simply, using wikis to engage students in collaborative problem-solving projects should be a natural fit for today's classrooms.

Structuring Classroom Wiki Projects

Perhaps the reason Wikipedia and Blue Shirt Nation are so appealing and powerful is that users independently self-select the kinds of contributions that they want to craft. Most begin by following the updates on topics that fuel their personal interests. They check new content for accuracy, correct mistakes, and polish formats. They insert links and challenge users who post inaccurate information. They serve as de facto custodians, policing the content that they care about—sometimes working alone and other times developing partnerships with digital peers who share the same passions (Tapscott & Williams, 2006).

Other users adopt specific roles that they fill across categories, inserting links, translating content, adding images, checking citations. Because these roles are self-defined, there is a high level of intrinsic motivation. No one is telling Wikipedia or Blue Shirt Nation users that they have to contribute, and yet the collective effort of a diverse group of users inevitably results in interesting final products containing extensive content (Tapscott & Williams, 2006).

While this uniquely organic model for the peer production of content works well for Wikipedia and Blue Shirt Nation, it can be a recipe for disaster in elementary, middle, and high school classrooms simply because teachers and students are often initially unsure of exactly what good wiki work looks like. Understanding the characteristics of successful projects, then, is a critical first step toward structuring any collaborative wiki efforts in your classroom. Those characteristics—introduced in greater detail to teachers in the "Exploring Wikis in Action" worksheet (pages 203–205) and to students in the "Characteristics of Quality Wiki Pages" worksheet (pages 206–207)—include accurate content, deep linking, evidence of group revision, and quality presentation.

Accurate Content

The initial fear that every teacher has when approaching work with wikis is the constant risk that students will learn to embrace a tool that may promote the sharing of inaccurate content or flawed ideas. With the much-publicized horror stories of false information appearing on Wikipedia, we've become hesitant to embrace wikis as a teaching tool. And in some ways, these fears are justified. Because wikis are open websites that can be edited by anyone at any time, the content on wikis is often changing. At any given time, wikis can contain information that is just plain wrong.

That same risk, however, can make wikis a valuable teaching tool! The most accomplished wiki educators don't shy away from inaccurate content posted on classroom wiki projects. Instead, they embrace it as an opportunity to teach students about the importance of judging the reliability of online sources. While they constantly push students to proofread for precision, and value accuracy in the products that are produced by their students, they also recognize that content errors are new opportunities to teach students about information literacy.

Deep Linking

Higher-level learning experiences require learners to read and react to information. Synthesizing and evaluating content created by others is essential before new understandings can be developed. In wiki work, evidence of synthesis and evaluation can be seen in the number and quality of resources linked to on a wiki page. As authors develop new content, they insert links from a variety of reliable sources to provide evidence supporting their thinking.

Deep linking in classroom wiki projects forces students to make connections between their own beliefs and external evidence. It also serves as an additional opportunity for classrooms to have conversations about judging the reliability of online sources. Wiki pages with extensive links to credible sources are more likely to be trustworthy than those with limited links to questionable sources.

Evidence of Group Revision

Wikis are designed for collaboration, plain and simple. They are tools that facilitate the asynchronous work of peers around content of shared interest. As a result, accomplished academic wiki pages have evidence of extensive group revision. Page discussion boards include ongoing conversations about quality and content, and a careful exploration of the page history button (generally found somewhere in the header or footer of each wiki page) will reveal an extensive collection of previous versions.

In many ways, group revision is the greatest challenge for teachers interested in incorporating wiki work into their classrooms because students are inherently tentative about making meaningful edits to one another's work. Used to largely isolated classrooms—where collaboration has generally been somewhat simple or superficial—peers generally use wiki pages as places to post their own content rather than to make changes to content posted by others. Over time and with constant modeling, however, students embrace the collective nature of wiki pages and start making meaningful revisions to the work of their peers.

Quality Presentation

Accomplished wikis are really no different from accomplished writing in any other format: they demonstrate the use of age-appropriate grammar, punctuation, and spelling. Writers recognize that effective communication depends on their ability to create pieces that are easy to understand and are unencumbered by mistakes.

For many teachers, wikis become natural forums for reviewing grammar and spelling rules with students. Because errors are almost always going to be present in constantly changing work being created by kids, wikis are built-in, real-world opportunities for proofreading practice. Accomplished wikis also demonstrate age-appropriate levels of visual presentation. Images and embedded video are often used to enhance wiki pages. Creators maintain a balance, however, between appropriate use of multimedia content and digital overkill, recognizing that interactive elements can distract readers.

Wiki Roles

Look carefully at nearly any Wikipedia entry, and you'll notice that the majority of this work is done by a small handful of people—over 50 percent of Wikipedia's edits are made by less than 1 percent of its users (Tapscott & Williams, 2006). In school-based wiki efforts, this level of unbalanced participation can be detrimental—especially when students are working on graded group projects designed to demonstrate mastery of required learning outcomes. In these situations, it is essential for teachers to introduce a defined set of roles for student participation. Not only can defined roles balance participation, but they can also serve as an introduction to the kinds of shared tasks that Wikipedians—who model successful collaborative efforts to create knowledge-based content every day—complete naturally.

The following roles, introduced in student-friendly language in the handout "Wiki Roles for Student Groups" (pages 208–210), can serve as a good starting point for your classroom's collaborative problem-solving projects.

Link Layer

As we described earlier, links are essential in wiki projects, because they allow authors to synthesize content and allow readers to explore on their own. The credibility of an entire site, therefore, depends on the quality of the links included. What's more, links help teachers quickly assess levels of understanding and common misconceptions about topics by comparing the assertions being made on a group's wiki page to the content included in their collection of links.

Successful student projects, then, depend on the Link Layer, who is responsible for reviewing every link included on their group's wiki pages. Link Layers should begin by identifying logical places to insert links in their group's work, find sources that align nicely with the conclusions of their collaborative partners, and check each site selected for bias or accuracy. Finally, Link Layers must be willing to replace any links to questionable websites that have been included in their group's work.

Flow Master

Often, the greatest challenge for students when collaborating on wikis is naturally blending the language styles and organizing strategies of multiple authors. Trained to work on a single piece from beginning to end, students rarely consider how well their contributions will work with the content already added by peers. The consequences: poorly structured pieces that are difficult to read and understand.

That's where Flow Masters—who are completely responsible for reviewing a group's wiki page—come in. Flow Masters read with a critical eye, looking for places where readers are likely to be confused. They polish language, ensure a unified voice throughout the piece, and check to be sure that content is organized logically. The challenge for Flow Masters is that wiki pages are constantly changing, which means that Flow Masters must constantly revise. Flow Masters make the kinds of revisions that improve the readability of their group's final product.

Spelling Cop

Chances are, your students take a lackadaisical approach to spelling, right? Today's teens rarely place a priority on precise language; they are surrounded by informal opportunities to communicate that are driven by speed and aimed at peers—text messages, Facebook updates, instant messages. The results include poor writing habits that lead to final products riddled with simple spelling errors regardless of their intended audience.

Collaborative wikis focused on important issues provide teachers with the perfect opportunity to stress the central role that accuracy plays in building credibility and earning the confidence of readers. Accuracy, however, depends on having a meticulous Spelling Cop in each group who is responsible for checking every word added to a shared final product. While the Spelling Cop's role appears simple, it requires persistence. Each new revision is an opportunity for another word to be misspelled, after all!

Discussion Starter

Like most of the work spotlighted in *Teaching the iGeneration*, good wiki projects start and end with conversations between students. The difference is that the conversations between partners in wiki projects are almost always focused on the steps necessary for efficient and effective peer production. Coordination is essential in any shared effort, and Discussion Starters are largely responsible for starting the kinds of conversations that can organize their group.

Discussion Starters live on the discussion boards of shared wiki pages. They are responsible for asking questions about what their group is producing. They must be good evaluators, comparing their group's product and progress against the work being done by others. They must also be good planners, helping their group set due dates and complete required tasks, and good motivators, capable of providing encouragement and direction whenever necessary.

Captain Spit-and-Polish

In chapter 3, we learned that visual influence is becoming increasingly important in today's world. Capturing the attention of iGeners—who've lived their entire lives connected to televisions, video games, and the Internet—depends on the careful use of graphics, images, colors, and font sizes. What's more, interactive content is remembered while static content is quickly forgotten.

Captain Spit-and-Polish is responsible for incorporating content that is visually appealing and capable of capturing the attention of viewers likely to scan first and read later. They use images, videos, and other embeddable content to support arguments and assertions. They also work to ensure that the layout of their wiki page is professional and interesting. The trickiest part of Captain Spit-and-Polish's job is remembering who the intended audience for a particular page is and making sure that all graphics, images, and layout decisions are appropriate for that unique group of people. The kinds of content that appeal to twelve-year-olds probably won't appeal to anyone over twenty-two!

Implementation Strategies for Wiki Beginners

Once your students are comfortable with the characteristics of good wiki work and are aware of a set of specific, defined roles for participation, you will be ready to start projects using wikis as a tool for the coproduction of content. To make this work more approachable and productive, consider the following suggestions.

Start With One Classroom Wiki

At their core, wikis are about sharing information. Students working together can use wikis to document what they are learning about concepts connected to the curriculum, to organize their thinking on topics of deep personal interest, or to generate shared solutions to problems built from the collective intelligence of a group. The challenge, however, is finding enough content to fill a wiki!

That's why it is best to keep your initial efforts simple and clean by creating wiki projects completed by entire classes instead of individual students. Consider having small groups design, monitor, and manage stand-alone pages in shared classroom wikis rather than creating and maintaining entire wikis on their own. Doing so will ensure that your wiki builds quickly without overwhelming anyone!

Model Classroom Wiki Projects Around Wikipedia Pages

Whether traditional teachers like it or not, Wikipedia will likely remain the most visible example of wikis in action for a long, long while. It has caught the attention of millions of users already, is built on simple and sustainable software, and taps into the natural human desire to share. Because of its size and influence—and because your students are likely to have used Wikipedia as a research source at some point in their school careers—consider using Wikipedia as a model for your own classroom wiki projects.

Creating a classroom encyclopedia covering the content you are studying or a comprehensive collection of solutions to one common problem will be a motivating and productive task for your students. Groups assigned particular topics to tackle, or charged with detailing the strengths and weaknesses of potential solutions, can create pages mirroring the format of Wikipedia entries. Conceptually, using Wikipedia as a model for your classroom wiki project will make your expectations approachable—and give students samples to refer to while completing their final products.

Provide Groups With Initial Structures to Follow and Content to Explore

While using Wikipedia as a conceptual model may provide your students with a sense of what you are trying to create, it may also completely backfire. Wikipedia is, after all, a vast resource with sophisticated and polished entries on an almost mind-boggling number of topics. Your students may end up absolutely intimidated when looking at your blank wiki on the first day of your classroom project and knowing that Wikipedia is the standard to be compared against!

To make initial efforts seem more doable, work to add extensive content to your classroom wiki ahead of time. Create page templates complete with tables of contents that detail required information—descriptions of problems, potential solutions, fatal flaws, final thoughts—for each group. Design one or two sample pages that students can refer to. Include extensive collections of supporting materials that students can use while researching. Share simple step-by-step directions for using the wiki tool that you have selected, post checklists and rubrics that can guide student work, and point to sources of embeddable content—photo warehouses, video sharing sites, free digital tools for creating interactive content—that students may find useful. Systematically front-loading your classroom wiki can help convince your classes that their efforts can produce an impressive final product rivaling Wikipedia.

Use Wikis to Enrich and Remediate

For many classroom teachers, finding differentiated learning opportunities can be an intimidating task. Classroom wikis, however—especially those designed to detail solutions to problems connected to required classroom content—can make independent work simple for everyone.

Because classroom wikis are constantly changing, they are natural sources of never-ending opportunities for students in need of differentiation. Advanced students can create new pages for your wiki and introduce challenging concepts in approachable ways. Students who finish work early can proofread content for accuracy, correct factual errors, add essential information, and point out flaws in the solutions proposed by their peers. Students in need of remediation can explore links embedded in classroom wiki pages to learn more about topics being studied. Using classroom wikis as tools for remediation and enrichment will help make the time and energy that you invest in organizing wiki work worthwhile—and will help your students see your wiki as a valuable learning tool instead of simply as a graded task to be forgotten.

Discuss Wiki Vandalism

The openness encouraged in communities that embrace wikis as a tool for knowledge building can also lead to the intentional destruction of content. Users with no real attachment to wiki projects sometimes decide to delete entire pages or add inaccurate—or inappropriate—content on purpose. Work that students have spent hours creating can literally be erased in an instant.

Users who intentionally destroy the work done on wikis are called vandals, and any teacher interested in wikis must reassure their students that vandalism is not a cause for major concern. Because wikis save every version of each page separately, work can be quickly restored as soon as vandalism occurs. While replacing damaged pages can be frustrating, it is important for students to know that nothing is lost forever on a wiki.

Keep Wikis Open for Viewing but Closed for Revision

All wiki services provide users with a wide range of viewing and editing settings. Wikis can be completely closed, requiring users to log in to see and edit content, or completely open, allowing anyone to view and edit without invitation. The best starting point for classroom wiki projects is to leave your wiki open for viewing, but to extend editing privileges to just the students in your classroom.

By doing so, you'll not only ensure that your students benefit from the motivation of creating work that can be seen by a larger audience, but also that the content created by your classes can't be destroyed by outsiders simply looking to cause trouble. Extending editing privileges to just the students in your classroom also means that you'll be able to monitor the kinds of work that each student is doing online. If you choose to grade contributions to classroom wiki projects, you can quickly identify the changes made under each student's username—and if wiki vandals strike, you'll be able to hold students accountable for their digital decisions.

Use RSS Feed Readers to Monitor Changes

Monitoring the content posted on—and changes made to—classroom wikis is often a concern that teachers wrestle with early in new digital projects. Wanting to ensure that students are acting responsibly, teachers worry when they are unable to see what kinds of work their classes are doing online together.

To make monitoring manageable, consider using an RSS feed reader (discussed in more detail in chapter 1) to track changes to individual wiki pages. While enabling RSS feeds on wiki pages will require that your wiki remain open for the world to see (a digital risk that some teachers are unwilling to take), you will quickly and easily be able to skim the contributions—new comments, edits, images, and content—being added by your students.

Name and Train Student Editors

Even after setting up RSS feed readers to track the content being added to classroom wikis, teachers may find that monitoring ongoing wiki projects for quality can be overwhelming, especially when students are highly motivated and making dozens of revisions per day. Uncomfortable with unmonitored pages and unable to find the time to keep up with the new work being added to classroom wikis, teachers end up pulling the plug on projects rather than risk being embarrassed by poor final products. To avoid this all-too-common end result, consider training student editors to be responsible for tracking the changes made to individual pages in your classroom project.

Student editors can visit wiki pages several times a week, checking new contributions for accuracy and appearance. When errors are found, student editors can make instant changes or can contact student authors and ask that they polish the work they've added. Page monitoring responsibilities can be assigned based on a student's demonstrated interest in a topic of study, motivation to revise and edit content, or willingness to take responsibility for a classroom's collective efforts. While page monitoring responsibilities will be limited as groups begin shared projects, class wikis are likely to cover enough unique topics over time that every student can take responsibility for one page of content.

■ ■

In addition to the checklist outlining the steps that teachers must take to successfully implement classroom wiki work ("Teacher Checklist for Wiki Projects," pages 211–214), the list of tasks that students must complete to create quality wiki pages ("Wiki Tasks for Student Groups," pages 215–216), and the scoring rubric that can be used to evaluate wiki products ("Wiki Scoring Rubric," pages 217–218) found at the end of this chapter, you can visit **go.solution-tree.com/technology** for a series of handouts and tip sheets to help you introduce wikis to students. There, you will find the online-only handout "Popular Wiki Services" detailing the features of three of the most popular wiki tools—PBworks, Wikispaces, and Wetpaint—designed to help you choose the service most appropriate for your purposes. You will also find step-by-step directions ("PBworks Directions for Teachers" and "PBworks Directions for Students") and screencast tutorials for using the popular wiki service PBworks (http://pbworks.com).

Final Thoughts

Asking students to solve problems is not a new concept for educators, but using technology to assist in the process or the product can add a new dimension to learning. Fortunately for the education community, software companies are looking at how to combine problem solving and collaboration to create programs that will engage students in a study of the skills, behaviors, and ideas important for success in tomorrow's world. One such company is Applied Research Associates (ARA). A research and engineering organization that specializes in everything from defense technologies to computer simulations, ARA has established a public/private partnership with NASA to create a video game called *Astronaut: Moon, Mars and Beyond* (www.astronautmmo.com/dmf/).

Astronaut: Moon, Mars and Beyond is a part of NASA's Learning Technologies project, an effort designed to identify ways that content can be delivered—and science, technology, engineering, and mathematics instruction can be supported—using new digital tools. What makes *Astronaut* engaging to students is that it is a Massively Multiplayer Online (MMO) game that introduces students to a series of space-themed problems that must be solved either by individuals or the cognitively diverse, independent, and decentralized teams that form in digital environments. Players begin the game by choosing a career path—roboticist, science officer, commander, space geologist, mechanical engineer—and then start a digital journey in which they protect imaginary space colonies from a series of dangerous situations (J. Heneghan, personal communication, January 11, 2010).

ARA game developers tried to specifically imagine the kinds of problem-solving behaviors that they wanted to encourage, and that students would need in order to advance in fields connected to science and engineering, when designing *Astronaut*. To succeed, *Astronaut* players first have to determine the nature of the problem they are trying to tackle and the resources that they need to find within the gaming environment in order to solve the problem successfully. Then, players have to consult other people on their digital team to design plans and craft potential solutions. Throughout, they are required to draw from their chosen career's development skills—introduced in the beginning of the game—to contribute to the solution (J. Heneghan, personal communication, January 11, 2010).

The whole idea behind *Astronaut* is to get students excited about science, technology, engineering, or mathematics careers, to introduce the skills and behaviors that support collaborative problem solving, and to provide a "coolness" factor that keeps players coming back for more. Rather than seeing video games as an intellectual wasteland consuming the after-school hours of today's teens—an attitude held by many prominent critics of the iGeneration—game designers see *Astronaut* as a way to reach students where they already are. If *Astronaut* succeeds in capturing the minds of its target audience, a new generation of scientists and engineers, who spent their afternoons online solving interesting problems together, might be born (J. Heneghan, personal communication, January 11, 2010).

Astronaut: Moon, Mars and Beyond is a glimpse into the future of how problem solving will be taught. Motivated to make connections and not limited by physical boundaries, students will be using new media tools—video games, wikis, discussion boards, videoconferencing applications—to collaborate on complex problems together. In the process, they'll study motivating content, explore new careers, and reflect on foreign situations. More importantly, they'll begin to look inside the minds of peers from all over the world, understanding that global challenges are seen through different lenses and recognizing that solutions cannot be nation-specific. Finally, they'll learn to see colleagues from other countries as allies whose intelligence and ability are only a mouse-click away.

Will your students be ready to problem solve in this kind of virtual environment? Better yet, are you ready to provide learning experiences that ask students to solve problems in an increasingly connected world facing a broad range of seemingly insurmountable, borderless challenges?

Understanding the Problem

The first challenge that any concerned citizen or world leader must face when tackling global challenges or controversial issues is to understand a problem as completely as possible before evaluating solutions. Understanding a problem begins by studying statistics, opinions, emotions, and impacts. Use this handout to shape your understanding of the global challenge or controversial issue we are studying in class. Remember to evaluate the sources you are studying for reliability and bias and to use http://snipurl.com to shorten Web addresses.

Type of Evidence	Evidence	Sources
Statistics are often the most convincing bit of evidence you can find when evaluating global challenges or controversial issues. By finding numbers that describe your problem today, over time, or in the future, you'll get a better sense of just how big the issue you are dealing with is.		
In an increasingly connected world in which people can publish their thoughts easily, there are going to be *tons* of different people expressing *tons* of different **opinions** about any global challenge or controversial issue that you choose to study. Some will try to explain the source of the issue or challenge you're studying. Others will detail potential consequences if your global challenge goes unaddressed. Reading through these opinions will turn you on to potential starting points for your solution planning.		
While statistics can be convincing and opinions can serve as starting points for your solution planning, **emotions** will always influence how important your problem really is and should always influence the choices you make when crafting solutions. After all, solutions are useless if they are wildly unpopular!		

page 1 of 2

Type of Evidence	Evidence	Sources
As you work through your research, pay attention to passions. What do people feel strongly about? Why? Are passions different depending on locations? How might this change your solution planning?		
In the end, the global challenge or controversial issue that you are studying has an **impact** on our planet in some significant way—otherwise it wouldn't be a global issue at all! While it is likely that you'll be able to find evidence of the impact that your global challenge is having on the world in the statistics, opinions, and emotions that you are collecting, it is important to create a clear, prioritized list of impacts before designing solutions. Otherwise, your work will be unfocused and careless.		

Summarizing Statement: After collecting statistics, opinions, emotions, and impacts related to the global challenge or controversial issue you are studying, write a paragraph summarizing important points to remember about your problem. Check with your group mates to see if you've left anything important out of your summary. Resolve any group disagreements by coming to consensus about what is most important to consider when developing potential solutions.

Evaluating Potential Solutions

Finding solutions for controversial issues or global challenges is a complex task that requires careful thinking. Use the following checklist to evaluate the quality of the solutions that your group is considering. Remember that the best research projects will review several potential solutions.

Name of Potential Solution:

1. How will your solution fix the problem we are studying in class? Can it be implemented everywhere, or will it only be effective for some people living in some places?

2. What is unique about your potential solution? Is it an idea that will catch the attention of leaders? Of businesses? Of individuals?

3. How difficult will it be to implement your solution? Are there obvious barriers that will cause your solution to fail, or is it likely that your solution will be an instant success? Why?

4. What kinds of costs will your solution carry? Will your suggestions be too expensive? Will your solution take too long to implement to be worthwhile?

5. Will your solution create any new problems? What are they likely to be? Are those new problems serious enough to make your solution essentially useless?

6. Is your solution something that individuals as well as towns, states, and countries can carry out on their own, or would large groups of partners need to work together? What kinds of groups would want to join together to see your solution succeed? Why?

7. What kinds of groups will naturally oppose your solution? Why? Are there legitimate reasons for their resistance? How will you address those concerns in your final proposal?

8. Are there any alternatives to the solution that you are studying? What are they? Would these alternatives be easier to implement? Would they carry fewer costs? Have fewer opponents?

9. Has your solution ever been implemented before? Where? What were the results? Do you have links to evidence of outcomes that you can share in your research project?

Rating Potential Solutions

While working with your partners to select the best solutions for the global challenge or controversial issue we are studying in class, you'll need a way to come to consensus with one another. Use the following rating scale to start conversations about each of the potential solutions that you are considering.

Rating: 5
This is a solution I believe in. It will be easy to implement by individuals, cities, states, and nations, and its costs won't scare people away. Better yet, this solution has no natural opponents or likely enemies. It's an idea that everyone can support. It's also a solution that I know can succeed—either because it has already been implemented successfully or because the potential barriers to the solution are simple to overcome. *I'm ready to recommend this solution to anyone, and I know it's going to work!*

Rating: 4
This solution has phenomenal potential. The barriers to implementing this solution seem relatively simple to overcome, and there are no natural opponents or likely enemies to our idea. What's more, the costs for this solution are not extraordinary. The only thing that causes me to hesitate is that this solution has never been implemented successfully before—which means that there are no guarantees that our idea will work! *I've got enough confidence in this solution to recommend it, however. Let's get started.*

Rating: 3
This solution hasn't convinced me yet. While there are some real strengths to pursuing this idea, there are also some real risks that I'm not sure can be resolved easily. We might be recommending an idea that is impossible to pull off because of the costs attached or because the barriers to success are too high. We might also be recommending an idea that people won't support. *I'll need more evidence before I'm willing to recommend this solution to others.*

Rating: 2
I've got serious doubts about this solution. Sitting here right now, I couldn't recommend this solution to others. There are too many risks and too few rewards. This solution might be too costly and/or too impossible to really pull off. What's more, there are probably going to be a bunch of people opposed to this solution, and without support, it's never going to get off the ground. Worse yet, I don't think this solution will be ready in time to solve the problem we're trying to address. *I'll move forward with this solution, but only with caution and only after doing a lot more research.*

Rating: 1
This solution seems like a bad idea. Our idea has never been tried before by anyone. What's more, there are obvious barriers that we're going to have to overcome if our solution is going to succeed—and I don't think it's possible to overcome those barriers. To work, someone is going to have to invest tons of time, energy, and money into our solution, and time, energy, and money are always hard to come by. What's worse is that I'm pretty sure our solution will create a whole new set of problems! *I don't think I'm willing to move forward with this solution.*

Rating: 0
This solution will never work. I can't believe that we're even considering this solution. There is tons of evidence to prove that this idea is too expensive or too impractical to even work. There are open enemies that we will need to convince before we'll even come close to getting others to believe in our solution—and even then, I'm pretty sure that this solution will fail. *There is no sense in even considering this solution.*

Problem-Solution Introductions

Writing about global problems and potential solutions requires a certain style. Writers begin problem-solution pieces by convincing readers that the problem being studied must be addressed and that there are practical solutions worth pursuing. To do so, they use several unique sentences in their writing, which include grabbers, backgrounders, persuaders, and closers. This handout will help you draft an introduction for your problem-solution piece. While the sentences don't have to appear in the order listed in the table, it's usually the best way to organize your introduction. In the final column, write more than one possible sentence and choose the best! In the "Gathering Feedback" portion, have a parent or a partner use the questions provided to rate the draft of your introduction.

Organizer for Problem-Solution Introductions	
Type of Sentences	**Possible Sentences**
Grabber sentences are designed to get your audience's attention! They come first in any paragraph on purpose. Without a good grabber, your readers are unlikely to even consider the problems or solutions that you're suggesting. Consider starting with a question, a quotation, or a particularly convincing statistic that you collected during your research. Example: *What would you say if I told you that almost 40 percent of the people in our world are currently living on land that will be underwater by the time that your children grow up?*	
Backgrounder sentences are designed to give your audience enough information to understand the topic that you are writing about. In the introduction of a problem-solution piece, backgrounder sentences work to describe the problem, but they avoid giving too much information about solutions. It is essential to mention the problem you are writing about in your backgrounders, if you haven't done so in your grabber. Be clear and concise so your readers have a solid understanding of the problem you are introducing. Don't ramble! Example: *That's definitely possible considering that 40 percent of our world's population currently lives within one hundred kilometers of a coastline and our seas continue to rise as a result of global warming.*	
Persuader sentences are designed to convince your reader that your problem is important and that it must be solved! Persuader sentences often point out to readers the ways that problems impact their lives today or will impact their lives tomorrow. Persuader sentences may also point out that change really is possible as long as people take action.	

Organizer for Problem-Solution Introductions

Type of Sentences	Possible Sentences
Remember that persuader sentences in an introduction should focus only on the consequences of the problem, not on solutions. Example: *If we don't find a solution for global warming, poverty will spread, inland cities will become overcrowded, and people will begin to fight over space. The good news is that with a bit of work now, we can avoid these problems later.*	
Closer sentences are designed to introduce readers to your stance on the problem. Closer sentences should also introduce readers to the solutions that you will be describing in the remainder of your piece. Remember that closer sentences should list the solutions in order from least important to most important, and should not give too many specific details about any one solution. Save that work for the remainder of your piece. Example: *By driving smaller cars, using less electricity, and changing the light bulbs in your house, you can do your part to protect our world.*	

Final Drafts

Sample Introduction	Your Introduction
What would you say if I told you that almost 40 percent of the people in our world are currently living on land that will be underwater by the time that your children grow up? That's definitely possible considering that 40 percent of our world's population currently lives within one hundred kilometers of a coastline and our seas continue to rise as a result of global warming. If we don't find a solution for global warming, poverty will spread, inland cities will become overcrowded, and people will begin to fight over space. The good news is that with a bit of work now, we can avoid these problems later. By driving smaller cars, using less electricity, and changing the light bulbs in your house, you can do your part to protect our world.	

Gathering Feedback

1. Which sentence do you like the best in the draft? Why?

2. Were there any sentences that left you confused? Which ones? How would you have changed these sentences to make them more effective?

3. Has the author left you convinced that addressing this global challenge or controversial issue is important? Do you understand his or her point of view? Can you name the solutions that he or she plans to recommend to readers?

Writing Solution Paragraphs

While the best writers rarely follow scripted templates, they almost always include the same kinds of sentences in their work. Similar to introductions, solution paragraphs in problem-solution pieces include grabbers, backgrounders, persuaders, and closers. The difference comes in the content shared. Use this handout to craft a draft of a paragraph explaining one of your solutions to an audience. While the sentences don't have to appear in the order listed in the table, it's usually the best way to organize your solution paragraph. In the right-hand column, write more than one possible sentence and choose the best! In the "Gathering Feedback" portion, have a parent or a partner use the questions provided to rate the draft of your introduction.

Organizer for Solution Paragraphs	
Type of Sentences	**Possible Sentences**
Grabber sentences are designed to get your audience's attention! They come first in any paragraph on purpose. Without a good grabber, your readers are unlikely to even consider the problems or solutions that you're suggesting. The grabber sentences in a solution paragraph must clearly state the solution that you'd like your audience to consider. By starting your paragraph with a clear statement of your solution, you're helping your audience follow your thinking. Grabber sentences in solution paragraphs answer the question, "What is most interesting or unique about this solution?" Example: *Fighting back against global warming really is as easy as changing a light bulb!*	
Backgrounder sentences are designed to give your audience enough information to understand your topic. In the solution paragraphs of a problem-solution piece, backgrounder sentences describe the solution that you'd like your audience to consider. Remember to keep your backgrounder sentences focused on one solution. Also remember that backgrounder sentences should be neutral. You're just trying to share information here—not persuade your readers. Backgrounder sentences in solution paragraphs answer the question, "How will this solution work?" Example: *That's because lighting accounts for 20 percent of the electricity that you use in your home, and a new type of light bulb called compact fluorescent uses 75 percent less electricity than old-fashioned light bulbs. Changing just one light bulb in your home can save you almost twenty-five dollars over the life of the light bulb. Each bulb that you change will keep nearly four hundred pounds of carbon dioxide from entering the atmosphere.*	

Persuader sentences in a solution paragraph are designed to convince your reader that your solution is worth pursuing and has a reasonable chance of succeeding. Persuader sentences can include personal reactions or opinions. They can also include specific examples. Persuader sentences in solution paragraphs should answer the question, "Why does this solution matter?" Example: *Imagine the amount of carbon we'd keep out of the atmosphere if every one of the world's 6 billion residents saved four hundred pounds of carbon dioxide each. With almost no effort or experience, we could change the world.*	
Closer sentences in the solution paragraphs are designed to convince readers to take action—whether that action is something concrete like making changes in their own life or less tangible like becoming an advocate in favor of the solution you are proposing. Closer sentences in solution paragraphs should answer the question, "What should readers do next?" Example: *The best part of changing light bulbs as a solution for global warming is that if you really care, you can take action today. Just head out to the local Walmart and pick up some compact fluorescent light bulbs!*	

Final Drafts

Sample Solution Paragraph	Your Solution Paragraph
Fighting back against global warming really is as easy as changing a light bulb! That's because lighting accounts for 20 percent of the electricity that you use in your home, and a new type of light bulb called compact fluorescent uses 75 percent less electricity than old-fashioned light bulbs. Changing just one light bulb in your home can save you almost twenty-five dollars over the life of the light bulb. Each bulb that you change will keep nearly four hundred pounds of carbon dioxide from entering the atmosphere. Imagine the amount of carbon we'd keep out of the atmosphere if every one of the world's 6 billion residents saved four hundred pounds of carbon dioxide each. With almost no effort or experience, we could change the world. The best part of changing light bulbs as a solution for global warming is that if you really care, you can take action today. Just head out to the local Walmart and pick up some compact fluorescent light bulbs!	

Gathering Feedback

1. Which sentence do you like the best in the draft? Why?

2. Were there any sentences that left you confused? Which ones? How would you have changed these sentences to make them more effective?

3. Has the author left you convinced that the solution presented is possible? Do you understand how his or her solution is supposed to work? Are practical steps for getting involved suggested? Do you know what to do next?

Rating Problem-Solution Pieces

Let's face it, not all problem-solution pieces are created equally! Some are more likely to convince readers to take action than others. Use this handout to rate the overall quality of the problem-solution pieces that you review.

Your Work Is Amazing

Your problem-solution piece is amazing. As I was reading your work, I was completely convinced that there was a real problem that needed to be solved. You included all kinds of evidence—both about the problem and the potential solutions—and you seemed to take any controversial emotions and opinions into account.

Most importantly, though, you made it seem urgent for me to take action and then provided a set of potential solutions that I can start working on—or see my city, state, or nation tackle—tomorrow.

You Got It

Your problem-solution piece was pretty impressive. You did a good job convincing me that there was a real problem that needed to be addressed and clearly outlining a set of solutions. There are good details and compelling language provided throughout. I'm not totally persuaded that all of your solutions are realistic, though. While they sound good on paper, one or two may prove to be impossible to pull off—either because they're too costly, too impractical, or opposed by too many people.

All in all, though, there are far more strengths in your piece than weaknesses.

You're Getting There

Your problem-solution piece has left me wondering. You mention a problem that I know is real. In fact, I've heard about it enough times that I really want to take action to help. You also mention solutions that I'll bet will actually work. They're certainly believable and interesting. Unfortunately, you haven't shared enough information to convince me to do anything!

I'd love to see more evidence—both to persuade me that your problem is urgent and that your solutions will work.

You've Got Work to Do

Your problem-solution piece isn't very convincing at all. To start with, you haven't really persuaded me that the problem you are tackling is that big of a deal. I know that I'm not ready to take action on the issue you're writing about. I'm also pretty sure that your solutions—which aren't detailed very clearly or supported with any real evidence—just won't work. I'll bet they would cost too much and have a ton of enemies.

Now, you might be able to change my mind, but you're going to need to do a ton of polishing before I'll be on board.

Celebrations and Suggestions

1. What can we celebrate about this particular piece? Has the author tackled an issue that other readers will believe in? Are there interesting solutions that just might work? What are they?

2. What suggestions do you have for improving this piece? Are there solutions that seem questionable? Places where you'd like to see more evidence provided? What next steps would you take if this was your work?

Exploring Wikis in Action

Often, the most challenging task for teachers interested in starting classroom wiki projects is imagining what's possible. Without a clear vision of how wikis can be used to facilitate the work they are doing with students, teachers can end up struggling to structure a successful wiki experience. Use this handout to evaluate several examples of student wiki projects and to collect ideas about the kind of projects that you'd like to pursue.

Carbon Fighters

http://carbonfighters.pbworks.com

This wiki was designed by a middle grades language arts teacher to give student groups the opportunity to write shared problem-solution essays on the issue of global warming. The final product for this project was an open letter to the governor of North Carolina arguing in favor of a range of alternative energy sources.

Criteria	Rating	Notes and Reflections
Accurate Content Quality wikis include accurate content and conclusions. Errors in thinking are few and far between.	☐ Above Average ☐ Average ☐ Needs Improvement	
Deep Linking Quality wikis include extensive links to reliable outside sources that serve to document student thinking and to validate student conclusions.	☐ Above Average ☐ Average ☐ Needs Improvement	
Evidence of Group Revision Quality wikis are shared efforts that include evidence of extensive contributions by all members.	☐ Above Average ☐ Average ☐ Needs Improvement	
Quality of Presentation Quality wikis include evidence of age-appropriate grammar and visual presentation.	☐ Above Average ☐ Average ☐ Needs Improvement	

Horizon Project 2008

http://horizonproject2008.wikispaces.com

One of the best-known student wiki efforts, the Horizon Project 2008, paired thirteen classrooms of high school students from six different countries in a collaborative effort to explore the major technology trends in college education in the next one to five years.

Criteria	Rating	Notes and Reflections
Accurate Content Quality wikis include accurate content and conclusions. Errors in thinking are few and far between.	☐ Above Average ☐ Average ☐ Needs Improvement	
Deep Linking Quality wikis include extensive links to reliable outside sources that serve to document student thinking and to validate student conclusions.	☐ Above Average ☐ Average ☐ Needs Improvement	
Evidence of Group Revision Quality wikis are shared efforts that include evidence of extensive contributions by all members.	☐ Above Average ☐ Average ☐ Needs Improvement	
Quality of Presentation Quality wikis include evidence of age-appropriate grammar and visual presentation.	☐ Above Average ☐ Average ☐ Needs Improvement	

The Monster Project

http://monsterproject.wikispaces.com/Welcome

A yearly effort to use wikis to pair students with one another, the Monster Project asks children in elementary school classes to draw digital images of monsters, craft written descriptions of their monsters, and ask peers in other classrooms around the country to recreate the same monster without any visual cues.

Criteria	Rating	Notes and Reflections
Accurate Content Quality wikis include accurate content and conclusions. Errors in thinking are few and far between.	☐ Above Average ☐ Average ☐ Needs Improvement	

Deep Linking	☐ Above Average	
Quality wikis include extensive links to reliable outside sources that serve to document student thinking and to validate student conclusions.	☐ Average ☐ Needs Improvement	
Evidence of Group Revision Quality wikis are shared efforts that include evidence of extensive contributions by all members.	☐ Above Average ☐ Average ☐ Needs Improvement	
Quality of Presentation Quality wikis include evidence of age-appropriate grammar and visual presentation.	☐ Above Average ☐ Average ☐ Needs Improvement	

Characteristics of Quality Wiki Pages

One of the first steps to creating a quality wiki page is to spend time exploring other student wiki pages. Working with your research group, use the following handout to evaluate at least one of the wiki pages listed below. Each was designed by groups of sixth-grade students who were presenting potential solutions to global warming—one of our world's greatest challenges. Remember to note what was impressive about the wiki page that you evaluate, any ideas you'd like to copy, and what you would improve about the work.

Wiki Samples:

The Solution to Pollution	The Green Squad	The Global (Warming) Girls
http://snipurl.com/srf2h	http://snipurl.com/srfrz	http://snipurl.com/srfys

Questions to Consider

1. Does the wiki page have an appealing layout that makes reading and exploring easy? Have subtitles or a table of contents been used to organize content? Were they needed?

    Your Response/Next Steps:

2. Is the content on this wiki page accurate and engaging? Have the authors included links to reliable external sources that you can explore to verify their information? Are you convinced by the arguments presented by this student group?

    Your Response/Next Steps:

3. Have interesting images and embedded content like videos or slideshows been included to catch the attention of readers? Would readers be drawn in or distracted by this extra content?

    Your Response/Next Steps:

4. Has the content on this wiki page been proofread carefully? Do typing errors or grammar mistakes get in the way of your understanding? Do you have to work to make sense of the content?

    Your Response/Next Steps:

5. Have the authors of this wiki page used the comment section in a meaningful way to plan their work? Is there evidence that this project was a collective effort, or does it look like most of the work was done by one or two group members?

   Your Response/Next Steps:

6. Does the page history of this wiki project show that this final product has changed significantly over time as group members added new content or made meaningful revisions to existing content?

   Your Response/Next Steps:

■ ■

Now that you've had the chance to explore wiki pages created by other student groups, work with your student research group to answer the following reflection questions.

Questions for Reflection

1. If you were to rank the three wiki pages in order from best to worst, what would your rankings look like? Why?

2. In your opinion, what are the characteristics of the best wiki pages? Why? Would your answer change depending on the audience that a wiki page was designed to reach? How?

3. In your opinion, what is the greatest mistake that student groups could make when creating wiki pages? What will your group do to avoid making those mistakes?

Wiki Roles for Student Groups

The following roles describe the work that needs to be done to make your wiki page truly outstanding. Divide up these tasks between the members of your group and work hard to make your final product amazing. Remember that you should visit your group's wiki page on a regular basis to complete your assigned tasks. Wikis change all the time—which means you're almost always likely to have more work to do!

Link Layer

One of the characteristics of high-quality wikis is the use of a multitude of links to outside sources. Links are essential on any website that you create because they allow readers to explore the topic that you're discussing on their own—and to validate that the information you share is accurate. The Link Layer of your group is responsible for all of the links included in your document.

Link Layers should begin by identifying logical places to insert links in your group's work. They should also check each source for bias or accuracy and be willing to replace any references to questionable websites that have been included in your group's work.

Flow Master

Have you ever finished reading a piece of text and been completely and totally confused? Have you ever had to read something three or four different times before you could even begin to understand what the author was trying to say? Frustrating, wasn't it?

The Flow Master of your group is responsible for reviewing your group's work to make sure that your readers aren't left confused. They should be on the constant lookout for sentences that don't make sense or places that make readers go, "Huh?" The Flow Master should read, reread, and reread again. After all, wikis change every day. If there are any text sections that need clarifying, the Flow Master should make revisions that improve the readability of your group's document.

Spelling Cop

Nothing ruins a good piece more than eight thousand spelling errors. It's simply impossible to be convincing when you can't spell anything correctly! Readers will stop thinking you're an expert after two—or maybe three—spelling errors.

The Spelling Cop of your group has a seemingly simple job: checking the spelling of every single word that is added to your group's document. The Spelling Cop had better be persistent, though—each new revision is another chance for a word to be misspelled!

Discussion Starter

Good group projects begin and end with conversations. After all, how can you really work together if you don't take the time to talk to one another about what you're producing? To make sure that conversations are a part of your wiki, you're going to need a Discussion Starter. Your Discussion Starter's home is going to be the discussion board of your group's wiki page. Their job: to ask constant questions about what it is that your group is producing.

Discussion Starters should be good evaluators, checking your page against the pages produced by other groups and finding ways to improve your work. They should also be good planners, helping your group set due dates and complete required tasks.

Captain Spit-and-Polish

Exactly how much time would you spend at a website that included no graphics or interactive features? How much time would you spend on a website that didn't include paragraph breaks or proper spacing between words? What about on a website that didn't look interesting? Right, none! Think about all of those pages that you land on and leave in two clicks. Your group's Captain Spit-and-Polish is in charge of making sure that doesn't happen to you! They need to find images and graphics that support the arguments your group is making and to make sure that your layout is professional and interesting.

The trickiest part of being Captain Spit-and-Polish is remembering who the audience for your page is—and making sure that your graphics, images, and layout are appropriate for that specific group of people. The kinds of pages that appeal to twelve-year-olds probably won't appeal to anyone over twenty-two!

Questions for Reflection

1. If you were to rank these wiki roles from the most important to the least important, what would your ranking look like? Why?

2. What types of special skills are needed to effectively fill each of these wiki roles? Is everyone in your group likely to be able to fill these roles without challenge? Why or why not?

3. If you had to choose a wiki role for yourself, which role would you pick? Why? Which role would you avoid at all costs? Can you design another role that would fit your unique strengths and weaknesses as a student and a person?

Record your wiki group assignments in the following table. Make sure that each group member has a copy of this handout and is aware of the roles that he or she is playing in your upcoming research project. There is room for a member's name, the role they will be taking on, and the reasons why they have been chosen for that role.

Member Name	Role Assigned	Explanation

Teacher Checklist for Wiki Projects

Like blogs, wikis are one of the most accessible tools available to classroom teachers new to digital projects. Teachers can often quickly and easily translate tasks that their students are already responsible for completing into wiki projects. These checklists will help you structure successful wiki experiences for your students. The following questions will help you determine whether or not you are prepared to facilitate wiki projects in your classroom. In the last column, consider including the names and contact information of anyone who can help you with this action step. Also, include the date when this action will be completed.

Technical and Procedural Preparations

1. Do your school or district's technology services specialists have a preferred wiki service? Have they made arrangements for students or teachers to have wikis using a particular service?

   Your Response/Next Steps:

2. Have you checked with your school or district's technology services specialists to learn more about any restrictions they have placed on the creation of digital work by students?

   Your Response/Next Steps:

3. Are you aware of any Internet safety policies or procedures in place at the school or district level that may influence your wiki project?

   Your Response/Next Steps:

4. Have you introduced your students to basic Internet safety practices—using pseudonyms, refusing to give away locations, never posting pictures of individuals? Are you convinced that they are prepared to write online responsibly?

   Your Response/Next Steps:

5. Have you informed parents that their children will be maintaining an online forum for content creation? Are you planning on asking parents to sign a permission slip before students can participate in your wiki project?

   Your Response/Next Steps:

6. Have you created an educator account for the wiki service that you are planning to use? Have you looked into whether or not the wiki service that you are planning to use allows teachers to create individual user accounts for each of the students in their classes or on their teams?

   Your Response/Next Steps:

7. Have you decided whether to make your wiki open to the general public for viewing and/or editing? Are you comfortable enough navigating the settings options in your wiki service to set viewing and editing permissions?

   Your Response/Next Steps:

8. Are you planning on using a feed reader (content aggregator) to monitor the new content being posted in your classroom wiki? If so, have you made your wiki available for public viewing?

   Your Response/Next Steps:

9. Have you developed a comfort level with the basic steps involved in creating content on your wiki? Can you add new pages? Do you know how to add images and links? Have you figured out how to upload files or to comment on pages? Are you comfortable with embedding content?

   Your Response/Next Steps:

10. Have you created a basic structure for your classroom wiki that includes an opening page introducing the purpose for your project and links to new pages where students will add content?

   Your Response/Next Steps:

Pedagogical Preparations

1. Have you thought through the kinds of pages you would like to see students creating in your classroom wiki? Will these pages focus on one particular predetermined theme, or will you open your wiki to a wide variety of student-generated content covering topics of deep personal interest?

   Your Response/Next Steps:

2. Have you introduced the characteristics of each type of wiki page that you are encouraging students to create? Are you planning on developing samples to guide their work?

Your Response/Next Steps:

3. Have your students explored wiki pages created by other students? Can they identify the characteristics of quality wiki work? Can they point out common flaws in student assignments?

Your Response/Next Steps:

4. Do your students understand that wiki pages are constantly changing and can include inaccurate information? Do they have a healthy skepticism of content posted online and the skills necessary for identifying sites that can be trusted?

Your Response/Next Steps:

5. Are your students prepared to give and receive feedback on written work? Will they be comfortable with peers revising and editing their contributions to shared wiki pages?

Your Response/Next Steps:

6. Do your students understand that the work done on wikis must be carefully edited and proofread in order to earn credibility with readers?

Your Response/Next Steps:

7. Do your students have the kinds of conversation skills necessary for working on collaborative projects with one another? Will they be able to do this kind of complex work in digital forums dependent on communicating through writing?

Your Response/Next Steps:

8. Are you planning on assigning roles to students working on shared wiki pages in order to structure their work? Do your students understand that quality wiki pages depend on a wide variety of contributions made over time?

Your Response/Next Steps:

9. Will your students work with one another on classroom wiki projects at school, or are you expecting all collaboration to take place online?

   Your Response/Next Steps:

10. Have you modeled the steps involved in starting new pages, adding links, inserting pictures, and embedding interesting content into the final products posted in the wiki service you've chosen to use with students?

    Your Response/Next Steps:

11. Do your students know how to use the links included in the page history of their wiki project to revert to earlier versions if their shared work is inadvertently—or intentionally—destroyed?

    Your Response/Next Steps:

12. Have you considered training a small cadre of student technology leaders to serve as student editors and page monitors? Do these editors have a clear sense of their responsibilities? Will there be any rewards for filling this role?

    Your Response/Next Steps:

Teaching the iGeneration © 2010 Solution Tree Press • solution-tree.com
Visit **go.solution-tree.com/technology** to download this page.

Wiki Tasks for Student Groups

One of the best ways for your research group to report about the controversial topic or global challenge that you are studying in class is to create a wiki page. After your teacher creates student accounts for everyone in your class and introduces you to the basics of wiki work, use the following checklist to organize your group's collective efforts.

Questions to Consider

1. Does every member of your group understand how to add content—text, images, links, video—and make edits to your shared wiki page?

   Your Response/Next Steps:

2. Is every member of your group comfortable with having their content revised by—and with revising the content posted by—peers, recognizing that wiki pages are constantly changing, shared final products?

   Your Response/Next Steps:

3. Have you worked out a process for solving disagreements—over content, links, or layout—that arise as your group's wiki page evolves?

   Your Response/Next Steps:

4. Does your group have a Link Layer, who will insert links to reliable external sources throughout your shared wiki page? Does your Link Layer know the characteristics of websites that can't be trusted?

   Your Response/Next Steps:

5. Does your group have a Flow Master who will edit your text for readability? Is this person an accomplished writer comfortable with making changes?

   Your Response/Next Steps:

6. Does your group have a Spelling Cop who will ensure that there are no spelling errors in your final product?

   Your Response/Next Steps:

7. Does your group have a Discussion Starter who will start conversations about the progress and quality of your group's work in the comment section of your shared wiki page? Will your Discussion Starter regularly visit the wiki pages being created by other student groups to collect ideas and make comparisons to your work?

   Your Response/Next Steps:

8. Does your group have a Captain Spit-and-Polish who will add images, manage formatting, and embed interesting content to make your shared wiki page more engaging?

   Your Response/Next Steps:

9. Has your group set a starting date and an ending date for adding content and making changes to your shared wiki page that everyone can agree to?

   Your Response/Next Steps:

Wiki Scoring Rubric

As your class begins to craft wiki pages designed to present potential solutions to controversial issues or global challenges, this checklist can be used by groups to self-assess their own products or by teachers to give final scores.

Questions to Consider

1. Has the group provided enough background knowledge on the controversial issue or global challenge for novice readers to make informed decisions?

2. Is there evidence that the group has considered a wide range of potential solutions for the controversial issue or global challenge before making final recommendations?

3. Has the group addressed the most common criticisms that are likely to be leveled against their chosen solutions?

4. Has the group used statistics, quotations, anecdotes, and/or stories effectively to express their point of view? Are readers likely to be influenced by this wiki page?

5. Has the group included extensive links to reliable outside sites designed to provide readers with evidence for central claims or sources for continued study?

6. Has the group used age-appropriate grammar and mechanics? Has the piece been carefully proofread to ensure that mistakes don't interfere with the reader's understanding?

7. Has the group included visual elements—pictures, charts, graphs, streaming video clips—to make their wiki page more engaging and their message more convincing?

8. Has the group used titles and subtitles—or embedded tables of contents—to organize their wiki page and to make navigation easy?

9. Is there evidence in the page history that this wiki was a collective project with significant contributions made by all members?

10. Does the page history also show evidence of extensive edits and revisions of one another's work? Has this page evolved over time, or has the majority of the content been added in final copy?

11. Has this group used the wiki's discussion board or comment feature to plan or review their work together? Do the comments in this discussion forum demonstrate active participation and ongoing reflection about the developing final product?

12. Will readers walk away from this wiki page knowing more about the topic being studied and the potential solutions that can be pursued?

Teaching the iGeneration © 2010 Solution Tree Press • solution-tree.com
Visit **go.solution-tree.com/technology** to download this page.

Epilogue

This book has been a journey through the mind of today's learner and an exploration of the kinds of skills that are being discussed in classrooms, workrooms, and boardrooms at local, state, national, and international levels. As we spend more time meeting with businesses and watching how the American economy is changing, we understand that the jobs of tomorrow are going to depend on students who can use technology to efficiently create, persuade, collaborate, communicate, innovate, and evaluate in knowledge-driven workplaces. Given this scenario, it seems apropos to end *Teaching the iGeneration* by hearing from a young learner with strong beliefs about just how schools should change.

Michael is a ten-year-old fifth grader living in the suburbs. His elementary school is only two years old and regularly posts some of the highest standardized test scores in the county. He is an above-average reader, an accomplished mathematician, and an all-around curious kid who should enjoy school. Unfortunately, even at the age of ten, Michael is already starting to find little value in the learning that takes place in his classroom and he's beginning to disconnect. In order to understand why he feels this way, it's important to look at the differences in how Michael learns at school and at home.

Learning at School

Michael gets dropped off at school each morning around 8:45, in plenty of time to make it to class before the Pledge of Allegiance begins at 9:05. When he enters the classroom, he has morning work to complete—editing a few sentences or completing a math problem or two. Once or twice each week, Michael has to write in his composition notebook. The rest of the day is chunked into blocks of time for math, reading/language arts, science or social studies, lunch, and specials (physical education, music, art, Spanish, or computers). Each block is full of either teacher-directed lessons or small-group instruction.

Michael's math classes look a lot like the math classes that his parents and grandparents sat through. Textbooks are opened, new problems are introduced, solutions are generated, answers are checked, and homework is assigned. Language arts lessons are worksheet driven as teachers push through county pacing guides designed to prepare students for end-of-grade exams. Sometimes projects are used to teach science and social studies content, but minutes are tight and most of the work assigned is completed at home. Class periods are dedicated to collecting information and taking notes. In short, Michael spends a lot of time in his classroom with work being directed at him and with very little choice in what or how he learns.

Michael's only experiences with technology in school come when he goes to the computer lab—a special scheduled once every other week. There are three computers wired for high-speed Internet access in his classroom, but they are rarely turned on. An interactive whiteboard sits in the media center, but it can only be used by the media specialist. While Michael lives in a community in which students have tons of digital devices at home, students are not allowed to bring their own technology into the school. Even if they could, however, their efforts would be pointless: their building doesn't have a wireless infrastructure yet.

For Michael's parents, homework time is always a treat. While they are both well-educated supporters of public schools, interested in classroom happenings, and capable of offering Michael help with learning almost any subject, his resistance to even trying to get through the required content can be exhausting. Challenging math questions are met with thrown pencils. Reading worksheets are met with tears. Twenty-minute assignments can take an hour's worth of coaxing and support—not to mention a healthy dose of consequences—to complete.

Michael's experiences with school are analogous to flying on an airplane. As you buckle in for the ride, you're directed to turn off all of your digital devices. Then, a highly trained pilot—seen as the only real expert on board—explains the plans for the flight, tells you to sit back and relax, and then does all of the real work. Sure, you've got some options—flipping through the wrinkled copy of *SkyMall* magazine sitting in your seat back, catching a quick nap, stealing a section of newspaper—but your choices are limited and completely uninteresting. Worse yet, even though you're less than six inches from a hundred other passengers, you spend your time largely alone and looking straight ahead. While you know that your trip is a necessary evil that you can't avoid, all you really want to do is get home.

Learning at Home

When Michael gets home, he usually makes a beeline for one of his family's game systems. The newest is an Xbox 360 with Xbox LIVE that lets him connect to the Internet. He's also got a PS2, a Nintendo Wii and DSi, and an iPod Touch—devices shared with his mom and dad and acquired over several years. When he's not playing with one of his video games, chances are good that he's curled up behind one of his family's four computers, which can all access the Internet wirelessly. Regardless of where he is, Michael is connected to the rest of the world, studying things that interest him, and making choices about what to learn—and his choices are as diverse as his interests.

As a part of the LEGO Network (http://mln.lego.com/en-us/network/status.aspx), Michael and his next-door neighbor have been climbing the rank ladder by designing blueprints and collaborating with other kids in a walled social network built around one of his favorite toys, LEGO bricks. While these kinds of opportunities to interact online seem extraordinary to Michael's grandparents, they are ordinary to him. After all, he's never known a Web on which he couldn't contribute, make friends, share resources, and upload information.

Michael's journey on the LEGO Network is surprisingly complex. In order to move up the rank ladder—an objective that Michael is intrinsically motivated to achieve—he has to figure out who to contact, what questions to ask, and how to acquire the resources that he needs to build the blueprints he has designed. All of the learning happening in the LEGO Network is directed by Michael. As he moves up in rank, he gains access to additional challenges and can help other people with his new status. When faced with particularly difficult problems, Michael tries many solutions before giving up and reaching out to his friend across the street or turning to YouTube videos for help completing the task. Unlike the homework headaches that are driving his parents nuts, Michael rarely quits on the LEGO Network or asks his mom and dad to do the work for him. He's proud of his level five ranking because he knows he's earned it himself.

When Michael is tired of the LEGO Network, he turns on his Xbox 360 and utilizes his membership to Xbox LIVE to connect to the rest of the world. Like most kids his age, Michael never plays video games by himself anymore. Instead, he signs on to the network and looks to see what games his neighborhood friends are already playing. He then responds to requests to join their games or invites them to join him. Many of the games that he plays require him to be part of a team and work toward defined goals with other people, mirroring the kinds of collaborative work done by his parents when they're at work.

If Michael had his choice, though, he'd play *Rock Band* all day long. After he slips the game disc into his Xbox, he starts a band as the drummer—his favorite instrument—and waits for a guitarist, bassist, and singer. After a handful of digital friends join his band—sometimes people he knows from school and other times people he's just met online—they take turns picking songs and playing sets of music. While his parents have turned the game's chat feature off in order to keep Michael safe, he still enjoys jamming out with people all over the world. It didn't take long for Michael to become an expert at *Rock Band*—or for his developing love of music and performance to extend into the real world, where he's now got his own drum kit sitting in the corner of his bedroom.

For the most part, Michael sees the Internet as a tool for staying connected and for finding information. He is still too young to join Facebook or MySpace, but he does spend time messing around on kid-friendly social networks. While his interests are always changing—which explains the ten different social sites that he's explored—Webkinz (www.webkinz.com/us_en/) and Club Penguin (www.clubpenguin.com) have kept his attention for a while now. Michael also likes to play learning games while he's online, but he doesn't think he's "learning" because he gets to pick the things he wants to study. His favorite has been *DimensionM* (www.dimensionm.com) created by Tabula Digita, which is teaching him algebra skills in an online video game environment. His parents are shocked because Michael refuses to give up when playing *DimensionM*. Instead, he turns to the help feature in the software to learn the math necessary to solve the problems that he can't figure out on his own and then goes back to mastering the level.

Michael literally does everything—from defining words and watching NFL highlights to designing virtual worlds and communicating with friends—online. His brain is wired to get information when he needs it and to use that information to solve problems or answer questions important to him. His network is vast, and he knows how to use it to direct his own learning.

The School and Home Gap

Without asking, Michael is also starting to bridge what he knows about technology with the work that he's doing at school. Recently, he was supposed to create a timeline detailing the lives of all of the presidents born in the Midwest. While this is a low-level thinking task, it could easily consume hours of research time poking through stacks of encyclopedias in the public library. In fact, that's exactly what his teacher wanted: her stated goal for the project was to teach students to research.

What she didn't realize is that Michael wasn't about to give up an entire Saturday for schoolwork. He immediately turned to Google Squared (www.google.com/squared) to assemble his data. After typing "U.S. Presidents" into the search box, Michael had an organized list of important information about every president. Then, he deleted all of the presidents that weren't born in the Midwest and sorted the eleven remaining presidents by birth date. He polished his writing—knowing that he had to put research facts into his own words—and emailed his final product to his teacher. The entire task took about ten minutes.

Michael's work was an "aha" moment for his teacher. She quickly realized that she was requiring students to master researching skills that were no longer needed. The kinds of information-gathering and sorting that were once done by hand could easily be automated and customized by individual kids if they just knew which tools to use. At first, she was embarrassed to have fallen so far behind. Over time, though, she realized that if digital tools could make students more efficient, there'd be more free time in class to wrestle with the kinds of complex tasks—problem solving, communication, collaboration, persuasion—that she'd pushed aside for so many years. *Twenty-first century learning*, a buzzword that she'd grown tired of, wasn't about replacing the work that she was already doing. Instead, it was about using digital tools to support and extend the kinds of cognitively challenging experiences that she cared about.

She knew, though, that making the most of digital tools was going to require structure and guidance on her part—she'd seen too many examples of teachers who simply turned their students loose with blogs and wikis only to find that the quality of the work produced was appalling—and she was ready for the challenge. Immediately, she began experimenting with ways to expose her students to new experiences built around important concepts. She was determined to set high standards for her students and was convinced that she could find a way to pair what she knew about good teaching with what Michael and his peers knew about technology. Her efforts are a work in progress, but she's taken the all-important first step, and we're convinced that she'll succeed!

Hearing From Michael

Knowing that we wanted to spotlight Michael's voice in the epilogue of *Teaching the iGeneration*, we asked him if he'd be willing to write an essay describing an ideal vision of schooling that we could share with our readers. Jazzed by the thought of "being published," Michael worked for months, crafting his thinking in countless conversations and writing more drafts than he's ever written for a school project. He's become a polished little presenter who knows more than most about what schools could be—and his essay painted a pretty convincing vision that impressed us enough to include it in full:

> The first thing I would do is make sure that everyone had a laptop so that when they need information or to learn something they could go out to the Internet and get it. You wouldn't have to go to the school building every day, maybe two days a week you could work from home or a place where you could get on the Internet. On the days that you didn't go to school you would have to work for at least seven hours, but you could choose the hours that you wanted to work. For example, you could get up at six o'clock in the morning and work until noon, take a two hour break, and then work one more hour.
>
> We would learn by working on projects. Some of the projects I would complete by myself, but most of the time I would work on a team to complete the work. When I was at school the teacher would still organize our day and help choose the projects that we worked on. The teacher would also help us when we had difficulty learning something we need to know. When we completed the projects we would present them to other students or teachers and that is how we would get our grades.
>
> The Internet could be used for learning games and to communicate with people in my group. I could also work with kids that weren't on my grade level if I needed help or someone needed my help. School would be really cool and I would just be learning all of the time (M. Garry, personal communication, January 18, 2010).

Teaching the iGeneration was designed to present many examples of how Michael's idea of learning can become a reality. We hope that you find value in the projects, resources, and ideas that we have shared and work diligently to create the kinds of learning environments that meet the needs of today's digital learners.

Technology Permission Slip

Often, teachers and administrators feel uncomfortable about introducing digital tools to students because of Internet safety risks that are widely reported in the media. These fears are completely understandable! In fact, moving forward with digital projects before articulating specific actions that parents, teachers, and students will take to keep safe online would be nothing short of irresponsible. Teaching students strategies for self-protection is a basic requirement for any educator interested in using digital tools to facilitate instruction.

This document outlines both the reasons that digital tools should play a larger role in classroom instruction and the behaviors expected of parents, teachers, and students in 21st century classrooms. It can be used as a permission slip to generate commitment to Internet safety before digital projects are started.

Teaching the iGeneration

Dear Parents,

Perhaps the greatest challenge facing parents and teachers is preparing students for a future that is rapidly changing yet poorly defined. New content and information are constantly being created, new partnerships developed across global boundaries are becoming commonplace, and new tools are connecting workers that once would have remained isolated.

Put simply, the work world that your children will inherit will be dramatically different than the work world of today! To properly prepare our students for that reality, we're planning to incorporate new digital tools into learning experiences here at school this year. Specifically, your child may have opportunities to use the following:

- **Tools for content creation**—Today's students must recognize that in a world in which new information is generated at a blinding pace, the ability to develop novel ideas after a careful process of synthesis and evaluation—and to edit and publish those ideas to wide audiences—is far more important than simply consuming knowledge generated by others.

- **Tools for communication**—Today's students must be able to engage in both collaborative and competitive dialogue. They must be able to understand different roles in complex networks of learners, respect multiple viewpoints, recognize how important listening is in productive conversations, and articulate a range of positions clearly. Today's students must learn to see communication as an opportunity to refine and revise their own thinking.

- **Tools for collaboration**—Because companies are becoming increasingly global, creating work teams of colleagues on different continents, it is imperative for students to begin collaborating with peers across classrooms, schools, communities, and oceans. They must be equal partners in the creation of documents and presentations and have ample opportunities to create shared final products. Ongoing experiences with collaborative exercises will help students learn the task management skills that are often prerequisites for successful participation in a world driven by joint endeavors.

- **Tools for information management**—Perhaps the greatest challenge facing today's students is sifting through the amazing amount of content being created and selecting what is truly useful. Where students of an earlier generation had access to a handful of sources while exploring new ideas, today's students have access to tens of thousands of sources. Students must learn to balance primary sources (interviews, blogs, surveys, personal data collection) with secondary sources (magazines, newspapers, websites, books) when collecting and organizing information.

Specifically, our students may be engaged in:

- **Reading and commenting on blogs being created by other students**—One of the best ways to motivate students to read is to provide them with opportunities to share their thinking with other students. Collections of classroom blogs make that possible. You can explore the blogs that your children will be exposed to by visiting this URL:

- **Creating a classroom wiki**—A wiki is an editable website that allows many writers to create content together. In education, wikis are generally used by students completing classroom projects. At our school, wikis are only editable by students in our building or by students in sister schools that we work closely with. Generally, our wikis are closed to outsiders—however, there are times when wikis are opened to the world. Here is a sample of a public wiki created by middle grades students: http://carbonfighters .pbworks.com

- **Joining in digital conversations with other students**—Middle grades students are social by nature, completely driven by opportunities to interact in ongoing conversations with one another. At our school, we plan to tap into this motivation by creating digital conversations connected to classroom content.

  These conversations are always closely monitored by classroom teachers, and all comments are viewed by teachers before they can be seen by students. What's more, participation in our conversations is limited to students in our school or in sister schools that we create partnerships with. Here is a sample of a conversation created by middle grades students: http://ed.voicethread.com/share/62276/

- **Writing entries for our classroom blog**—Student writers are generally motivated by having an audience and receiving feedback from their peers. At our school, those goals are often accomplished by creating classroom blogs. Blogs are public websites on which content can be posted and comments left by readers from around the world.

  To ensure that inappropriate content is not added to classroom blogs, all new entries and comments are reviewed by teachers before they are seen by students. What's more, students use pseudonyms while writing and are taught to never reveal their identity or their location. Here is a sample blog that has been maintained by middle school students: http://guysread.typepad.com/theblurb

Addressing Internet Safety

Students of the 21st century are exposed to dangers different from those faced by earlier generations. With nothing more than a few simple mouse clicks, children can stumble upon inappropriate content or participate in potentially unsafe interactions with other users.

Students must be skilled at self-advocacy and protection. They must learn to guard themselves and their identities while creating, communicating, and collaborating in virtual environments. They must recognize—and have an action plan for removing themselves from—dangerous situations. They must also understand and respect the line between one's public and private life.

Age-appropriate guidance, monitoring, and guidelines assist students as they learn to take responsibility for their own behavior when using online resources. Providing controlled educational environments focused on learning helps students utilize new tools responsibly while giving educators and parents the required safety and security.

To help prepare our students to be responsible digital citizens, we will consistently emphasize and enforce the following rules for Internet safety in our classrooms and community:

- **Students participating in any digital project are expected to act safely by keeping personal information private.** They are expected to never share their family names, passwords, usernames, email addresses, home addresses, school names, city names, or other information that could make identification possible.

- **Students participating in any digital project will let teachers or parents know anytime that a digital interaction seems unsafe.** They are expected to help police their classroom projects by pointing out undiscovered, inappropriate comments or interactions to parents or teachers.

- **Students participating in any digital project are expected to treat the project as a classroom space.** They understand that speech inappropriate for class is also inappropriate for our digital projects. If inappropriate language is posted in digital projects, students understand that they will be referred to the office for consequences. Students also understand that repeated instances of inappropriate language or content will result in the closing of all classroom projects.

- **Teachers understand that *all* content created by their students must be monitored and moderated.** A primary responsibility of all teachers interested in using digital tools in the classroom is ensuring student safety. The first step to making digital learning experiences safe is monitoring and moderating all content posted in digital projects. Teachers accept responsibility for reviewing and approving all comments added to blogs or digital conversations before they are made available to student readers. Teachers also accept responsibility for reviewing content created by students on an ongoing basis and closed projects that are no longer active.

- **Teachers take active steps to review Internet safety rules with students frequently throughout the course of the school year.** Teachers understand that students need consistent reminders and reinforcement about safe online behaviors. As a result, they regularly introduce short mini-lessons on digital safety in their classrooms. One website that is regularly used to develop minilessons is NetSmartz, the website on Internet safety created by the National Center for Missing and Exploited Children: www.netsmartz.org

- **Parents recognize that they have an obligation to monitor digital activities and behaviors beyond the school day.** The greatest risks to students engaged in digital projects come from unsupervised participation in online activities. While the faculty and staff will carefully monitor student involvement in classroom projects, parents understand that we cannot effectively monitor student activities beyond the school day or beyond the scope of school-sponsored activities.

  Therefore, parents accept responsibility for monitoring the online lives of their children away from our school. One of the first steps that proactive parents often take is ensuring that the family computer is in a public location, making monitoring easy!

- **Parents accept responsibility for learning more about Internet safety.** There are amazing resources available online that can be used by parents to learn more about keeping their children digitally safe. A growing collection of these resources can be explored by visiting: www.childnet-int.org/kia/

Permission

Before your child may fully participate in our technology experiments, I am asking for you and your child to agree to the Internet safety rules and to acknowledge your consent by signing and returning the following form.

I have read and understood the rules for keeping students safe while working on digital projects. I agree to abide by each of the rules, doing my part to make digital learning experiences both fun *and* safe at our school.

Student Name (please print):

Student Signature: Date:

Parent Signature: Date:

References

Adler, M. (1998). *The Paideia proposal: An education manifesto.* New York: Touchstone.

Alpert, J., & Hajaj, N. (2008). We knew the Web was big [Weblog post]. Accessed at http://googleblog.blogspot
.com/2008/07/we-knew-web-was-big.html on January 21, 2010.

Bauerlein, M. (2008). *The dumbest generation: How the digital age stupefies young Americans and jeopardizes our future
(or, don't trust anyone under 30).* New York: Penguin.

Berdan, K., Boulton, I., Eidman-Aadahl, E., Fleming, J., Gardner, L., Rogers, I., et al. (Eds.). (2006). *Writing for a change:
Boosting literacy and learning through social action.* Somerset, NJ: Jossey-Bass.

Bettelheim, M. (2007). Tentacled tree hugger disarms seventh graders. *Inkling.* Accessed at www.inkling
magazine.com/articles/tentacled-tree-hugger-gets-legs-up-on-twelve-year-olds/ on January 21, 2010.

Bloom, B. (Ed.). (1956). *Taxonomy of educational objectives, handbook 1: Cognitive domain.* Reading, MA: Addison-Wesley.

Boss, S. (2009). Pocket entrepreneurs benefit from teenage philanthropists. *Edutopia.* Accessed at www.edutopia
.org/microlending-global-philanthropy-fundraising-entrepreneurs on January 21, 2010.

boyd, d. (2007). Why youth [heart] social network sites: The role of networked publics in teenage social life. In
D. Buckingham (Ed.), *Youth, identity, and digital media* (pp. 119–142). Cambridge: Massachusetts Institute of
Technology Press.

boyd, d. (2008). *The Economist* debate on social "networking" [Weblog post]. Accessed at www.zephoria
.org/thoughts/archives/2008/01/15/the_economist_d.html on August 20, 2009.

boyd, d. (2010). Friendship. In M. Ito et al., *Hanging out, messing around, and geeking out: Kids living and learning with
new media* (pp. 79–115). Cambridge: Massachusetts Institute of Technology Press.

Brown, D. (2005). The writing classroom as a laboratory for democracy: An interview with Don Rothman. *Higher
Education Exchange,* 43–55.

Brown, G. (Speaker). (2009). Wiring a web for global good [Video file]. In *TED: Ideas worth sharing.* New York: TED
Conference. Accessed at www.ted.com/talks/gordon_brown.html on March 20, 2010.

Cashmore, P. (2009). YouTube: Why do we watch? *CNN Tech.* Accessed at www.cnn.com/2009/TECH/12/17/cashmore
.youtube/index.html on January 21, 2010.

Champ, H. (2009). 4,000,000,000 [Weblog post]. Accessed at http://blog.flickr.net/en/2009/10/12/4000000000/ on January 21, 2010.

Common Sense Media. (2009). *Is social networking changing childhood? A national poll.* San Francisco: Author.

Cookson, P. W., Jr. (2009). What would Socrates say? When technology pairs up with Socratic inquiry, students have an opportunity to start a purposeful conversation—with the world. *Educational Leadership, 67*(1), 8–14.

Copeland, M. (2005). *Socratic circles: Fostering critical and creative thinking in middle and high school.* Portland, ME: Stenhouse.

Creative Commons. (n.d.a). About: History. *Creative Commons.* Accessed at http://creativecommons.org/about/history on January 21, 2010.

Creative Commons. (n.d.b). About: Licenses. *Creative Commons.* Accessed at http://creativecommons.org/about/licenses/ on January 21, 2010.

Davidson, H. (2004). Meaningful digital video for every classroom. *Tech & Learning.* Accessed at www.techlearning.com/article/2166 on January 21, 2010.

Dewey, J. (1910). *How we think.* Boston: D. C. Heath & Co.

Dobbs, M. (2004). Swift boat accounts incomplete: Critics fail to disprove Kerry's version of Vietnam War episode. *Washington Post.* Accessed at www.washingtonpost.com/wp-dyn/articles/A21239–2004Aug21.html on January 21, 2010.

eMarketer. (2009). User content creation around the world. *eMarketer: Digital Intelligence.* Accessed at www.emarketer.com/Article.aspx?R=1007440 on January 21, 2010.

Fallows, D. (2008). Search engine use. *Pew Internet.* Accessed at www.pewinternet.org/Reports/2008/Search-Engine-Use.aspx on January 21, 2010.

Ferriter, B. (2007). Re: Another failed "shock and awe" campaign [Weblog comment]. Accessed at http://teacherleaders.typepad.com/the_tempered_radical/2007/04/a_report_releas.html#comments on January 21, 2010.

Ferriter, B. (2008). Statistically speaking... [Weblog post]. Accessed at http://teacherleaders.typepad.com/the_tempered_radical/2008/04/statistically-s.html on January 21, 2010.

Ferriter, B. (2009). Learning with blogs and wikis. *Educational Leadership, 66*(5), 34–38.

Ferriter, W. (2005). Digital dialogue. *Tech & Learning.* Accessed at www.techlearning.com/article/4224 on January 21, 2010.

Fox, S., & Vitak, J. (2008). Degrees of access (May 2008 data). *Pew Internet.* Accessed at http://pewinternet.org/Presentations/2008/Degrees-of-Access-(May-2008-data).aspx on January 21, 2010.

Getzels, J., & Csikszentmihalyi, M. (1967). Science creativity. *Science Journal, 3*(9), 80–84.

Getzels, J., & Csikszentmihalyi, M. (1976). *The creative vision: A longitudinal study of problem finding in art.* New York: Wiley.

Gillies, J., & Cailliau, R. (2000). *How the Web was born: The story of the World Wide Web.* New York: Oxford University Press.

GRABstats. (2008). Video game statistics/Video game industry stats. *GRABstats.com.* Accessed at www.grabstats.com/statcategorymain.asp?StatCatID=13 on January 21, 2010.

Hampton, K. N., Sessions, L. F., Her, E. J., & Rainie, L. (2009). *Social isolation and new technology: How the Internet and mobile phones impact Americans' social networks.* Washington, DC: Pew Research Center.

Hargadon, S. (2009). *Educational networking: The important role that Web 2.0 will play in education.* Pleasanton, CA: Elluminate.

Heath, C., & Heath, D. (2007). *Made to stick: Why some ideas survive and others die.* New York: Random House.

Helft, M. (2009). YouTube's quest to suggest more. *New York Times.* Accessed at www.nytimes.com/2009/12/31/technology/internet/31tube.html?_r=1&ref=media on January 21, 2010.

Hess, F. (2008). *Still at risk: What students don't know, even now.* Washington, DC: Common Core.

Hoffman, R. (2004). Swift veterans quotes. *Swift Vets and POWs for Truth.* Accessed at www.swiftvets.com/staticpages/index.php?page=Quotes on January 21, 2010.

Horrigan, J. (2008). *Home broadband usage.* Washington, DC: Pew Research Center.

Horrigan, J. (2009). *Wireless Internet use.* Washington, DC: Pew Research Center.

Horst, H. A., Herr-Stephenson, B., & Robinson, L. (2009). Media ecologies. In M. Ito et al., *Hanging out, messing around, and geeking out: Kids living and learning with new media* (pp. 29–78). Cambridge: Massachusetts Institute of Technology Press.

Huston, T. (2009). Making sense of the dumbest generation. *Huffington Post.* Accessed at www.huffingtonpost.com/tom-huston/making-sense-of-the-dumbe_b_192948.html on August 31, 2009.

Ito, M., Horst, H., Bittanti, M., boyd, d., Herr-Stephenson, B., Lange, P. G., et al. (2008). *Living and learning with new media: Summary of findings from the Digital Youth Project.* Chicago: MacArthur Foundation.

Junco, R., & Mastrodicasa, J. (2007). *Connecting to the Net.Generation: What higher education professionals need to know about today's students.* Washington, DC: National Association of Student Personnel Administrators.

Junee, R. (2009). Zoinks! 20 hours of video uploaded every minute [Weblog post]. Accessed at http://youtube-global.blogspot.com/2009/05/zoinks-20-hours-of-video-uploaded-every_20.html on August 9, 2009.

Kirkley, J. (2003). *Principles for teaching problem solving.* Bloomington, MN: Plato Learning.

Krane, B. (2006). Researchers find kids need better online academic skills. *UConn Advance, 25*(12). Accessed at http://advance.uconn.edu/2006/061113/06111308.htm on January 21, 2010.

Lee, J., Grigg, W. S., & Donahue, P. L. (2007). *The nation's report card: Reading 2007.* Washington, DC: National Center for Education Statistics.

Lenhart, A., Kahne, J., Middaugh, E., Rankin Macgill, A., Evans, C., & Vitak, J. (2008). *Teens, video games and civics: Teens' gaming experiences are diverse and include significant social interaction and civic engagement.* Washington, DC: Pew Internet and American Life Project.

Lenhart, A., & Madden, M. (2007). *Social networking websites and teens: An overview.* Washington, DC: Pew Internet and American Life Project.

Lenhart, A., Madden, M., Smith, A., & Macgill, A. (2007). *Teens and social media.* Washington, DC: Pew Internet and American Life Project.

Li, C., & Bernoff, J. (2008). *Groundswell: Winning in a world transformed by social technologies.* Boston: Harvard Business School Press.

Lipsman, A. (2009). *YouTube surpasses 100 million U.S. viewers for the first time* [Press release]. Accessed at www .comscore.com/Press_Events/Press_Releases/2009/3/YouTube_Surpasses_100_Million_US_Viewers on January 21, 2010.

Lipsman, A. (2010). *November sees number of U.S. videos viewed online surpass 30 billion for first time on record* [Press release]. Accessed at www.comscore.com/Press_Events/Press_Releases/2010/1/November_Sees_Number_of_U.S._Videos _Viewed_Online_Surpass_30_Billion_for_First_Time_on_Record on January 21, 2010.

Littleton, C. (2009). Hulu ascends higher in 2009. *Variety.* Accessed at www.variety.com/article/VR1118013207 .html?categoryid=13&cs=1&ref=bd_film on January 21, 2010.

Madden, M. (2007). *Online videos go mainstream: Most Internet users—and three-in four-young adults—now watch them.* Washington, DC: Pew Internet and American Life Project.

McKinsey & Company. (2009). *The economic impact of the achievement gap in America's schools.* New York: Author.

National Academy of Sciences. (1996). *National science education standards.* Washington, DC: National Academies Press.

National Association for Sport and Physical Education. (2004). *Moving into the future: National standards for physical education* (2nd ed.). Reston, VA: Author.

National Commission on Writing. (2009). *Letters to the president: Student voices.* New York: College Board.

National Council for the Social Studies. (1994). *NCSS curriculum standards for social studies.* Silver Spring, MD: Author.

National Council of Teachers of English. (1996). *Standards for the English language arts.* Urbana, IL: Author.

National Council of Teachers of Mathematics. (2004). *Principles and standards for school mathematics.* Reston, VA: Author.

National Education Association. (2008). *Access, adequacy and equity in education technology: Results of a survey of America's teachers and support professionals on technology in public schools and classrooms.* Washington, DC: Author.

National Writing Project. (2008). Letters to the next president: A real-world purpose for student writing. *National Writing Project.* Accessed at www.nwp.org/cs/public/print/resource/2719 on January 21, 2010.

New York State Education Department, Curriculum, Instruction and Instructional Technology. (1998). *Social studies standards.* Albany: New York State Education Department.

Newman, A. A. (2009). A campaign for clothes by a guy not wearing any. *New York Times.* Accessed at www.nytimes .com/2009/10/29/business/media/29zappos.html on January 21, 2010.

Nielsen Company. (2009). *How teens use media: A Nielsen report on the myths and realities of teen media trends.* New York: Author.

Norris, P. (2001). *Digital divide: Civic engagement, information poverty, and the Internet worldwide.* New York: Cambridge University Press.

North Carolina Department of Public Instruction. (2006). *North Carolina social studies standard course of study: Sixth grade.* Raleigh, NC: Department of Public Instruction.

Oblinger, D., & Oblinger, J. (Eds.). (2005). *Educating the Net Generation.* Boulder, CO: EDUCAUSE.

Oxfam Development Education Programme. (2006). *Education for global citizenship: A guide for schools.* Oxford, UK: Author.

Partnership for 21st Century Skills. (2009). Framework for 21st century learning. *Partnership for 21st Century Skills.* Accessed at www.21stcenturyskills.org/index.php?option=com_content&task=view&id=254&Itemid=120 on July 20, 2009.

Patterson, K., Grenny, J., Maxfield, D., McMillan, R., & Switzler, A. (2008). *Influencer: The power to change anything.* New York: McGraw-Hill.

Perlstein, L. (2007). *Tested: One American school struggles to make the grade.* New York: Henry Holt and Co.

Porter-O'Donnell, C. (2004). Beyond the yellow highlighter: Teaching annotation skills to improve reading comprehension. *English Journal, 93*(5), 82–90.

Prensky, M. (2009). Re: The larger lessons [Weblog comment]. Accessed at http://weblogg-ed.com/2009/the-larger-lessons/#comment-70619 on July 19, 2009.

Rapaport, R. (2009). The new literacy: Scenes from the digital divide 2.0. *Edutopia.* Accessed at www.edutopia.org/digital-generation-divide-literacy on January 21, 2010.

Ravitch, D. (2009). The partnership for 19th century skills [Weblog post]. Accessed at http://blog.commoncore.org/?p=88 on July 26, 2009.

Richardson, W. (2008). What do we know about our kids' futures? Really [Weblog post]. Accessed at http://weblogg-ed.com/2008/what-do-we-know-about-our-kids-futures-really/ on July 19, 2009.

Richardson, W. (2009). New reading, new writing [Weblog post]. Accessed at http://weblogg-ed.com/2009/new-reading-new-writing/ on January 21, 2010.

Rotman-Epps, S. (2008). *The fragmentation of yesterday's newspaper.* Cambridge, MA: Forrester Research.

Sage, A. (2009). Evian roller babies attract record 45m hits. *Times Online.* Accessed at http://technology.timesonline.co.uk/tol/news/tech_and_web/article6919017.ece on January 21, 2010.

Samuels, H. (2009). Focusing a research topic. *CRLS Research Guide.* Accessed at www.crlsresearchguide.org/08_focusing_a_topic.asp on January 21, 2010.

Santa, C. M., Havens, L. T., & Valdes, B. J. (2004). *Project CRISS: Creating independence through student owned strategies* (3rd ed.). Dubuque, IA: Kendall/Hunt.

Shah, A. (2009). Poverty facts and stats. *Global Issues.* Accessed at www.globalissues.org/article/26/poverty-facts-and-stats on January 21, 2010.

Shirky, C. (2002). Weblogs and the mass amateurization of publishing [Electronic mailing list message]. Accessed at www.shirky.com/writings/weblogs_publishing.html on January 21, 2010.

smartinez. (2010). you can't *buy* change, it's a process, not a purchase. the right shopping list won't change education #edchat [Twitter post]. Accessed at http://twitter.com/smartinez/status/7421752814 on January 21, 2010.

Smith, R. A. (2009). Two dowdy clothing brands go for vogue. *Wall Street Journal.* Accessed at http://online.wsj.com/article/SB10001424052748703510304574626740978607998.html?mod=djemPJ on January 21, 2010.

Steele, J. (2008). *Score reports 6.5 million Americans watched mobile video in August* [Press release]. Accessed at www .comscore.com/Press_Events/Press_Releases/2008/10/Mobile_Video on January 21, 2010.

Surowiecki, J. (2004). *The wisdom of crowds.* New York: Doubleday.

Tapscott, D. (1998). *Growing up digital: The rise of the Net Generation.* New York: McGraw-Hill.

Tapscott, D. (2009). *Grown up digital: How the Net Generation is changing your world.* New York: McGraw-Hill.

Tapscott, D., & Williams, A. D. (2006). *Wikinomics: How mass collaboration changes everything.* New York: Penguin.

Texas Education Agency, Curriculum Division. (1998). *TEKS for social studies.* Austin, TX: Author.

Three loud cheers for the father of the Web. (2005). *The Telegraph.* Accessed at www.telegraph.co.uk/news/uknews/1482211/ Three-loud-cheers-for-the-father-of-the-web.html on January 21, 2010.

Tucker, J. (2009). Social networking has hidden costs. *San Francisco Chronicle.* Accessed at www.sfgate .com/cgi-bin/article.cgi?f=/c/a/2009/08/10/MN9T1954T7.DTL on August 31, 2009.

United Nations Children's Fund. (2008). *The state of the world's children: 2009.* New York: Author.

Weeks, L. (2008). The fate of the sentence: Is the writing on the wall? *Washington Post.* Accessed at www .washingtonpost.com/wp-dyn/content/article/2008/06/12/AR2008061202258.html on August 31, 2009.

Wikipedia. (2009). Wikipedia: About. *Wikipedia.* Accessed at http://en.wikipedia.org/wiki/Wikipedia:About on January 21, 2010.

Winn, P. (2009). Technorati's state of the blogosphere: Introduction. *Technorati.* Accessed at http://technorati.com/ blogging/article/state-of-the-blogosphere-introduction/ on January 21, 2010.

World Bank. (2008). *Dollar a day revisited* [Policy Research Working Paper 4620]. Washington, DC: Development Research Group, World Bank.

Index

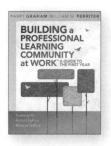

Building a Professional Learning Community at Work™ : A Guide to the First Year
Parry Graham and William M. Ferriter
Foreword by Richard DuFour and Rebecca DuFour
This play-by-play guide to implementing PLC concepts uses a story to focus each chapter. The authors analyze the story, highlighting good decisions and mistakes. They offer research behind best practice and wrap up each chapter with practical recommendations and tools. **BKF273**

21st Century Skills: Rethinking How Students Learn
Edited by James Bellanca and Ron Brandt
This book introduces the 21st century skills movement, the Partnership for 21st Century Skills, and the Framework for 21st Century Learning. Chapters focus on why these skills are necessary, which are most important, and how to best help schools include them in their repertoire. **BKF389**

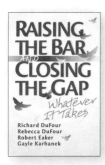

Raising the Bar and Closing the Gap: Whatever It Takes
Richard DuFour, Rebecca DuFour, Robert Eaker, and Gayle Karhanek
This sequel to the best-selling *Whatever It Takes: How Professional Learning Communities Respond When Kids Don't Learn* expands on original ideas and presses further with new insights. Foundational concepts combine with real-life examples of schools throughout North America that have gone from traditional cultures to PLCs. **BKF378**

On Excellence in Teaching
Edited by Robert Marzano
Learn from the world's best education researchers, theorists, and staff developers. The authors' diverse expertise delivers a wide range of theories and strategies and provides a comprehensive view of effective instruction from a theoretical, systemic, and classroom perspective. **BKF278**

Literacy 2.0: Reading and Writing in 21st Century Classrooms
Nancy Frey, Douglas Fisher, and Alex Gonzalez
Literacy 2.0 is where traditional literacy and technological literacy meet. Benefit from the authors' extensive experience in secondary literacy 2.0 classrooms. Discover precisely what students need to be taught to become proficient in the literacies associated with information and communication technologies. **BKF373**

Solution Tree | Press
a division of
Solution Tree

Visit solution-tree.com or call 800.733.6786 to order.